FROM BRICKS TO BEANS

29. 11. 2010

FROM BRICKS TO BEANS

Surveyor to Grocer

by

ROGER A. OWEN

With Best Wishes

R.

The Memoir Club

© Roger A. Owen 2010

First published in 2010 by
The Memoir Club
Arya House
Langley Park
Durham
DH7 9XE
Tel: 0191 373 5660
Email: memoirclub@msn.com

British Library Cataloguing in
Publication Data.
A catalogue record for this book
is available from the
British Library

ISBN: 978-1-84104-507-8

Typeset by TW Typesetting, Plymouth, Devon
Printed by JF Print, Sparkford, Somerset

To Lena

For twenty eight years of support, encouragement
and just being there, through the hardest, most
challenging period of my working life, to come out at the
other end, still with half a smile and now free to enjoy the
fruits of what we have worked towards.

To Glen and Jason

Through our time together you have never been a
moment's trouble other than the usual parental worries of
exams and so on, all of which has left me free to
concentrate on my career. Thanks, guys!

Contents

List of Illustrations ix

Preface xiii

Acknowledgements xv

Chapter 1 The End 1

Chapter 2 Country to Town and Cross Border Liaisons 10

Chapter 3 Early Years 16

Chapter 4 Further Education and Career Start 29

Chapter 5 'Call Yourself a Surveyor . . .' 37

Chapter 6 Off With the Jeans and On With the Suit 49

Chapter 7 Bricks to Beans – The Conversion Begins 64

Chapter 8 Sandcastles and Cricket 74

Chapter 9 The Morrison Years 1976–1979 Red Rose County,
Exit Door and Promotion 79

Chapter 10 Consolidation in Many Ways 1979–84 90

Chapter 11 Other Travels 104

Chapter 12 On Market Street 1985–87 120

Chapter 13 The Big Reward and Meeting 'God' 1987–90 133

Chapter 14 This 'Sporting' Life and 'The Knights' 152

Chapter 15 By Bus and York Museums 1991–94 168

Chapter 16 Pushing the Boundaries 'Darn Sawf' 1995–98 175

Chapter 17 The Brink of Greatness 1998–2002 187

Chapter 18 Oh Dear, We Are Big – 2002–5 195

Chapter 19 Never Trust A Dutchman 2005–06 210

Chapter 20 The Big Decision and Massive Change 2006–08 218

Chapter 21 Bradford City – Disaster and Pride 236

Epilogue 246

List of Illustrations

Between pages 48–49

1. Home from the war – how it all started. Phyllis Thompson and leading aircraftsman Stanley Owen, at the end of World War Two.

2. Cross border liaisons – the Big Date.

3. Anyone for the Grand National?! – Bridlington aged two and a half.

4. The scarecrow aged four and a half.

5. Opening the batting for Lancashire at Cleveleys, August 1955.

6. Founder member of the Wolf Cub pack.

7. Holidays further afield, Bournemouth, 1959.

8. The Bournemouth trolley bus on its turntable at Christchurch, 1959.

9. Year one at Bingley 'Tech', 1960.

10. Growing older and full of testosterone! The same group, 1963–64.

Between pages 112–113

11. Students union ID for final year, October 1971.

12. Jethro Tull meets the Bay City Roller, me and Andy Sedgwick in our final year, complete with tie dye t-shirt.

13. The original Girlington Supermarket.

14. The 'new' Victoria supermarket, 1969–70.

15. Keighley, 1968.

16. The original Mayo Avenue, Bradford store, on conversion from a laundry, with Sylvester Ramsden's famous chimney, yet to be felled on the cornflakes! (Picture courtesy of Bradford Industrial Museum).

17. Two great guys! Ken Morrison, presents Ron Curry with his retirement gift, May 1987.

18. Ron's legacy – a full spec Trinity House lighthouse, at Preston's Riversway, July 1987.

19. The Morrisons Petrol station at Preston.

20. The interior of the Preston store.

Between pages 176–177

21. The Ben Cruachan hydroelectric scheme, on a school visit from Bingley, opened October 1965.

22. Beep beep! Same bus but not me driving, the Hanson School of Motoring PSV, on which I learnt to be a 'knight of the road'.

23. Best man to my best mate, me and Keith on his wedding day, 1977.

24. The flying machine! Shame about the brakes, me and special Morris Marina with MG engine, spring 1974.

25. Lena's 'brothel on wheels', the purple Capri, with me and Keith Whawell in the Yorkshire Dales, 1977.

26. Former Rex Procter colleague Geoff Emmett in a motley crew of Round Tablers from Haworth and Banbridge, County Down, in the early eighties.

27. Never mind the Knights of the Round Table, what about the cavaliers? – charity collection, Christmas, 1978.

28. I was reading the words on the card – honest! Eve of Newark store handover and fortieth birthday, October 1988.

29. As rare as hen's teeth – A social gathering of the Morrisons Board, to celebrate Ken Blundell's retirement, together with wives.

30. One of the many visits to Euroshop.

31. Glen's proud day, graduation from Nottingham University.

32. Four years later and here comes Jason, leaving Cambridge, proud day number two.

33. Long time friend Bob Dyson.

34. Another proud day, Glen and Helen marry, March 2002.

35. Just happy! Jason, me, Glen and Lena, after the knot had been tied.

Between pages 240–241

36. Hillsborough – opened April 1991 – our fiftieth store and a superb conversion, of an 1854 Barrack building.

37. Interior of Hillsborough.

38. Enterprise Five, Bradford, opened October 1987 – one of the early Market Streets in the largest store in the group.

39. A more modern day Market Street. Willenhall 2009.

40. 'Bring me sunshine' – Eric Morecambe sponsored statue on the promenade of his birthplace.

41. After unveiling Eric, Her Majesty met the other Erics.

42. 'The train now arriving' – David Mach's brick masterpiece steams into Morton Park, at Darlington.

43. The Jarrow March becomes more than just a picture in the paper. Graham Ibbeson's bronze sculpture.

44. The third store at Victoria shopping centre, Bradford, opened in 2000, after its predecessors in 1961 and 1969.

45. Bet you can't get your trolley round this lot of trouble – Safeway, Downpatrick, Northern Ireland.

46. 'Never trust a Dutchman' – the brand new produce depot, at the Hook of Holland.

47. The New Corporate Headquarters, opened Summer 2006.

48. The Hilmore House winning team.

49. The last 'team', pictured in 2007.

50. One year after joining the Board.

51. One year before leaving it. Draw your own conclusions.

Preface

'It has been an ever-changing scene, we have always moved forward at pace and there have been a lot of landmarks along the way. What has driven me through the years is a determination to succeed in doing the job properly. I also had a great team behind me and support from colleagues throughout the business to help make it all happen.'

'There has been much over the years to give me grounds for satisfaction, I look back with pleasure on locations where we have been selected to build a store because of our level of care and attention to detail.'

'I leave behind a tremendously experienced property team that is highly regarded in the industry.'

'I have enjoyed a career sprinkled with tremendous experiences and some great characters, more than enough for me to think about writing a book!'

Extract from interview, for Morrisons' *Fresh News* February 2009.

Acknowledgements

Firstly, to Clare Horrocks for all the typing, putting up with the many alterations and inserts and not complaining (at least not to me!). To Morrisons for the use of the photographs and to Andrew Depledge for putting them together.

I have come across and worked with far too many people in my career to acknowledge each one individually. Some are mentioned here and not in the body of the script and vice versa, but I do specifically want to mention the following:

At Bingley Secondary School – the late John 'Jock' Cockburn, for his fantastically interesting drawing lessons that got me interested in construction in the first place, at the tender age of fourteen.

At Rex Procter and Partners, the late Frank Palmer for his sage advice, John Burnley who trained me, Peter Wilson, Geoff Emmett, Peter Hutchinson, Steve Watkins, Steve Norman, Colin Swift, Mike Hartley, Ian Armitage, and many others who were part of a phenomenal team and who went on themselves to gain even greater success, either in the practice or elsewhere. Without them I would not have set off on the proper road to where I finished.

At Morrisons, Sir Ken Morrison for giving me the chance in the boardroom, Bob Stott, George Buttle, Bob Emmott, Martin Ackroyd and the more modern group of Marc Bolland, Mark Gunter, Richard Pennycook, Martyn Jones, together with so many others who supported me through some tough times, coupled with others no longer with us, Ken Blundell, John Dowd, Keith Hutchinson and David Hutchinson in particular.

Within my own team, I have seen the development of many names who have moved on and been successful elsewhere, too many to mention, but specifically I acknowledge the contribution made over the years of my closest management team, Chris Evenson, David Wade, Russell Walker, Graham Carter, Paul Hooper, Chris Ferguson, Carl Conlon, Vic Sephton, Kevin Tiernan, Keith Atkinson and others who have not served as long, but who have performed just as well.

Finally, it would be remiss not to specifically mention the late Bob Monkman and Wilson Wrigglesworth, both now departed, who were in at the start and who supported me so well, and last but by no means least my PA and Office Manager Glynis Wilkinson, loyal, discreet, reliable. My minder and enforcer who, like me, is now enjoying her autumn in the sun, sometimes undervalued, always appreciated.

Saving the closest to last, the late Ron Curry who started me at Rex Procter, took me to Morrisons and made a lot of what I am today. He saw some of the success at first hand and probably watched over the rest from afar.

Thanks to you all!

CHAPTER 1

The End

IN THE SIX MONTHS OR SO prior to my retirement from full time employment on 1 February 2009, I was increasingly the subject of comment from my friends, business associates and other quarters, which all headed in the same direction: 'You should write a book'.

Having mused on this for some time, I eventually decided, around September 2008, that I would do just this, and the following month, on the date of my 60th birthday, I was presented by my PA Glynis Wilkinson with a birthday present of what was called 'the complete writer's kit', and a message along the lines of 'you'd better get on with it.' I didn't open the birthday present and read it in any great detail until after I retired, but the seeds were well and truly sown and I found myself increasingly occupied during the periods of otherwise boring driving, rail or air trips with thinking about the format of this book. I have always believed in orderly writing, whether it is a letter, a report, a Proof of Evidence, or anything along those lines. My simplistic rule was to start at the start and finish at the end.

All of my ordered plans were turned on their head when, whilst driving along in November 2008, some three months before my retirement, I happened to hear an interview on the radio which featured Britain's premier female comedy writers and actors, Dawn French and Jennifer Saunders. The pair were reviewing their career in writing and acting ahead of a series of Lifetime Achievement awards which capped off their time together, and the interview featured comments and probing of Dawn around her then recently released autobiography entitled *Dear Fatty*.

The interview went along quite well until it came to Jennifer's turn! Miss Saunders jolted my mild interest into sharp focus by declaring that she always read the last chapter of autobiographies first, simply to find out whether everything turned out well for the writer. Generally speaking if the final chapter did not capture her attention, then she usually did not read the rest of the book. There then followed a one-woman campaign to have the end as the start. So therefore in the forlorn hope that Miss Saunders purchases this diary of my life, this chapter is dedicated to you Jennifer.

The issue as to whether it all turned out well is largely one for others to judge of me, rather than for me to judge for myself. I have never been an '*I am*' type of person and my experience of those people is that they are often long on talk and short on substance. My advantage is that there are numerous piles of bricks around the United Kingdom which have my name on them. Inside those piles of bricks is a throbbing, vibrant community, of people involved in making their living and the living of a very successful company. How successful is to be judged by the company's shareholders and the stock exchange, and I will leave it at that, for now.

If I were to be a little self-indulgent I would recount the experience I had on my very last away trip from the office prior to retirement. At the back end of 2008, Morrisons had tendered for a number of stores which were to be disposed of by the Co-operative Group, as a consequence of the fallout from their acquisition of Somerfield. Subject to Competition issues being resolved and approved we had been notified that our offer on various properties had been accepted, and these stores came into the umbrella of the Morrison Group during 2009. The Co-op then decided that there were other units which they would consider disposing of and I felt that I should look at a number of these and give my views prior to retirement. On 20 and 21 January 2009, roughly one week before I retired, I spent time in Scotland looking at potential acquisitions in the North and acquisitions already contracted to make. The outposts visited included Fraserburgh, Banchory, and Montrose, and then on to Glasgow for my last overnight hotel stop at the Hilton in the City Centre, a place that I had come to quite enjoy, despite Lena's aversion to it on several trips we made together.

On the morning of 21 January, I was drawing a line and putting the final 'dot' in my diary and preparing for a sprint to Edinburgh, back in time for lunch with Archie Gilroy, a former director of Bone Steel, who had provided and erected structural steel for the company for some fifteen years. Thereafter the very final dash to Helensburgh and Alexandria, before returning to Glasgow Airport for the last flight back to Leeds. As I idled my way through the *Daily Mail* I came upon the horoscope page, complied by a chap by the name of Jonathan Cainer.

Sitting in the Hilton's restaurant with nothing much else to do I idly consulted the page. I, like many of you reading this no doubt, have over the years been a cynic and regarded horoscopes as mumbo-jumbo. For example, I had never won the football pools or the lottery when I was told I was getting a windfall. When I was told I was entering a calm and successful period of my life, all hell usually broke loose. When told I was in control, I usually discovered that one word from me and everyone did as they liked, so it was only with passing interest I looked at the star sign Libra and jolted back in my seat as the words leapt off the page;

> Stand up. Take a bow. Sit Back. Take a break. You can't do both at once, but you can do both in reasonably rapid succession – and you should. You have something of which to be proud. You have worked hard to achieve something many might have given up on. We may live in troubled times, but you are used to dealing with trouble and you've accomplished much that's important. Yet while remaining diligent and straightforward, you also need to give yourself some rest and reward.

I wonder if that horoscope prediction which so accurately reflected my working life on the week before it finally came to a close will be good enough to convince Jennifer Saunders to read further.

I'd expressed a desire to Marc Bolland, my Chief Executive and my Board colleagues that I should quietly drift away when the time came. I'd also told my own senior management team that I wanted no presents and no fuss. One of the reasons for my trip to Scotland the week before finally finishing had been to keep out of the way as well as try and do some good work.

Later that week Lena and I held a dinner for my senior departmental staff which went very well and thereafter my Scottish trip was put to use with a meeting between myself, Marc Bolland, my Chief Executive and Peter Marks, the Chief Executive of the Co-op Group, a good old Bradford boy and Bradford City fan, like myself, at the Co-op's Head Office in Manchester. Thereafter I entered the final week of my full employment.

The last week was a quiet affair, but punctuated by two notable events. Firstly, I attended my last Plan Review meeting with my colleague Mark Gunter the Store Operations Director and three members of the senior management team, David Wade, my Construction Director, Paul Pleasance, Retail Services Director and Andy Newton, who worked alongside Paul. More of the Plan Review meetings later, as they were central to the delivery and success of the Company's post Safeway acquisition period.

On the Thursday of my last week I attended and chaired my final Environment Group Corporate Social Responsibility meeting and handed over the chair to the Group Distribution Director, and received some very warm and touching comments from the team, which comprised a cross section of the Company's business.

Friday 30 January was my last working day and I had decided that I could not possibly fulfil a full day in the office. The emotion would have been too much to bear, so as the following Monday saw the opening of a new store at Rothwell, a village community to the south of Leeds, I decided I would spend the afternoon in the company of my Project Manager Paul Taylor, whom I had recruited from school and seen through college and professional qualifications. The project was not completed to our satisfaction and was part of a major town centre redevelopment. The state of play gave me the excuse not to be in the Head Office I had built and opened some two and a half years earlier, so I made it known I would be disappearing at lunchtime.

My staff assembled, at least those based in Bradford, and Chris Evenson, my loyal, well respected and very competent deputy, made a short speech and presented me with a very funny photograph album, representing one development for each of my twenty-two years on the Main Board, with comments from various people and a summary of other developments completed in the individual years covered, a useful reference for this book.

I sort-of half managed to make a speech, not a very good one, and not one which included everything I wanted to say, but after thirty four years and twenty two 'at the top' it was very difficult. After that off I went.

On the evening of my last day at work, I attended the Annual Dinner of the Bradford Society of Architects and Surveyors, at the noted Bradford Club as a guest of my initial employers, Rex Procter and Partners. The Annual Dinner has taken place for many, many years, of a Society that has its roots in the architecture of many of

Bradford's fine buildings and woollen textile mills. I was received quite royally by a number who knew of my career change that day and with almost ironic coincidence one of the first to shake my hand was John Burnley, my old boss and tutor. One of the first ever to shake my hand on my first day of work was one of the last to shake it on my final day.

I had been rewarded previously with a dinner for the full board, sometime prior to my retirement, as Marc Bolland very sensibly said that he would not have me caught up around the time of my departure and organised a super event the second week in February, when a group of twenty of us had an excellent meal at the Hotel Du Vin in Harrogate. Marc spoke some nice words and this was then further backed up when Chairman Sir Ian Gibson took me for lunch the following week. Ian had been unable to attend my formal dinner and again some really rather nice words were spoken, by a man I have significant respect and admiration for, particularly in his achievements in the automobile industry.

The day after my retirement I was invited to be a guest at the opening of the new Rothwell store I mentioned earlier. The site was not finished to our satisfaction, but fortunately, as my colleague Mark Gunter keeps reminding me even now, it snowed and a lot of the builder's rubble was covered in a blanket of the white stuff. To my relief, Honorary President and former Chairman Sir Ken Morrison arrived for the opening and commented on what a great job 'Roger's team' had done in clearing the snow, apparently not accepting Mark Gunter's comments that the snow was actually rubble! I was flattered to see my photograph super-imposed on one of the many historic record photographs placed around the store showing locations of local interest, which will forever remain in the store, at least until the first refurbishment.

Turning back the clock slightly, I concluded many years ago that in academic terms I was a late developer. I recount school and college education later in the book, but I feel that I really started to 'spring to life' in my final academic year after a period of fairly intense industrial training in the Bradford office of the Leeds based Quantity Surveyors Rex Procter and Partners, and I have acknowledged elsewhere the tremendous assistance I got from various people. That was the introduction to working as a team no matter what the task, be it washing the office car, putting together Bills of Quantities for tender, working as a chain gang or just simply the day-to-day work.

The client list was very varied and therefore so was the work, ranging from Public Sector projects for the Government and Local Authorities to Private Sector work for the Building Societies, commercial developers and my first introduction to Morrison Supermarkets.

I simply left because I was unsure as to whether or not I would eventually make Partner.

Did I make the right decision to move to Morrisons in 1975? Definitely, yes.

I joined Morrisons when there were twelve stores within a fifteen mile radius of its Head Office in Bradford, together with one warehouse, I left it with over three hundred and eighty stores stretching from Inverness to Gibraltar and with numerous depots, produce pack houses, food factories, abattoirs and a brand new Head Office. In addition I had put in place the acquisition and construction of some fifty further retail outlets and two distribution centres.

I joined with a job description which challenged me to develop a good estate and expand the rent. When I joined, rental income was in the order of £45,000 per annum, when I left it was approaching £45 million per annum. I have recruited, educated and promoted numerous people and have developed an excellent team, which was led from the front. I have been fortunate in making many friends in the property and construction world and beyond. I have been fortunate to have had professional external advisers who have 'joined the cause' and fought alongside us, often rare these days when some consultants are more concerned with their fee income than the service they provide. I have worked alongside one of, if not *the*, retail great, in Sir Ken Morrison, and I have witnessed the dramatic and successful effect of his successor Marc Bolland who is to be congratulated for many achievements in a short period.

I have paid tribute elsewhere to my wife Lena and two sons Glen and Jason, they have all made a major contribution to a stable domestic life which much reflects into your ability to do your job better.

I consider that I was extremely lucky to meet Lena. She already had some form of stability of domestic life, tough as it was, having been previously married, and for the seven years prior to our marriage bringing up two young boys from the age of six in the case of Glen and two in the case of Jason, all on her own, fitting in trips to school with a full time job. Money was very tight, as indeed it was when we were first married, but she soldiered on and brought up two boys who were an absolute credit to her, making my life as it was to unfold with her all that much easier.

When we married in 1981, Glen was thirteen and Jason was nine and I took on the responsibility of seeing them through the rest of their schooling and academia. Whilst they were both very well liked by their peers they were never wild, in the sense of getting into trouble, except between themselves with the usual sibling rivalry, which still exists even today.

They both attended, in their turn, the same schools, and their secondary education was undertaken at Rhodesway Comprehensive, quite near to the house we moved to after our first twelve months of marriage. They worked their way through school in a conscientious and diligent manner and, unlike me, it seemed to come annoyingly easily to them. Lena and I often exchanged words as the stress of GCSE and then A-Level examinations loomed, but I worried needlessly. Both of them obtained a whole stack of GCSEs at good levels and then went on to obtain very good pass levels at A-Level. At that point their paths diverged.

Glen firstly went on to Nottingham University, to study Electrical and Electronic Engineering. Then, having finished went to work for the computer company ICL, in Stoke, before returning to education, taking a Masters Degree at Edinburgh University in Artificial Intelligence (the thinking computer). Both courses of study were concluded with high level Degree passes, a 2.1 at Nottingham and a high level Honours at Edinburgh.

Jason, to our amazement, came home one evening and said that Cambridge University had invited a group from school to go one Saturday and look around and learn something about the university, as Oxford and Cambridge 'had the word' from Government to be more inclusive across the social strata. We were nervous about this but off he went. His appetite whetted, he applied for and was granted a place to study General Engineering at Corpus Christi College, where he duly obtained a First Class Honours degree. This was followed by work for leading Highway and Transportation and Civil Engineers Halcrow Fox in Leeds, who financed his Masters Degree at Leeds University. Like his brother before him, he passed with flying colours.

Both then moved on to work. Glen, in small business first of all, in Nottingham, then Leicester, prior to moving to Germany for four years working for Deutsche Telekom, a time he enjoyed.

This was followed by a period of soul searching, after which he took himself off for ten months sailing around the world, where he met his now wife, Helen. More of this later.

Jason, worked for Halcrow in London where he met another Helen and then he moved to work with his father, David Keedy, in the latter's caravan sales business at various sites along the South Coast of England, living in Chichester for a while. And as the clock turns full circle, the two brothers are now back together again, but more later, suffice to say that in my eyes and those of their mother, they have achieved what every parent must surely want for their children, which is to do better than you did yourself.

I finished my career well rewarded and in my view, with little unfinished business.

I have consistently worked, over the years, ten hour days, with a minimum of a five-day week and often more. During the Safeway acquisition of 2004 and before, I was working fifty per cent more than that, as a minimum. I do not claim uniqueness, but I do claim unique tiredness.

Did I do it? – Not for me to answer, but I do know that I have no regrets in any aspect of my life. I can now take holidays when and where I please, I can drive a nice car, I have two wonderful grandchildren, I can look at taking non-executive directorships, that suit me, I am unpressured and above all I know that I am a very lucky individual on the one hand, but on the other hand, as the famous golfer Gary Player once said when accused of being lucky, 'it's strange, but the harder I practise the luckier I get', and it seems to me that the parallel of this for me is that the harder I worked, the luckier I got.

Whilst I have no regrets about aspects of my own life my single biggest regret with Morrisons is that the Board of the day did not accept my recommendation that my Development Director, Chris

Evenson, be appointed as my successor. I had flagged this for over two years prior to my retirement and had been hinting at Chris for longer than that. Chris is an exceptional guy, well respected with the people we employed professionally and in the Property world, but for some reason various people, in their turn: Ken Morrison, Marc Bolland, Sir Ian Gibson and most surprising of all, my Executive colleagues, did not fancy him for the 'top job'.

Notwithstanding this Chris was thought good enough to be the caretaker manager after my departure and was rewarded to do so. I took the rejection from my recommendation to be a major smack in the mouth from people I thought were loyal to me and I take no pleasure in discovering, as I finish this book, that the Company is still largely working through the development programme which myself and Chris left, and has apparently caused chaos in some construction areas and is probably getting what is deserved. After 22 years at the top, to have your judgement and opinion thrown over was rather harsh, but Morrisons today is a big company, and therefore joining the big company circus of constant change and revolution and evolution of Senior Management who do not stay, but pick up large bonuses and move on.

Chris Evenson, for his part, quietly moved away to a position with a well-respected development company on the same or very similar terms that he was employed by Morrisons and is a very happy lad. I am both sad for him and delighted for him at the same time.

Judge for yourself whether this is a balanced view or not, in the chapters to follow. Are you still with me Jennifer?

CHAPTER 2

Country to Town and Cross Border Liaisons

PHYLLIS THOMPSON, AGED 24, and Stanley Owen, aged 33, were married at Shipley Parish Church in Yorkshire on 9 September 1946, and on 21 October 1948, Roger Anthony Owen came into this world at the maternity hospital not a hundred yards away from my parents' marriage location. Both the Owens and the Thompsons came from very regular backgrounds.

On my mother's side, that meant parents from farming stock on the Wolds of East Yorkshire. Ernest Thompson and Nellie Wilkinson were both born within a narrow radius of Pocklington, east of York, three years apart, in the last decade of the nineteenth century, and both came from families of farm labourers. Life was hard and there was a definite need for thrift, culinary skills and hard work.

My grandmother, Nellie, was seen by her parents to have some abilities. Equally having been seen to have not much prospect out in the open countryside of achieving anything other than following in their own footsteps, she was packed off to Shipley in the West Riding of Yorkshire. She went into what was then called 'service' as a housemaid/general assistant to one of the many wealthy textile people, a family sufficiently well off to live in a nice leafy area of Shipley in a big house with a big garden, away from the constant pollution and grime of the woollen textile mills in Bradford some three miles away. Here my grandmother polished and honed her skills and became a first class cook, a talent which she maintained long into her life, indeed I have kept one of her recipes for Christmas pudding which I believe, in the right hands, is absolutely priceless. It's a Christmas pudding to die for.

The lure of the big town and no doubt, more importantly, my grandmother, brought Ernest Thompson to Shipley, where the couple were married, and in February 1922 my mother was born. She was to be the only child. At this time the Thompson family lived a tough life in a back-to-back terraced house not far from the centre and slums of Shipley, with my grandfather working in a local engineering works, until, one day, tragedy struck and he was badly injured, by an escape of molten metal, which left him bed-bound for many, many weeks and lucky to escape with his life. Once recovered he was unable to go back to the heavy work and the better money which the family had previously enjoyed and in those days there was no Welfare State or any other benefits, but he was fortunate to obtain a position as the Caretaker of the Shipley Parish Church school, with which came accommodation for the family. This necessitated a move of a few hundred yards from the old home, which was retained and rented out, in turn subsidising the loss of income to my grandfather.

Mother was an intelligent girl, who qualified for a place at the Grammar School, whose name was given by the benefactor of the nearby Saltaire village, Sir Titus Salt, where she studied and obtained her School Certificate of Education. She was also a talented pianist and obtained exam passes with the Royal College of Music.

Again, times must have been hard, most children were working by the age of fourteen or fifteen and it must have been quite a sacrifice and a struggle for my grandparents, but the better standards of education paid off and my mother joined the Civil Service. During the War years she moved away from Shipley to work for the Air Ministry (latterly Ministry of Defence) in Harrogate, where she was responsible for a lot of the parts and materials which went into the mighty Spitfire fighter plane, which played such a major part in winning the Battle of Britain in the Second World War.

Mother's pride in her job and the aircraft was enjoyed to the present day and her room has embroidered pictures of that famous warplane on the wall.

Stanley Owen (neither of my parents had middle Christian names), was from a different stock altogether. A Lancastrian, he was one of a family of two other brothers, older and younger, and a younger sister, whose history was steeped in St Helens.

My grandfather, William senior, was someone whom I met but never really knew, and I have no recollection whatsoever of my grandmother Margaret, who with a family of four was, not unnaturally, a housewife, since my grandfather was first a labourer and then glass polisher at the St Helens plant of Pilkington's, the glass makers. Their marriage gave issue to three brothers: William junior, Stanley, my father, and Ronald, the youngest who never married; and my aunt Elva. Like the Thompson side of the family, they lived in a back-to-back house in Charles Street, St Helens.

St Helens was and still is, a tough town of hard working, honest people who at that time were either at Pilkington Brothers or down one of the various pits which formed the Lancashire coalfield. Newton-le-Willows or Sutton Oak in St Helens itself was probably the biggest candidate for St Helens miners. Some people no doubt also took the relatively short trip to work on the docks in nearby Liverpool, or the chemical works of Widnes.

My eldest uncle, William Junior, followed his father, as many did in those days, into Pilkington's, in the same production areas, developing his trade as a glass cutter, something you had to learn very quickly, as witnessed by Uncle Bill's part missing finger.

Pilkington Brothers had another large plant at Kirk Sandal just outside Doncaster, and there was a constant movement of staff between the two plants. Doncaster was a much more attractive proposition for living and Kirk Sandal was surrounded by open countryside, although of course, it did also have the South Yorkshire coalfield. Whilst the family were resident in South Yorkshire the three younger siblings grew up and my father and younger brother were fortunate to attend Grammar School. My father was ultimately employed by Pilkington's in an office type capacity, which qualified him to be the scorer for Pilkington Works Cricket team as it played fixtures around the Doncaster, Sheffield and coal mining areas. Dad was later to get out of the Pilkington's syndrome.

My youngest uncle Ron was probably the most intelligent of the whole family, studied hard and became a qualified electrical engineer, going back into Pilkington's and working for the group his entire working life. In latter times Pilkington's developed a patented system of glass production known as 'Float Glass' which did away with a lot of the old required skills such as glass cutting, and Ron was selected by Pilkington's to travel to some fairly far flung places, particularly in Africa, to set up Float Glass plants under licence from Pilkington's in the emerging countries.

The family (minus Bill and my dad and, for a time, my aunt who was married, gave birth to my cousin Daryl and then divorced), moved back to St Helens, on the same street, but a different house. 137 Charles Street is a place I visited many times in my earlier years and I remember the fear and trepidation on one occasion when the Pilkington-employed 'knocker-up' came down the street in his clogs at 5.00 a.m. tapping on windows to let the loyal servants of PBs, as it was known, know that it was time to get up for another day in the dirt and heat.

My uncle and aunt, together with my cousin, who is slightly older than me, moved into the family home in Charles Street and lived there for a number of years before striking out to a very nice village at Billinge, between Wigan and St Helens, where they stayed, after my cousin married and moved away, until my uncle's death.

So much for the Owen family history.

During the Second World War, my father served and became a Leading Aircraftsman in the Royal Air Force, in Africa and for a time in Italy, and was therefore not involved with my mother's beloved Spitfire.

After the War, my father joined the Civil Service; the couple met, were married and for a very short time lived in Harrogate before moving to the very predictable terrace house in Castle Road, Shipley, which was their address when I was born, on Trafalgar Day 1948. Like my mother I was to be the only child.

Whilst I have no early recollections of the Owen family, I do remember and indeed we still do have photographs of me 'helping' my Grandad Thompson barrow coal from the large stock to the boilers which created heating and hot water for the Parish Church school. I seem to remember, although only three, the wide open spaces of what I thought were massive playgrounds and having the run of them when there were no other children about. But all this was to come to an end in December 1951 when without any real warning my grandfather passed away with heart failure. Although I do not know too much about it I suspect that he was very much a changed man following his near tragic accident in the Engineering Works from years earlier, which had left him much weakened and no doubt struggling to perform his tasks.

My grandfather, no doubt encouraged by his country roots and to help the family budget, took an allotment in Shipley, which was a haven from working life, and which provided his home and then more latterly my parents with produce. It also provided my father with his first interest in gardening, something that he pursued for many, many years, until in later life it became too much for him.

Grandfather's death came like a bolt out of the blue and of course, left my grandmother with a very difficult situation. The house was the property of the Education Authority and the old family house in nearby Barrett Street, which was leased, gave the sitting tenants legal protection against any form of eviction on lease termination. Therefore it was decided that my grandmother should come and live at our house.

Our house at the time was really quite large, although it was a terrace. It stood four storeys tall, including a cellar and an attic, which was extremely good for sleeping during the warmer summer months, as I grew older, but no good in winter, as insulation levels were not what they are today.

The basement cellars were used for washing, storing coal and also storing food on a very large stone slab, which acted as the 1950s version of a refrigerator. If you included the two attics the house would have accommodated five bedrooms, which was massive for its time although the downside was it initially had an outside toilet, very cold during the winter months and often supplemented by a paraffin heater to stop the water freezing in the pipes. This is the stuff of which many stories by the likes of Michael Parkinson are made.

My grandmother stayed with us until she was hospitalised shortly before her death in November 1980 and was generally acknowledged by both mother and father to have been a significant strain on our family life. My grandmother was born of a generation which expected their families to look after them in old age. When she moved in with us she ceased to pay for any expenses, other than her own holidays with friends, which put an extra burden on my parents and caused no end of strain for my father in particular and possibly even on my parents' marriage.

Mother and Father never particularly included me in any of their thoughts and conversations on the subject, even when I was considerably older, but I know that my father, before his death, confided many of his problems to Lena, and my mother in particular was keen to stress at various times during our marriage that when she got old she did not expect us to do the same thing. Consequently, when at the age of 87 mother became too frail in both mind and body to continue to live alone, we moved her into very nice residential accommodation, ironically only some fifty yards away from the house where her own mother had been in service as a child. Everything goes around in circles!

Being born to a family who were effectively involved in the Wars of the Roses, father from Lancashire, mother from Yorkshire, there's always been a friendly rivalry. In sport, of course my dad influenced me significantly, more of this later, but in life Lena has always said both to him and my mother that he had to come out of Lancashire to find anyone decent.

Decent of course is something that often goes with humility, and coming from humble backgrounds my parents certainly exhibited this.

CHAPTER 3

Early Years

M Y EARLY YEARS WERE HAPPY, but largely uneventful, at least until I started school for the first time, aged five. I always used to think when I was younger that I remembered being born, certainly there was a recurring dream of some struggle, then a blinding flash of light; and then nothing for probably two to three years sticks in my mind.

The earliest recollection I have of anything had to be dramatic, and indeed it was, when aged three or four I struggled with a tin of paint out of our cellar area at the family home in Castle Road Shipley and managed to spill it, having dropped the heavy weight at the top of the stairs. The paint stain stayed on the York stone paving until we left the house some thirteen years later, and I remember the scolding I received from my father.

My first school was the Albert Road Infant School at nearby Saltaire, some mile or so from the family home, which was a good choice, even better considering we had the Northcliffe Infant and Secondary Modern School only a hundred yards from our home. My parents did well to get me in, but little did they know the fuss I would create on the first day. At this time my mother was working for a foundation garment company in Shipley, which was a five minute or so trolley bus ride to the school, set on the very edge of what is now a World Heritage site, the old mill village of Saltaire, founded by Sir Titus Salt. We went on a 'dry run' prior to me starting, but I had led a quite sheltered life, safe in the comparative luxury that although both my parents worked, my grandmother was at this time living with us so I never had the problem of being with a childminder, or anything similar, and indeed this isolated me a little. Sure, I had friends in and around where we lived, but they were going off to other schools.

I set off to Saltaire in a good frame of mind.

I remember this vividly, because of what happened next. My mood changed on the trolley bus ride from home and by the time I had arrived at the school gate I was largely a shaking, screaming wreck, a state which persisted throughout the entire morning of my first day. The obligatory one-third pint of milk did not calm matters, but I did remember I had to make my way to the roundabout at Saltaire to await my mother arriving from her work. Alas, she missed the bus and the continuous sobbing turned to almost hysteria.

In hindsight I think this was probably one of the penalties, if that is the right description, of being an only child. I had no one to beat me up, or to be beaten up by me, and therefore school had intervened in what was really quite a soft life. Eventually calm was restored when my mother, breathless, arrived on the next bus, and from there on things calmed down. I made friends and some of those friends remained with me through my secondary school days, moving onto Grammar School, and I occasionally see some of them, even now. I think the longest acquaintance was one Terence 'Terry' Lister, who joined me at junior school, I then joined him at Grammar School and I believe he is now a teacher at an English School in Frankfurt. Although by the time this book is published, he may well be retired. I am not a great believer in Friends Reunited, or school reunions, for that matter.

Whilst in the Infant School, I developed something of an interest, which has remained throughout my life, to the present day: the nerdy subject of buses. Bradford City Transport had a bus depot at Saltaire, this had originally been a tram depot, but was converted to trolley buses when the more efficient vehicles arrived, and every morning before school, two or three of us leaned over the wall, watching those vehicles coming off rush hour duties, being washed and turned around in the depot. I visited the depot several times over recent years, now turned into a fashionable style of pub/diner, euphemistically known as the 'Tram-Shed'. With my knowledge of structures, vague as it is, I have often marvelled at the apparently very slim structure, supported what seemed to me to be a mass of electrical cabling.

From the Infant School, I moved up to Albert Road Juniors, where I attended from the age of seven to eleven. The Junior School shared the same site as the Infants, but had separate playgrounds and again, as with my initiation to education, my first week at the new school proved somewhat disastrous. At 4.00 p.m. leaving time, within two days of starting, there was an almighty surge of pupils trying to get into the one cloakroom at the same time as those coming out. Of course when you are seven, pushing against people four years older, there is a significant difference, and the eleven-year-olds won, with the result that one Roger A. Owen was pushed out along with others and went head first into a cast iron radiator, seeing stars and drawing blood from a quite small but quite deep cut over the eyebrow. At that time the Saltaire village had its own cottage hospital to which I returned, having initially been taken home by my teacher. Two stitches were inserted by a very gruesome casualty sister, without anaesthetic, and boy did that hurt. I was off school for about a week and apparently during my absence the riot act was read to other pupils and by the time I returned, some sense of order had been established in the cloakroom push. It was while I was at Albert Road that I first started to take an interest in writing, composition as it was called then, and using grammar to the best of my ability. I delighted in the usual post summer holiday essay of 'What I did on my summer holiday', and also developed a firm interest, or at least as much as you can at that age, in Geography, often spending time learning where towns and cities were in our country as well as abroad.

My interest in sport, particularly football and cricket, had taken off some time earlier, but more of that later, and in my final year, the Eleven Plus examination year, I was selected to play for the school in goal.

In those days there were no leagues at that age group and a series of three or four friendlies were usually arranged at the end of each season with neighbouring schools, the key opponents being the Roman Catholic St Walburgas, who always seemed to have good footballers.

We finished that season with one win, one draw and two defeats. Although it had to be said that Albert Road's goalie was not at fault with the defeats.

Playing in the same team as me was the very same Terry Lister, together with one or two others who went on to become quite notable in local football, in particular a rather prolific goal scorer by the name of David McBain.

Slightly prior to this time had seen my first involvement in anything 'social' which took me out of my school environment.

Unbeknown to me, Mum had been quite actively working away at the Parish Church towards the formation of a Wolf Cub Pack. In her time, mother had been involved herself in first Brownies, then Guides, and then on from there had also involved herself as a Sunday School teacher, and she was clearly anxious to extend these activities. Begging and scraping, she managed to get together the bones of a Wolf Cub Pack and someone to lead it, one Alan Marriot, and with the blessing of the vicar, the uniquely named John Keys Fraser, the fledgling Cubs was launched, with me as one of their members.

I was later to transfer to the Scouts, but never really had the same enthusiasm for Scouting, although I did enjoy the rough and tumble of 'wide games' and also the relatively infrequent camping trips and attendance at the area's camping competition.

I well remember our first mammoth trip away from the local Bradford area Scouting campsite at nearby Cottingley, when we were taken in a van to a remote site at Stainforth, near Settle at the top end of the Yorkshire Dales. Transport was provided by Arthur Pellitt of Baildon and we caused much hilarity by hanging out of the back door of the old truck, with the mobile toilet seat over our heads, rather like the 'gurners' of Cumberland. People travelling through the Dales to the resorts of Morecambe and so on found us highly amusing.

Mr Pellitt and his subsequent family have transported literally hundreds of Boy Scouts from around the Shipley area to campsites over the years and the business is now carried on by his grandson, who rather curiously was responsible for moving some of my mother's furniture, early in 2009, when age and health meant she was better accommodated in Residential Care.

The final year at Albert Road saw the group of us sit our Eleven Plus examination. I had previously been entered for the entrance examination to Bradford Grammar School by my parents, who were eager for me to progress and had clearly made provision to pay the school fees, but unfortunately (or rather fortunately, as it turned out), I failed the examination on both occasions I sat it. I suspect that my mind might have been on that afternoon's FA Cup Final, which always seemed to coincide with the examination.

I had my mind and heart set on a place at Grammar School either in Bingley or Saltaire village, where my mother had previously attended along with several notables, the most famous of whom was one Jim Laker who went on to be something of a record breaker playing for England at cricket.

Imagine the scene when the Eleven Plus results came out and I discovered that I had failed and been selected to go to Northcliffe Secondary Modern School, not a hundred yards from our home. I was devastated and heart-broken as to how this could have happened. Northcliffe had something of a reputation for being a tough school, where the pupils generally speaking went onto more manual type jobs. Nothing wrong in that, but my parents felt that I ought to have a better chance and had concluded in their own minds – parents are always biased, aren't they? – that I was not very good at sitting exams.

My father lodged an appeal at the Local Educational Authority and I was granted a place at Saltaire Road County Secondary School, which gave me an opportunity to sit GCE O-Level examinations. It seemed this opportunity was short-lived however, as to my absolute delight, we were advised that I had been awarded a place at Bingley County Secondary School, which was divided into what were called Technical and Modern wings. I had been awarded a place in the Technical wing, which allowed me to take GCE O-Level exams in due course and which was one step below Grammar School. At that point I think we all realised that I had been quite close to achieving a Grammar School place, but clearly that was not to be and with hindsight it was actually the making of me, for Bingley Tech, as it was known, set me on the path to my Surveying career.

I joined the incoming throng and some 1,300 other pupils in September of 1959, including the regularly featured Terry Lister and others from my time in Saltaire, Alan Grange, Peter Hudson and a number of others, and it was there I first met my best and life-long friend, one Keith Richard Whawell.

Keith was one of four boys and lived on the edge of a local beauty spot, Shipley Glen. His father was a commercial representative and they lived in a big house with a tennis court on the lawn and a double garage, quite removed from the Owen terrace house.

Keith was several days late arriving at school as he had been away on holiday with his family, and the one thing that struck me immediately about him was the size of his feet, which were enormous, something I always teased him about in later life. Being the second of the four brothers, he was also somewhat into hand-me-downs from his elder brother Peter, and the first games session saw Keith turn out in a pair of football boots of rather dubious age and condition.

The discipline at the school was, to an eleven year old going on twelve, fearsome. The staff wore gowns for school assembly every day, the Headmaster was a rather daunting character, but of quiet nature, by the name of Sanderson, and everyone wore school uniform.

My first year form master was a tall, thickset individual with a booming voice by the name of Bob Green, also my first year Maths Teacher. Bob of the booming voice was also a thespian of some note with the local Bingley Little Theatre, membership of which he fulfilled throughout his working life and curiously came back into my life, in a minor way, only a few years ago.

Bob, like many local Bradford people, had invested in Morrisons when it first went public in 1967 and had occasion to write to Ken Morrison on one issue or another, the communication being circulated at a Board Meeting. Ken asked for volunteers to respond to the letter which, I recall, was kind in its content, but I do not recall the subject. When my turn came to read the script I saw the signature 'B R Green' and immediately declared that this person had taught me at school. After the laughter died down I volunteered to write the response and decided to hand deliver it. To my surprise this was the same Mr Green. We spoke for some time and I was subsequently invited to address the local group of retired gentlemen of which Bob was a member about the development of Morrisons. The teacher finished up being taught!

Bob has now sadly lost his wife of many years but remains a tangible link with my first touch of senior education.

For the first year or so I stayed for school dinners, but later in my time, I took to going home, which was not too much of a chore, as students living outside a certain radius of the school had bus passes, and this gave me the opportunity to ride the savoured red buses of the West Yorkshire Road Car Company, later to become part of the National Bus Company, or the blue trolley buses of Bradford City Transport, which later in my school life were to be replaced by rather tetchy diesel double-deckers.

Perhaps stung by the disappointment of not achieving Grammar School status, my first two years at Bingley, now known as Beckfoot Grammar School, were really quite good academically. After a gentle pep talk from my parents about getting down to things and stuck-in, rewarded by my first new bicycle and a season ticket to Bradford City Football Club, I duly knuckled-down, finishing fourth and eleventh out of thirty-some, in my first two years, and it was at that point that the construction bug started to bite.

In year three, aged thirteen going on fourteen, my class of all boys was split into two. There was a commercial class, of all girls except for one Michael Brindle, and they studied commercial issues such as shorthand and typing, a language and needlework, whereas us rough toughs took building or engineering drawing and studied woodwork or metalwork, depending on whether you were a 'builder', or a 'engineer', I chose the former.

One lesson a week was devoted to building drawing, under the tutilage of John 'Jock' Cockburn, a fearsome Scot who was third in line to the Headship. I fell in love with the subject immediately. Drawing various brick walls of varying types of bonding, English, Flemish, English garden wall and so on, was really no problem to me and I thoroughly enjoyed trying to understand how these various components of everyday life were put together. Joining me in the builders group was my friend Keith Whawell, who later went on to achieve a BSc Degree in Construction and worked at various locations including, during his industrial training, building the M6 motorway near Kendal, where you could suffer from frostbite one day and sun stroke the next, if of course you were not being washed away by the torrential rain in between.

Others to join along those lines were Peter Hudson, who eventually took over his father's joinery business, Alan Grange who went on to work with British Telecom and others who were perhaps less academically minded, who went on to work for the utilities such North Eastern Gas and Yorkshire Electricity.

I believe we had a classic grounding and a classic education, whereby those who could do and those who could not do quite so well found their niche in the more practical arenas. This, to my mind, is sadly missing today where everyone, regardless of his or her abilities, is encouraged or even pushed into further education, where many pupils waste their time, learning meaningless subjects with total lack of interest when they could be doing something more vocational. Bingley Secondary School was different.

At school in those days the philosophy of proper exercise with three games sessions each week was well enmeshed. The school played competitive sport, particularly soccer in the Bradford Leagues, and there was corresponding competitiveness for the girls.

In its time Bingley School produced one or two notable footballers who went on to join the professional ranks, or who played for the collective Bradford Boys School Team in national competitions. The school soccer leagues had two year groups, under thirteen (on the first day of winter term) and under fifteen (on the same basis), therefore you played in your school colours in the second and fourth years.

As I have already recounted from my junior school days I had been a goalkeeper and quite fancied the prospect again, until our first games lesson, when my classmate Brian Bell, a veritable giant of a guy in both height and weight terms, pronounced that he was a goalkeeper. I have to say that up until then, during my first week of secondary school, I had thought that Brian would be anything but a sportsman, but he went on to confound everyone's private thoughts by playing for the school's first team at both under thirteen and under fifteen levels and doing so with some accomplishment.

My first appearance for the under thirteens, was in the school's second string, which came as a big disappointment to me, but I had, by then, made a transition from goalkeeper to outfield player, which came as something of a shock. But our first game resulted in a victory, whilst the first team lost, and thereafter I replaced my great friend Keith Whawell, usually on the right side of the defensive back four, as it would be called today, but in the old positions I played at right back.

My first game was at home to a school called Highfield. I was very, very nervous but surrounded by some really good players who were worthy in later years, in my opinion, of Bradford Boys representation. Amongst these was the ever recurring Terry Lister and in particular Steve Knight and Michael Donahue. Steve was a no-nonsense, hard-tackling centre half who skippered the team at both age group levels, whereas 'Donny' was a small guy, but quite quick and very tricky, who played wide on the right. Both of these in later life went on to play local league soccer for many years and then went into coaching. Indeed, Steve's father Bob Knight founded the quite noted Crag Road United, who still to this day play in local league football. At that time they were founded to play Sunday youth league matches and their biggest opponents of that era were Pudsey Juniors, who were something of a nursery team for Leeds United and who featured many who went on to play in Leeds' first team over the years.

I always felt that Steve Knight, in particular, should have played for Bradford Boys and could quite conceivably have gone on to make a professional, or semi-professional career. Steve was a great guy, who you always wanted alongside you if there was any trouble, but his domestic circumstances perhaps accounted for the fact that academically he did not achieve as much as maybe he was capable of, and he consequently left school before taking GCE O-Level exams and went to work first for a local dye-works and then for a very long time and still today, for the Royal Mail.

Saturday mornings were something to look forward to. Firstly, teams were summoned on Friday morning break to hear the team selection and be given shirts for the following day's match, followed by the match itself and then a hasty washing of the kit by Mum, to be returned, cleaned and ironed, for the following Monday, just in case you were dropped for the following week's game.

In my third first team game I fell foul of a bit of gamesmanship, which even to this day I remember and am quite ashamed of. The opposition were attacking, when the winger I was marking overran the ball and it went for what I thought was a goal kick for our team. I trotted after the ball to retrieve it for Brian Bell, only to hear one of our science teachers, a Mr Sykes, I cannot remember his first name, indicate that he had awarded a corner. With that I duly turned and came away leaving the ball where it was.

Sykesy was a strong disciplinarian and immediately gave a long blast on his whistle, called me over and gave me the mother and father of all bollockings, in front of both teams. I was told in no uncertain terms that I would report to the Head Master the following Monday and if he had anything to do with it I would never play for the school again.

As I recall we won the match, but I spent a very quiet weekend brooding on my fate.

Monday duly arrived and I was accompanied by the same Sykesy to the Head's office to be given a further dressing down and a lecture on the morals of sportsmanship. I was told in no uncertain terms that if any member of staff ever had any cause to reprimand me for a similar incident in the future I would suffer some fairly dire consequences. This was not me, the little lad who had been brought up with manners, and the lesson was duly learnt and the actions never repeated, at least not until I was into my twenties and playing Sunday morning pub football!

Whilst we were a decent team, at both under thirteen and under fifteen levels, we were never going to win promotion to the top division and we were never in danger of being relegated. I believe that not being in the top division positively deprived the likes of Steve Knight of representative honours, and possibly one or two others, as well.

At under fifteens, we had to step up to a slightly higher league and play different schools, the then Bradford Grammar Schools of Hanson, Grange and Belle Vue were our opponents and they had some really good players, some of whom went on to play professionally. The most notable of whom, I guess, was one Bruce Ian Bannister, who started his career with my beloved team at Valley Parade and then went on to form a quite notorious striking partnership, known as 'smash-and-grab', at Bristol with another striker by the name of Alan Warboys.

Bruce now runs a quite successful mail ordering direct sales sports shoe company in Bradford and can be seen at Bradford City home games.

These opponents were quite testing for us but we managed to hold our own and actually progressed in the Bradford Schools Cup to be on the fringe of a semi-final place when we came up against Eccleshill School, a tough secondary modern in the middle of a large council estate, which had a reputation. The match was at home and because of adverse weather, had to be played late in the season after school, one evening. We actually got quite a good crowd, encouraged by the then new Head Master G J Farmer-Little, who was a fiery Welsh man, more keen on Rugby Union than soccer, but was keen to encourage school participation. We had our chances, but did not quite manage to take them and drew the match, which was then to be played again after school at Eccleshill.

We duly arrived to be greeted by outgoing pupils, most of whom declared that they were a brother, or even in some cases, a sister of one of the Eccleshill players and that if we won, we would not get off the site in one piece. The whole match was played in a quite intimidating atmosphere with incidences such as being tripped up by the spectators as we went to collect a loose ball for a throw in or a corner, spitting and so on. We lost the game and our chance of glory had gone, but if nothing else we were a team and stuck together.

Cricket at school was not quite as strong and although I was interested in it, I never really got the chance to play until my GCE O-Level year, when I was approached by classmate Wilf King to go and play for Windhill, in the Bradford League Junior section.

The Bradford League is a very successful league even today and was then likely to feature many Yorkshire County cricketers, who were not in the first team, or who had a vacant date in their diary. Along with the Lancashire leagues, the Bradford league had pioneered professionalism and had attracted a number of West Indian Test Cricketers, such as Constantine and others, to play in it. Indeed, the same Jim Laker who famously took nineteen wickets in an Old Trafford test match and who had gone to the same school as my mother also played in the league for a while and it was not unheard of, even at junior level, to find a few bob in your shoe if you had done well. Unfortunately, Windhill were not one of the star performers and although I went primarily as a batsman, batting at three, four or five in the order, I had a really very poor season. I had never quite fathomed to this day why that would be, but at my first session in the nets I suffered from an attack of what cricketers call the 'yipps' and found I could not get my arm to go over when bowling properly, a situation which persisted with me for almost my entire cricketing life. My batting was not much better and I don't think I achieved double-figures on more than one occasion during the whole season, of about ten games. In hindsight I might have been better not playing and concentrating on studying for my O-Levels, but I saw the cricket, once a week, as a diversion.

The one up-side of playing for a 'big name' cricket team did curry me some favour back at school, where I appeared for the school team in a number of friendly games and was picked to play against the staff. I suppose now, looking back, I realised in those games just what a difference there was, even at junior level, between playing in a league as noted as the Bradford League and just pure local school cricket, as I was reasonable successful in the school games.

Life moved on and my final year (or at least as it was planned) started on a rather low note.

The relatively new Head Master G J Farmer-Little, was as I said a rather fiery, bubbly Welsh man, who brought a whole new atmosphere to the school. On the one hand, he was less formal than his predecessors, a point which I feel was initially resented by the teaching staff, judging by the change in demeanour, which even at fifteen/sixteen years of age we all picked up on. One of the Head Master's first moves was to announce that school prefect positions, which had normally been awarded by staff, on merit, would be determined by a school election, and he went about encouraging hustings type meetings and posters and so on. At that time I was an extremely shy and retiring individual when it came to anything outside of my comfort zone with my classmates, I was not particularly interested in socialising with the opposite sex, and being in a class of all boys, of course, this was not necessary even on an accidental basis. The consequence was that I was not one of those voted for, and as a further consequence of apparently not making the effort to try to be elected I was also passed over on the limited number of teacher picks. Not a bad result for someone who two years earlier had been touted as a potential Head Boy!

Through my school time I had achieved a rather peculiar notoriety. The school entered and ran various competitions in conjunction with outside bodies. I seem to recall that there was a national art competition, run by Typhoo Tea, which was regularly won by Colin Swift, a year older than me, but who was later to become a colleague in my early Quantity Surveying career at Rex Procter and Partners.

I was not the artist that Colin Swift was, but I developed something of an art for the unusual pastime of cake baking. At that time one of the National Flour Manufacturers held a school competition, in various categories and various years, for the best of different types of cake.

A number of challenges were thrown out between teachers and pupils as to who could bake the best cake, with bets often being squared with sweets and so on – all very non-controversial – and it was here that my grandmother's country baking skills and knowledge came into being.

Guided by, but most definitely not helped by, my grandmother I proceeded over three successive years to win the prize for best-in-year and best-in-school Victoria Sandwich cake, and once my classmates got in on the fact that I had some hidden talent, bets were flying all over the place and my class annually 'cleaned-up', in the 'pound of sweets' stakes.

The bets had a very big side-effect for the Owen family, for at this time my mother had gone into partnership with one of her former workmates Marjorie Moorhouse, and ran a sweet and tobacconist shop on the opposite side of Bradford to where both families lived. This was an exciting time for me as at weekends I would go to the shop to spend most of my pocket money on various goodies and on winter Saturdays would punctuate the visit with a trip to Valley Parade, the home of my footballing heroes. Mum's shop became supplier of the cake baking prizes.

Time now seemed to pass more quickly and thoughts turned to GCE O-Levels and what I might be doing as a career in the future.

CHAPTER 4

Further Education and Career Start

IN MY FINAL YEAR AT BINGLEY, I duly sat mock O-Level examinations and to my surprise and to some extent, disappointment, I was entered for nine O-Level examinations. I thought that this was rather wrong, as I was absolutely hopeless at Art.

During the course of my final year my parents were regularly asking me what I thought I would do for a job or career, since, as I have said, I was very interested in construction, but really had no idea at all. One night my father, on returning home from work at the Ministry of Defence in Harrogate, said he had met a young man who was doing some measuring work in and around Dad's office. Upon questioning, it had materialised that this young man was a Quantity Surveyor! I had no idea what one of these was, but Dad filled me in and in the absence of any other attractive thought I decided that this might be worth pursuing, after all. The young man involved had advised that the job entailed a lot of travelling, working outdoors and on different types of projects in the construction world. Consequently, at a careers evening at Bingley School, I met John Jackson, who was Departmental Head at what was then Leeds College of Technology and discovered what I needed to do to get a place on the college course, which would give part exemption from the professional examination of the Royal Institution of Chartered Surveyors, ending up with up letters after my name!

Armed with the knowledge that I needed to pass five GCSE O-Levels, including Maths and English Language, I duly applied for and was granted a provisional place at the College for the academic year commencing October 1965. All seemed well, until my O-Level exam results landed on the doormat. At this time I had obtained my first working job with a pay packet, in the Parks Department of the then Shipley Urban District. This was a wonderful six weeks of weeding, brushing bowling greens, watering hanging baskets and working with real every day 'muck and bullets' guys who made me most welcome. One man in particular stands out, a certain Thomas

'Tommy' O'Hara. Tommy was a very small man in stature but someone I regarded as having an enormous heart.

Standing about five foot six, Tommy had, as I recall, a false or defective eye. He came from a very humble household and immediately after work each evening he would go and sell the local evening paper, the *Bradford Telegraph & Argus*, around the streets. He even working on a Saturday evening, winding his way through the streets of Shipley town centre, including the Owen household, selling the pink *Yorkshire Sports*, with his raucous bellowing voice, which was surprising for such a little man, dressed in his gardener's dirty and torn raincoat and often with a flat cap. He would arrive at work with his packed lunch and 'mashings' which comprised a folded piece of the previous night's evening paper with some tea leaves and sugar bound up inside. When break time came, wherever we were, Tommy would disappear and knock on an adjacent householder's door to ask if they could boil up a kettle for him to mash up his break-time or lunchtime drink.

We had several discussions over those weeks and indeed the following year, when I went back for a second session of horticultural entertainment. Tommy taught me one important lesson, which was no matter where you came from, or how humble or poor you were, you should always try to do your best for your family and loved ones and have ambitions for them to do better than you. I might be wrong but I seem to recall that at least one of his family, I believe his eldest daughter, eventually went on to University and greater things. If that were not the case, then it would certainly not be for want of trying. I thought Tommy O'Hara was life itself encapsulated in a little unassuming man and I was to meet more of his kind in other jobs later.

I returned from a family holiday with my parents, I cannot remember where, to find the fateful envelope on the doormat. It was my O-Level results.

My optimism evaporated immediately, as for the second time in my examination career, I was devastated to find that instead of the required five passes, and I had achieved only four and had failed my Maths examination. Having built up my hopes for a place at Leeds Tech I was absolutely crushed, the new school year was only a week or so away, Leeds Tech were advised that my grant application, which had been approved by the West Riding County Council Education Authority, was cancelled and I went back to Bingley school to first ask for and then be accepted into a repeat class to re-sit three O-Level examinations at the November examination board. I was joined in this by the same Keith Whawell, who at that time had set his eyes on a career in construction and had similarly failed to achieve the necessary passes.

In hindsight this was the best thing that could have happened to me at the time, as I believe that what followed changed, not my career, but certainly the way to achieving it.

I returned to Bingley School in September 1965 and determined that I would work very hard to achieve the alternative pass requirement of six GCE O-Levels at two sittings. I retook Maths, Geography and Physics, the latter of which was never a favourite subject, in the November. In January 1966, I achieved the required two further passes but once again the door was closed in my face.

During the course of autumn and immediately after my O-Level re-sits, I made plans to obtain a job which would take me through from January to October 1966 in the construction industry and attended various interviews for Site Surveying assistants and so on. Just as I thought I would be hitting the road to earning a wage came the news from Leeds Tech, that the professional institution, the RICS, as I shall refer to them from now on, had upped their requirements to GCE A-Level standard and had changed the Leeds course accordingly, but in return had granted an exemption from all the Intermediate RICS examinations, the only examination being the Finals. This was a far better way forward for me, as in the earlier days the Institution had an Intermediate and then two final examinations, which I would have had to sit externally through my college career with my O-Level Qualifications. This was now swept away and the doors were opened, even if the doors were slightly further away than they had been before my O-Level examinations.

After the November re-sits, Keith and I obtained Christmas employment with the Royal Mail. He was working at Shipley railway station unloading bags of mail from the various trains travelling between Leeds and Bradford and other points to Scotland, and I was working on parcel delivery and collection. The first week of my time was manna from heaven, as the parcels were delivered on a luxury coach, which brought me back to my fascination with the bus industry.

We had some real fun, two of us students working with two Royal Mail men and being driven around Shipley in a coach operated by Feather Brothers of Bradford, later to be brought into the Wallace Arnold Coaching Company. Now, sadly, swallowed up by Shearings of Wigan.

We generally managed to get round very quickly, which was a godsend to our driver as he was invariably involved in Christmas Dinner works outings in the evening and had to clean the coach during the afternoon. We found a nice niche for this, parking the bus up behind a cinema at Saltaire, whilst the four of us quietly slid into the local coffee bar listening to the latest Beatles and other Merseyside artists, while our driver mopped out the bus and placed cardboard for us to stand on. This worked very well for two or three days, until the Supervisor caught us and I was moved at that point onto parcel delivery and collection in what would today be described as a 'man and a van' operation. This was not quite as pleasant, as it involved collections from local Engineering works around Shipley, often with heavy pieces of metal castings to be transported.

My O-Level results being favourable when received in January then left me with a dilemma, of how I was to obtain A-Level passes, any two would do, in order to progress to Leeds Tech. I went for a discussion with Mr Gray, who was the Head of Salt Grammar School in Shipley, my mother's old school, but now relocated to new premises, and was accepted onto the A-Level course for History, Geography and Engineering Drawing, but with the very stern warning that the Head Master thought I had no chance of catching up six months and that I may well have to do a repeat year in the Upper Sixth.

I duly moved to Salt Grammar in January 1966 and was reunited with the very same Terry Lister and others that I had been with at Bingley, such as Tony Atkinson, Andy Jowett and some from the girls' side, Judith Lawson, Carol Holden and even some others going back to my infant and junior days, such as Steve Exley, an exceptional footballer, Margaret Burton and some new friends, Rob Midgley, Lynn Petty, Maria France and notably one Glynis Franks, who twenty years later was to become my PA and Office Manager at

Morrisons and who was to work for me for my entire career on the Board.

Having to catch up six months with the ringing endorsement of the Head that I wouldn't do it was a major task. I was lucky in that I was able to borrow the notebooks of Paul Turner and others over the upcoming half term holiday and I spent six hours each day copying up notes to bring me up to date with what was involved.

The Grammar School was totally different to Bingley and the A-Level course was significantly removed from O-Levels, here you were expected to do more thinking for yourself, there was more debate in open sessions and the whole atmosphere was different. The Sixth Form common room was relaxed, but discipline was strong. Full school uniform had to be worn, and at that point I gave up my paper round!

I had delivered papers from the age of fourteen, around the same back-to-back streets of my grandmother's original home, spreading further afield when I graduated to morning delivery, which included my own home, no tips at Christmas! In the course of my round I delivered papers to a certain Wilkinson family whom I was to come across later in life but whom I knew through other mutual friends. Ian Wilkinson, the eldest brother, was to work alongside me for a time at Rex Procter and Partners and is still practising today as a Quantity Surveyor, whereas David, the youngest brother, was eventually to marry the same Glynis Franks who later became my PA – what a strange web life is!

My end of year examinations went the way of the work I had put in and to the surprise of many I was allowed to go forward to the Upper Sixth for A-Levels, necessitating a new application to Leeds Tech, for the updated Quantity Surveying course.

Life in the Sixth Form in my final year was again very different. Unlike Bingley, everyone in the Sixth Form was automatically a school prefect, having to wear different coloured ties and responsible for enforcing discipline throughout the school. We were treated as adults, although we didn't always behave as such.

Come the Christmas break I was given permission to again conduct the Christmas post with the Royal Mail, but this time I had no luxury of the coach and had to hot foot it around a very large round, up hill and down dale, in one of the more select areas of

Shipley, which at least brought me one or two tips, on the good side, but on the other side, my rather shy and retiring one, even at this age, it brought me one or two other 'tips' in the form of rather scantily clad housewives who answered the door for recorded delivery post!

The postman on my round went sick after two days and I ended up working all day delivering a full round, which was exhausting but financially rewarding, and at the end of it all I was treated to my first trip to a Public House, arriving home having sunk five pints of Hays (brewed in Bradford) mild and thinking there was nothing to it, until my parents' dining room suddenly started spinning. Happy days!

We were a happy bunch in that Upper Sixth Form, very together and good friends.

At the Christmas of our final year, 1966, we put on a concert for the rest of the school, which was a skit on school life and life generally, I remember one of my sketches was, together with two others, to mime the Supremes recording of 'Baby Love' whilst dressed in a flimsy negligee donated by one of the larger girls and which only just fit – all good stuff!

Sport at Salt Grammar was also different, it was a different league since we continued to play soccer, and in my final Sixth Form year I was captain of the school Second Eleven, with the famous Terry Lister and others such as Steve Exley playing for the first team. We were not in leagues at this time, as a lot of schools did not go to A-Level age, so we played a series of what were euphemistically referred to as friendlies, but that did not excuse the twice-weekly training sessions. The absence of close-knit networks of A-Level studying schools meant that we had to travel further for away games, to the dizzy locations of Burnley, Holmfirth and Leeds, and this was done on my favourite mode of transport, a 'luxury' coach belonging to Samuel Ledgard of Leeds and Otley. Ledgard's were later bought out by the West Yorkshire Road Car Company, later part of National Bus, and were notorious for acquiring second-hand machinery, which was then 'tickled and fettled' to keep running. I remember one such trip to Burnley where in addition to receiving a hammering from the home team who were light years ahead of us, we only just made it back home for me to visit Valley Parade with a whining rear axle and some very suspicious blue smoke coming from the rear of the bus.

Towards the end of that season we played a friendly game with Buttershaw Comprehensive in Bradford. Buttershaw is a tough area, which was the venue for the domestic comedy drama film *Rita, Sue and Bob Too*, and you can imagine what sort of reception the 'big-time Charlies' got when they arrived in their luxury coach, which the driver said he was going to promptly remove as he was frightened it would end up on bricks! On that occasion our Upper Sixth female colleagues accompanied us as they were playing a hockey match against the same school. We ran out winners and the coach was stoned as we left the school grounds.

A number of educational visits were undertaken in our last year, usually on a Friday afternoon, again involving coach travel, and one particular trip sticks in the mind, to Shaw Cross Colliery, near Dewsbury.

A small group of about ten or fifteen of us went and were taken underground to the coalface. Here we made our way on all fours, under creaking timber pit props, to the face and saw the coal cutting machine travelling across in front of us, all well and good until a few seconds after the passage of this machinery, a large chunk of the roof fell away, all very safe but to us extremely scary.

We duly surfaced to find coal dust had penetrated ever corner and opening of our bodies and although I personally had no sympathy for the way 'King' Arthur Scargill conducted the miners' strike of the 80s, I had tremendous admiration for the guys below ground who made their living in such rough conditions. Experiences like this, the Royal Mail and the Parks Department show you the other side of life, set against your own relatively cosy and comfortable existence and in my case, I believe, taught me some humility and tolerance and in later life I believe I have always got on well with the men on the site, the men driving trucks and the men working in the warehouses, normal guys doing a normal, but important, job.

The end of Sixth Form came, I sat my A-Levels and passed the required two subjects, which would get me into Leeds Tech. I remember driving out into the countryside to the Devonshire Arms at Bolton Abbey with a number of my friends, including Michael Bridgman who was later to do some consultancy work for me and became a close friend before that in his catering career. During the course of that summer I graduated from the world of manual labour

during holidays, to clerical, when my mother got me a position with
the Inland Revenue at her office in Bradford. I was accepted for my
Quantity Surveying course at Leeds Tech and so a new phase of my
life commenced.

CHAPTER 5

'Call Yourself a Surveyor . . .'

I ENTERED LEEDS COLLEGE OF TECHNOLOGY in October 1967 to join the College Diploma in Building Economics course, which had superseded the previous RICS sponsored courses.

The course, regrettably, in some cases, was only to last for two years, being further superseded by a BSc Degree course in Quantity Surveying, so I was to miss out on the 'cap and gown' routine, unlike my two stepsons in their lives. The new course coincided with the College upgrade to Polytechnic status.

My course colleagues were a cross section of new incomers and three of four who had failed the previous year on the old RICS course. One student stood out on day one – Stephen Norman, who attended in jacket, shirt and tie and continued to do so throughout his entire college career, a mark that I thoroughly admired in him. Steve was the only one on our course to own a car, as I recall a Ford Anglia, which was immaculately kept and which he advised us, somewhat to our surprise, was required so he could visit his girlfriend Susan, who lived in Ripon, at weekends.

Steve was a very proper grammar school boy from Bradford and I am sure he will not mind me describing him as such, for as time progressed, he would become a working colleague at Rex Procter and Partners, graduating first to Associate and later to full Partner, before going off on his own, a career which he is still pursuing today. Other notables on the course were Tom Fincham, who went on to become Partner in a Leeds practice, Roger Symes, who achieved some successes for himself, and a good old boy from Cowling, near Keighley, one Malcolm Ramsden, who is now Senior Partner in another Bradford based practice Michael Eyres and Associates, and who I still see from time to time, at various business gatherings.

As with my Sixth Form studies, life was different again, you were expected to do more research, not be lectured at, but be tutored to and in the common knowledge of Further Education, they 'weed you out early'.

I found college life quite agreeable, but one orf two of the subjects were hard. The maths was very much based on A-Level standard, which I did not possess, and some of the more physics-orientated subjects were very much a struggle. In addition there were new topics, such as law and so on, but I thought I did reasonably well.

We parted for the summer holidays at the end of June and were to reconvene in October. We were 'advised' to obtain construction related summer holiday jobs, if we could, even if this meant digging ditches. Steve Norman and myself applied to the two leading Quantity Surveying practices in Bradford, namely R G McCaffrey and Rex Procter and Partners. We were both granted interviews at the latter and I duly arrived at 117 Little Horton Lane, Bradford 5, towards the end of the academic year to be interviewed by the Senior Partner, one Ronald Lawrence Curry, with whom my relationship was to last over the next twenty five years.

117 Little Horton Lane was a house that had been converted to offices, as had a lot of the Victorian stone-built dwellings of Bradford, as the wealthy moved further out and the wool textile industry and engineering industry associated with it declined.

The building was shared with an electrical contractor and was an offshoot of the main Rex Procter office in Leeds. Other offices were based in York and London and were to be later supplemented by branches in Newcastle and as I recall, Milton Keynes.

The entrance and waiting area was the old entrance hall to the Victorian house and I was greeted by the receptionist, Carol Brown, who had lived not ten doors away from the Owen family in Castle Road, Shipley. After a brief wait I was shown into the Senior Partner's office and had trouble actually seeing him at the start. The office was extremely dim and was illuminated by what appeared to me to be a forty-watt bulb, dangling over Mr Curry's desk. He was a quite formidable character, large in build and gruff in voice, but the interview went well and I was offered a temporary position in the summer holidays. I was told in no uncertain terms that in the 'old days' my parents would have had to pay for me to work there, but times had changed and I was to be paid the princely sum of six pounds per week, and that this amount would 'cost us money'.

Steve Norman and I duly arrived in early July of 1968 and commenced work.

I was put to work in what was euphemistically described as 'the back office' under the direction of Michael, 'Mike' Hartley and his small team, which included the noted Bingley artist Colin Swift. I spent the first week and a half being taught how to fold drawings and do photocopying, which involved dipping the pieces to be copied in developer. No fancy toner in those days! Photocopying was ok provided that you had not nicked your finger with a piece of paper, in which case it was extremely painful.

My first week at RP & P, as it was more popularly known, or for those in the know 'Sex Procter and Partners', was eventful from two points, firstly, I very soon got a trip out with Gerry Price, Associate Partner, who was to become Full Partner in due course and later leave the practice for the Church. We went to an old mill property near Batley, in West Yorkshire, famous for its Batley Variety Club, where all the stars appeared and Eric Morecambe had his first heart attack. We were to do a Schedule of Condition, which meant us being out for the whole day, and at lunchtime Gerry said it was normal practice to just go to the pub for a sandwich and a beer. I took this as a trick question and just to be on the safe side, drank lemonade.

Later in the first week, I was involved in my first piece of 'taking off', a technical term and nothing to do with the nickname of the practice. I was measuring some lead-lined X-Ray partitions for the Bradford Royal Infirmary for Peter Wilson, who was also later to become Associate and then Partner.

Peter was the smoothy of the office, being in possession of a Ford Lotus Cortina in its classical white and green colours. Peter was also a member of Round Table, which gave him an added air of superiority, for some reason. I shall return to the Knights of that particular organisation later, based on my own experiences.

Peter Wilson was quite a 'jack-the-lad' at this time and occupied a small office at the rear of the first floor of our building, which he shared with the temporary measurer Roger A. Owen, but more permanently with Peter Hutchinson, who was later to go to greater things in Property Development and construction around Bradford, and John Blackburn, a maniac car driver, who was later to move on to bigger things in Local Government. Peter always seemed to have a nose for what was going on outside the building, although he did not occupy a window seat and in my time in his office would regularly jump up without warning, rush to the window and announce that the current entertainment was 'on'. This usually comprised the arrival of one or more ladies of dubious occupation to one of the terrace houses facing our office, where the aforementioned ladies would spend an hour or so with the resident Asian bus drivers. I don't think they were servicing the trolley buses! Our attention to the arrival and departure of these young ladies was often met with a volley of obscenities, which only served to heighten our rather schoolboy humour.

Whilst I was doing my first measuring work for Peter, everything suddenly became dark and Bradford suffered one of its worse storms in living memory, the thunder and lightning crashed around, the hail, the snow and the rain came and the entire city centre of Bradford, being in a bowl surrounded by hills, just like Rome but without the style, filled with water.

The day before the storm, one of Procter's big jobs had started, which was the construction of the first block of the National and Provincial Building Society or, simply, the Provincial, as it was known in those days. The boys in the office took a walk into the city centre at lunchtime, to find subways totally submerged, with police divers in place and the driver of the piling rig on the Provincial site sitting on his cab roof, marooned and surrounded by flood water; it was some hours before he could be rescued. An interesting start.

At this time RP & P were moving offices from their then current address, to 123 Little Horton Lane, which was some three doors further up the same road, a very similar property to the one they already occupied, but due to the expansion of the Bradford office we had acquired the entire building, which was being gutted and refurbished. This was my first and lasting brush with Ron Curry.

I was summoned to the office of the forty-watt bulb and told that I was to go and measure the mat well for the rear entrance door to the offices, in order that a mat could be ordered. As I was to find in later life Ron Curry very often did things in his own style and to a non-standard answer. When I explained to the boys in the back office what my task was, I was very quickly appraised by Mike Hartley that coconut doormats came in standard sizes, so it would it be a case of getting the nearest standard size to the mat well frame, as they were not purpose made. I walked the fifty yards or so to the new offices, measured the mat well depression and discovered, to my horror, that it was not to a standard size mat, thereafter reporting to the Senior Partner the nearest standard size that would fit. Two days later I was summoned again to the office of the forty watt bulb to discover a Senior Partner with eyes bulging, who greeted me with the classic line 'call yourself a Surveyor, you couldn't survey Jack Shit'. I then got a lecture on how to measure and a telling, in no uncertain terms, that my career as a Quantity Surveyor would be very short, if I worked on the same basis throughout my working life, as I had with the coconut doormat. My protestations that mats came in standard sizes were met with deaf ears and a sharp response questioning as to whether I had ever heard of customised doormats, clearly I had not. The experience lived with me for a couple of days, until as the building work finished and we started preparing to move. To my surprise I found the 'offending' mat well had been 'blocked in' to fit a standard coconut mat and was told the original size was a builders' error! 'Call yourself a specifier, you couldn't specify . . .'

In and amongst all of this I received the results of my first year college exams and immediately became convinced that the 'yipps' had spread to my academic career. For the third time on major tests I had failed and there was no opportunity to re-sit the two subjects I had come up short on. I promptly contacted the college, went to see John Jackson and was told that if I could fund my own fees and cost of living I would be granted a place on the upcoming year's entrance, which was to be the third and final year of the College Diploma studies, after which the entrance qualifications had gone up again to accommodate the BSc grading of the course. I accepted, and after discussion with my parents, it was agreed that I would stay at home and travel each day, my parents would pay my college study fees, which were nowhere near as steep as they are for students today, and that I would fund out of my own savings any other issues. The next academic months were a complete study lesson in frugality.

I returned to the now Leeds Polytechnic in the October of 1969, to join my new classmates, who featured individuals such as John Davy, who later went on to Partnership level in a Leeds practice, John Hinchcliffe, who also achieved further success, and others. We were a very close-knit group of about thirteen, including a mature student by the name of John Aneurin Jenkins, obviously a Welsh man. This particular one was older than us, married with one child and another on the way, a former customs officer from the Gower Peninsula, near Swansea, who had decided on a career change and dragged his wife Margaret and then only child Rebecca from the beauty of the Gower to the dirt of Leeds. John and I, together with others such as Andy Sedgwick were to become good friends and I marvel even now at how John managed to get through college, during which time his first son came into the world. John took all sorts of part-time jobs, including filling station attendant and so on, just to make ends meet, often studying in the filling station kiosk during quiet times. They surely found it very, very tough, but John as I know was a very determined individual, who upon completion of his studies joined Leeds City Council and then embarked on a globe trotting life, working for various Government Departments in Jamaica, the Bahamas, Sri Lanka and in practice in the Middle East, culminating in setting up his own Loss Adjusting/Insurance Advisory service in Sussex.

My first year re-sit at college was slightly better, simply because I knew what was coming, but my exam results were not that great and I was becoming obsessed with the real fear of failure.

During my second sojourn at Rex Procter, I remember confiding in the Associate who was training me, John Burnley, that I had some doubts. I was advised in no uncertain terms, as I recall, to keep going on the basis that passing exams only shows you can do certain things on certain days.

Steve Norman my earlier college compatriot was now a year ahead of me and was undertaking a fifteen months Industrial Training period with Rex Procter, so our paths diverged at this point, although we usually met two or three times each college term for a beer to catch up with things at RP & P and college. By now, Steve was thoroughly enmeshed in his relationship with Sue and his continuing trips at the weekend to Ripon. They had met and become school childhood sweethearts when their schools were thrown together on a skiing trip to the Alps around the age of seventeen, and I know that Steve was totally besotted with the girl, who was to become his wife before he tragically lost her, leaving him to bring up his young daughter. So sad.

During my second summer period at Rex Procter, I got involved with more wide ranging work, and although, of course, my educational knowledge was no wider than it had been twelve months earlier, the practical experience that I was receiving stood me in good stead. I worked on some good projects, including work for Morrisons, on their then new Head Office.

Senior Partner Ron Curry was also at that point the part-time Property Director on the Main Board of Morrisons and consequently RP & P were in prime position for Morrisons work. At that time Morrisons was a small company, which had just gone Public, but had been a record number of times over-subscribed on the Stock Exchange, a record which lasted for many, many years and may indeed still be live, even today. Days working in a location, better than the back office, allowed me to see clients' cars arriving and Ken Morrison's silver grey Aston Martin was a regular visitor.

I returned to college for my second year to be joined by one of my initial colleagues Dave Butler, a super lad who lived in a village to the East of York and who had been struck down with pleurisy the previous year, which meant he could not take the exams. Dave was a good footballer in local York Leagues, regularly netting a hat-ful of goals every Sunday, which was quite amazing, considering he spent most of every Saturday night in the pubs and clubs of Scarborough, often returning just in time to pick his boots up and go and play a match. The second year passed uneventfully and this time I managed to negotiate the exams at the end of it, leaving me free to take up RP & P's offer of fifteen month Industrial Training period, Steve Norman at this time was to return to college for his final year and I took up a lot of where he left off. I remember thinking that I should now be in good shape to finish my academic studies, remember the phrase, 'at Further Education they weed you out early'. This was shattered by a visit from John Jackson early into my Industrial Training period.

We sat down in the meeting room at Little Horton Lane and John, completely out of the blue, without any warning at all said to me 'do you really feel you are cut out for this career?', I questioned as to why and he rattled off my first year exam failure, my stuttering success on the re-sit and my not too spectacular pass at the end of year two. I was absolutely devastated by his comments and blustered very quickly that I would show him in the fullness of time what I was made of.

To his credit he accepted my word and simply said that he looked forward to being proven wrong.

During my Industrial Training Period I had a super time, RP & P were, and still are, without doubt one of the premier Quantity Surveying practices in the country, in my opinion, providing a wide range of services to a wide range of clients, and I got the full monty in terms of experience. I worked on a number of Morrison projects, including the construction of a new store, from negotiated tender with Gilbert Ash Contractors to the hand-over of the building. I worked on private sector and public sector works. I worked on Works of Maintenance for the Department of the Environment, as it was then, and much, much more. I measured Bills of Quantities and I handled final accounts. I could not ask for any more experience than I got and I returned to college in October 1971 a changed person and full of confidence.

Social life at RP & P was great for bringing someone who was basically shy out of their shell. We had bowling and cricket evenings during the summer and we had indoor football and other events during the winter. We almost always finished up in some nightclub or other in Bradford and the team spirit and bond between what was not a great number of people was fantastic.

During my Industrial Training period, I met for the first time someone who was to be, in client/consultant terms, my guardian over the many years to come: one of the most competent and able Surveyors I have ever come across, Steve Watkins. Steve, like me, reported to John Burnley, who in his turn was one of the youngest ever Surveyors to become Chartered and along with other young guns on the office, such as Geoff Emmett, Peter Hutchinson, Mike Bowmer and a host of others, we were really a quite formidable and well oiled unit. And at this time that I should refer back to my old Bingley School compatriot Colin Swift.

Colin was a year older than me and as I have said before, a brilliant artist. Late in 1972, this was demonstrated in pure technical terms, when we were all involved in the measurement of the tender documents for the then Bradford and Bingley Building Society Head Office in Bingley, euphemistically referred to as either the Hanging Gardens of Babylon, or the Wedding Cake. Designed and supervised by the now extinct Bradford architects, John Brunton and Partners, the project was huge. It was also to be built at break-neck speed, which meant that the tender process too was at break-neck, so much so that the amount of overtime I worked paid for my first ever new car, a Ford Escort, which was registered to me in November 1972.

As with most tender documents a lot of detail has to be worked up by the Surveyor and Colin produced an entire plumbing and sanitary wear layout in 3D for the building, drawn freehand and then to be measured off the architect's dimensioned drawings. I remember to this day the details of the work, which should have been framed and kept for posterity, and Colin's efforts were an exercise in preparing properly and then executing well.

This was the time I started to meet individuals and characters in the construction industry on my own.

The first individual I met, in an industry which seemed to be full of peculiar characters, was one Sylvester Ramsden, a noted Bradford steeplejack and Demolition Contractor.

Around the end of the 1960s and early 1970s the woollen textile industry in Bradford was dying. Cheap imports and cheap manufacturing abroad in emerging nations such as those in Asia were killing the industry and consequently many mills closed down, fell into disrepair or were simply bought for redevelopment. Sylvester was an acknowledged skilled steeplejack, the forerunner perhaps of the famous Fred Dibnah, who did to the Lancashire cotton mills and their chimneys, what Sylvester did to the Yorkshire woollen mills and their chimneys. He knocked them down.

Sylvester's technique was very simple, he would erect his ladders on the outside face of the chimney, scale to the top and then straddle the open funnel of the chimney while he worked his way around on his bottom, knocking out brick after brick after brick, until eventually he reached the ground still straddling the chimney. He was regularly seen pushing his ladders on a handcart around Bradford with a cheery smile, his face caked in soot and the obligatory flat cap.

I was selected to measure the final account for a Morrison store at Illingworth, on the outskirts of Halifax, a very rough slum clearance created estate of the 1960s, with many social problems. As I left Morrisons in 2009, the company was on the point of redeveloping the store in total, although it had been extended since its original build date.

During this contract, I met one Tim Garnett of local and noted northern demolition and earth moving contractors Ogden's of Otley. Tim was to go on from being a Surveyor with the firm to running their property development side and marrying one of Ogden brothers' daughters.

The form of contract for this quick build was based on what was known as the Bovis Fee System, which had been developed by Bovis to cater for numerous fitting out contracts of stores for their client Marks and Spencer. It was a noted development in the construction industry and was based on the client paying the net cost of carrying out the work, in terms of bricks, mortar, materials and labour, plus an agreed management fee which was based on the cost of a tendered document rather than the actual costs as invoiced.

The theory was that the contractor had the incentive of building at the lowest cost price, but on measurement achieving a high management fee, which would be paid irrespective of whether or not the contractor was able to reduce the construction period.

As a consequence of this, the Quantity Surveyor had to measure and agree all the separate domestic sub-contractors' accounts direct with them and not with the main contractor. Usually the Quantity Surveyor becomes involved in agreement with final accounts with Specialist Nominated Sub-contractors for works such as suspended ceilings or flooring, or mechanical and electrical services, but here we were involved with re-measuring everything.

Once the excavation had been complete, I duly met the aforementioned Tim Garnett and learned a very quick lesson.

One of the ways to accurately measure areas and thereafter calculate volumes is to triangulate irregular shape sites in order that you can accurately get the measure of an irregular shaped boundary. The area of a triangle, of course is calculated by multiplying the base by the height and dividing by two. In trying to agree the excavation final account, I discovered that there was a major discrepancy between my measure and that of Tim Garnett's and we sat in the contractor's office for over an hour with him trying to convince me I had measured it wrong, when the penny suddenly dropped, that he had calculated a number of large triangles, the dimensions of which I agreed with but he had not divided the result by two, in other words he had measured a rectangle, not a triangle. When I pointed this out to him, I was simply met with a wry smile and the quote 'well it was worth a try'. I never forgot that particular lesson.

The Morrison store was built in twenty two weeks, although it was a very basic and cheap finish and cost in the region of £220,000. The site cost £49,000 to buy in its initially stages, although the site was extended, together with the store some years later. What would you get for that sort of money today I have to ask?

The store was handed over to our client just one week before I returned to college for my final year.

During the course of my Industrial Training Period with Rex Procter, which spanned from the summer of 1970 to September 1971, I found I had more free time outside of work. The work was certainly challenging and the days were full but I found myself thinking of ways to supplement my income to see me through the relative hardship of an unsalaried final year at college. RP & P were not paying much, but it was more than nothing, even after the mandatory deduction for 'keep' to my Mother each week.

Why not combine income earning with pleasure? And so it was I returned again to the real life fascination of bus transport and decided to take what was then known as the PSV licence, a course I embarked upon in late autumn 1970.

My driving tuition was taken with the Huddersfield based haulage and bus Company, Hanson. This was part of the vast Lord Hanson empire which seemed to touch everything and every part of life in the town of Huddersfield, where it was based. The Hanson driving school was based in a suburb on one of the surrounding hillsides at Marsh, where the instruction vehicle, a beaten up, vintage single deck coach was garaged alongside the Hanson funeral fleet. At least, I thought, if I caused an accident and was unfortunate the appropriate vehicle would readily be on hand! The single deck vehicle represents nothing of what buses are about today. There was no power steering for a start, which resulted in stiff shoulders, after the first two or three lessons. The gear box was heavy duty and required a double declutch operation to change both up and down. The phenomenon of double declutching means that the clutch is disengaged between gear shifts as the gear level is moved into neutral, the foot is then lifted off the clutch pedal and then depressed again before engaging the next gear. Usually when changing down through the gear box this process was accompanied by a blip on the accelerator pedal to rev the engine and assist with smoother gear changing. There were no air brakes on this baby, only hydraulic, and the hand brake was the old hand-pull ratchet type. If you pulled it too far on it was a pig of a job to get it back off again.

After several lessons I was duly entered for and passed the test in early 1971, being awarded the famous driver's badge for display in a jacket lapel button hole. My licence number was BB64051, with the perimeter border emblazened with the word 'driver'.

Some of you will well remember the 1970s comedy films 'Confessions of a . . .', often thought as a sequel to the Carry On films. Far from boring you with my exploits, I would recommend a book which I recall, The Weekend Coach Driver written by a chap who is famous in the world of vehicle preservation and writing, David Weyman, who went down a very similar path to myself. Maybe my exploits are for another version!

1. *Home from the war – how it all started. Phyllis Thompson and leading aircraftsman Stanley Owen, at the end of World War two*

2. *Cross border liaisons – the Big Date. Red Rose Owens to the left, William Junior, William Senior, Ronald, Elva and Margaret, the happy couple, proud mum Nellie Thompson, Vivien (William Junior's wife), proud dad Ernest and Stanley Thomas, husband of Elva*

3. *Anyone for the Grand National?! – Bridlington aged two and a half*

4. *The scarecrow aged four and a half*

5. *Opening the batting for Lancashire at Cleveleys, August 1955*

6. *Founder member of the Wolf Cub pack*

7. *Holidays further afield, Bournemouth, 1959*

8. *The Bournemouth trolley bus on its turntable at Christchurch, 1959*

9. Year one at Bingley 'Tech', 1960, I'm back row, fourth from left, with Steve Knight, next but one on my left, Wilf King who introduced me to Bradford League cricket next to Steve, lifelong friend Keith Whavell, middle row, over the teacher's left shoulder, Terry Lister, next to him and budding footballer Michael Donohue, second from left, front row, with form master Bob Green

10. *Growing older and full of testosterone! The same group, 1963–64. Wilf King back row, first left, Steve Knight, back row, fourth from right, Michael Donohue, standing, fourth from left, Keith Whavell, front row, left, me and Terry Lister, front row, third and fourth from left*

CHAPTER 6

Off With the Jeans and On With the Suit

I RETURNED TO LEEDS POLYTECHNIC for my final year of study in October 1971, hugely encouraged by my time at RP & P, for my Industrial Training and the range of work I had been involved with. My confidence had lifted as an individual, being exposed on a day-to-day basis to some very, very competent people. I also had the added bonus of being the student rep for the department and was to attend several meetings during the year with tutors and others regarding the Polytechnic's plans for future development.

Part of my final year study was a unit which was allocated to a specific project and the students had to pick, have vetted and approved and thereafter produce a project on a particular construction related subject. The final version would find a copy being sited in the Polytechnic library. I picked Contract in its Varying Forms and set out to analyse the differences between the various construction contracts for building, civil engineering and so on and provisions for various elements. This brought me to my first notice of the 'God' of Contract Law in construction terms, one Donald Keating QC, who later was to become Sir Donald, now deceased, but a man who I would come into direct conflict with in my early days on the Morrison Board, more of which later.

The final college year for the now diminished group of twelve seemed to pass very quickly. We were tutored by an extremely competent Quantity Surveyor, by the name of Ray Whitrod, who together with one of his former partners had written a book on measurement. My project tutor was Alan Spedding, who went on to be a Senior Lecturer at other colleges, and in addition to working hard we had a quite good social life, including my very first business venture, in partnership with the aforementioned Andy Sedgwick and another man of the North East, Paul Davison. Andy came from Northallerton and was a staunch Middlesbrough fan, whereas Paul was Darlington born and bred and a big 'Darlo' fan.

I cannot remember the exact facts as to whether Middlesbrough had drawn with Manchester United, at Old Trafford, or whether the Cup match concerned was simply a tie at the old Ayresome Park, but the three of us decided that there was opportunity to subsidise our finances by becoming ticket touts for the match.

Consequently, the three of us squeezed into Andy's MG Midget, drove to Old Trafford, purchased quite a few tickets and duly presented ourselves outside the gates of Ayresome Park, for what was an afternoon kick-off, midweek, caused by the uncertainty of power supplies and therefore the availability of flood lighting. We all three strolled around outside the ground trying to look suitably furtive and suspicious, with my student beard, Andy's long hair and our various assortment of jackets, looking very much the part. Unfortunately, we had counted without the problems of an afternoon kick-off and people being unable to break from work to attend the match and ended up having to sell the tickets for face value, resulting in us being minus the petrol costs and other sundry expenses, such as beer at Old Trafford and so on. We did see the funny side of it.

I had been told that a full-time job awaited me back at Rex Procter in the summer of 1972, subject to my exam results, and the year passed very quickly with me turning in what even I would describe as some quite good work.

My dissertation of Contract and Contract Law was typed up by Mum, who polished up some of her old skills for the project, and I finished the year in second place, jointly with the same John Jenkins, from the Gower, with us both missing a distinction by only fractions of a percentage. So much for John Jackson's prophecy and suggestion that I was not cut out to get through the course.

I joined RP & P full time at the beginning of June 1972 and my new life started.

Initially things were very much to be picked up as I had left them off, including finalising some of the Final Accounts for projects that I had been working on prior to my return to college. The practice was extremely busy and numbers were short. There was also the added complication that there had been a national construction industry strike during the early months of 1972, which had delayed all sorts of projects and led to various contractual disputes, which the Quantity Surveyor is always the front line for settling.

I returned to work under the tutelage of the same John Burnley and was promptly given the Final Account for a Morrison Superstore in the Merrion Centre in Leeds, a relatively modern shopping centre, which had been extended to include a new store. The building strike had caused delay and my first two visits were somewhat hairy, having to pass through the lines of picketing builders, indeed, my first visit saw me arrive in the safety of the site cabins covered in spit, not a pleasant experience. Fortunately, the strike finished within the first couple of weeks of my full time employment and matters returned to normal, but the delays were not recovered.

The Morrison project brought me my first brush with Morrison management and in particular Main Board Director Ken Blundell, who was responsible for the stores, and his Area Director, George Buttle. It was the latter who got me into trouble, although the trouble was largely of my own making.

I had attended site to agree the measure with the painting sub-contractor, not an easy task as the store had no suspended ceilings and therefore all the profiles of the various steel sections, the roof decking, the ventilation trunking, service pipe work and so on and so on had to be measured, in addition to the flat surfaces of the external walls. The two of us duly set about the measure and I had to keep my wits about me, as the director of Crown Point Decorators was indeed a wily old fox. As we reached the end of the first wall of the building, I noticed a painter still working away applying a gloss finish to some timber batons and as I was about to enquire as to what this work was, a voice behind me firmly said 'don't be measuring that, he's a Morrisons painter and we are paying for it'. I turned round to see someone I didn't know, but who it later transpired was the same George Buttle.

I am not one for boring readers by giving blow-for-blow accounts, suffice to say that on no less than three separate occasions, as myself and the painter walked around the store, the same George Buttle interrupted with the same phrase of 'don't measure that, we've painted it'. By this time the young Owen was getting somewhat exasperated. I did actually know what was in the contract and what wasn't and on the third or fourth such interruption, I rather snappily advised Mr Buttle that I did know what I was doing.

George Buttle had been brought up very much from day one in Morrisons and if a halfpenny could be saved on a penny, he and the rest of the management team would move all they could to ensure that it happened, and George was certainly demonstrating to me that he knew how to do this and that this was his task. I didn't begrudge him advising me but really did not need the constant reminders, and clearly George took my rather short answer as being one of dismissal. For my part I thought no further of it, until I returned to the office.

'Don't take your coat off, go straight up to Mr Curry' were the words which greeted me in the reception area as arrived back in Bradford from the Morrison site. I duly knocked on the door, was greeted by a bellowed 'Come in, shut the door, what the f****** hell do you think you are playing at!' This was followed by a series of sentence upon sentence of expletives, far too many to mention here, which alluded to the fact that my boss had had his colleague on the Morrison board and client of RP & P on the phone, questioning the dismissive attitude of a young Surveyor called Owen at the Merrion Centre store. I was told that the last thing you did was upset clients, my protestations to the contrary went unheard and I was instructed to get into my car, go to the client's office immediately and do whatever was necessary to apologise to an apparently very upset Ken Blundell 'who is paying your wage'.

I duly drove the one and a half miles or so and presented myself to the rather daunting receptionist, Mrs Hartley, who also doubled as Ken Blundell's secretary. I was then directed to his office, which was to me very large, had his desk in the corner diagonally opposite the main entrance door, and a stunning white carpet. As I entered Ken, who was later to become my colleague on the Morrison Board, looked over the top of his glasses. Ken Blundell was a man of few words, who had a very serious bark and as I found out in later life a potentially lethal bite when he chose to use it, which, fortunately, was not very often.

I was firstly invited to sit down and then asked if I wanted a cup of tea, which I declined on the basis that my trembling hand might spill it over his pristine white carpet. I was then asked to explain my actions and I started by profusely apologising if I had upset Mr Buttle, that it would not happen again, and more to the point that I did actually know what I was supposed to be measuring and what I was not.

I sat back and waited for the volcano to erupt. Ken looked over the top of his glasses again, smiled rather urbanely, as he was prone to do, and said he was sure I knew what I was doing, but he often liked to make the point with Ron Curry, as 'I know how to wind him up'. He went on to say that nevertheless it was important that costs were not incurred twice, that Morrisons ran a very tight ship, that every penny counted, then very graciously accepted my apology on behalf of himself and George Buttle and proceeded to spend the next thirty minutes asking me about my college life and what my ambitions were at RP & P. He said he felt we ought to spend some time, as if I returned to the office too quickly, Ron Curry would not be convinced that I had had a suitable bollocking and further that Ken was sure 'you will look suitable chastised when you next see Ron'. We shared the secret as indeed we shared others over the years. I know that George Buttle was in on it and he and I often joked over our years together at Morrisons, about that first meeting.

RP & P at that time were involved in some quite large projects. In addition to the Bradford and Bingley Building Society HQ, which had part paid for my first new car, the practice was involved in a large scale shopping development in Leeds, known as the Bond Street Centre, numerous school rebuild projects, commercial office development work throughout the North and the bread and butter stuff of rebuilding bridges for British Rail, as well as Department of the Environment work in Post Offices, Sorting Offices, Telephone Exchanges, Tax Offices . . . the list was endless. We never seemed to be short of work and the Partners' preferred business model of not overstaffing but working consistently hard was a major bonus to me, as it threw me into all sorts of experiences and very solid grounding of working for various clients, with various different methods of reporting requirements and so on.

John Burnley, to whom I reported, was very much the rising star of the practice. He was absolutely brilliant and was kept as the retained contact for all Morrisons work, so in addition to the work I carried out on the new Morrisons store in Halifax during my Industrial Training Period I was quickly thrown into other work, primary involving an extension to the fairly recently built Head Office and Distribution centre in Bradford. This was not a large job and John, very confidently, decided that I should be able to manage most of the Tender Documents myself and thereafter managed the Final Account.

About this time two large-scale projects came on stream, in the wilds of East Yorkshire in Scarborough. These were to be commercial redevelopment projects of two former hotels, the Balmoral and the Pavilion, which had fallen victim to the decline experienced in many British holiday resorts. They were past their best and not fit for redevelopment or refurbishment.

The Balmoral development was to be carried out for a London client by the name of Parking Management, whilst the Pavilion Hotel scheme was to be carried out for Teesland Properties, an offshoot of the Bovis conglomerate, as I recall. This brought me into contact with another noted (and I use the word advisedly) Bradford based demolition contractor, Arnold Marriott, and this was to start a relationship that lasted for many years, through to my Morrison days. Arnold will crop up from time to time in the following chapters, but I devote a section to him here.

I have previously described the working methods of the famous Sylvester Ramsden, whose reign with RP & P finished when he was demolishing the chimney of an old laundry, purchased by Morrison supermarkets and converting into a new store in the Bankfoot area of Bradford. The store had opened and the clients had decided that the old laundry chimney should come down for safety purposes. Sylvester, for reasons best known to himself, did not demolish in his usual bottom shuffling manner around the perimeter of the chimney, but decided to fell the chimney in one go, resulting in most of it falling into the supermarket's warehouse. Then there followed an insurance claim, the client's insurers did not want the damaged products and Sylvester, it is rumoured, spent the next two months eating three square meals a day, of cornflakes. Thus ended his chapter.

Arnold Marriott and his partner Barry Gomersal were a different kettle of fish altogether, they had mechanical plant! They came on the scene at a point in time where West Yorkshire's prime demolition and excavation contractors Ogden's of Otley were pricing themselves out of the market and looking to diversify into other areas such as property development. Arnold had worked in demolition for other contractors, before setting up his own company DCD, more fully known as Demolition and Commercial Disposals. As a reader of this you will need to recall, or perhaps take yourself back to days where Health and Safety did not rule as it does today. Short cuts were taken based on the demolition man's experience and knowledge of buildings and for the most part these short cuts were successful. Many of the people employed in the industry however were, by nature, somewhat itinerant and drifted from contractor to contractor, leaving behind them a trail of unrepaired damage, or in some instances even worse.

I was appointed by John Burnley to administer the final accounts of the Scarborough projects: the Balmoral, to be carried out on a tradition JCT form of contract and the Pavilion, to be carried out on the Bovis Fee System, with which I had become quite familiar through my experiences on Morrison projects.

The Balmoral was to comprise a small shopping mall and multi-storey car park together with a larger store, which was to be occupied and operated by Tesco, a company who, even in those days, were notoriously aggressive in their business approach, and their Property Director Francis Kreja was noted as being quite ruthless and more than capable of overturning tables in meetings and so on. The client was essentially a one-man commercial property company which lacked major experience and had employed a very small architectural practice and equally small engineering practice, the latter of which was nevertheless very competent.

Arnold Marriott's company were appointed to carry out the demolition on both sites and he also won a third contract to demolish another hotel in the town, the Cambridge, for a third client, unconnected with my work at RP & P.

Work commenced, but needless to say the boys from Bradford very quickly became distracted by the bright lights of the seaside, the visiting day trippers, particularly of the female variety, and of course the local girls who were more than happy with the influx of new company. Work very quickly fell behind programme and industrial unrest was threatening the country.

Not long into the contract I visited the Balmoral site, with Arnold's large crane and concrete ball well in action swinging away madly and creating a huge gap in the streetscape of the Yorkshire holiday resort.

A small group of his men were gathered around a brand new tipper wagon which had its cab angled away from the norm, and two heads perched over the engine. Upon questioning I was told that the engine refused to start but not to worry they were going to tow it off the site and bump start the vehicle. I was not particularly well versed in the system and vagaries of air brakes, but I did know that they were designed to fail safe, which meant that if the pressure dropped the brakes would go on and not come off again. I was quickly assured the brakes were disconnected and that upon the engine firing the tow truck would stop and all would be well. Arnold, of course, forgot one key thing, that having disconnecting the air supply to the brakes there was no pressure, and true enough the engine did fire as the wagon was being towed across the site, by Arnold's fourteen year old son driving another vehicle. A toot on the horn signalled the tow truck to stop, where upon the following vehicle, brand new or not, crashed into the back, spilled its windscreen all over the site and did various other damage.

Undeterred by what would have been a disaster to most people, Arnold calmly announced that the brand new truck would remain in service as a site run-around and would be repaired on its return to Bradford. This remained the case for the balance of the contract period, which was finished weeks beyond its due date.

Whilst running backwards and forwards to Scarborough, on one particular afternoon, I spied the damaged truck being towed out of Scarborough through a small village called Seamer at about 3 p.m., and as I returned back to West Yorkshire in the early evening I discovered the truck in a lay-by just outside the same village. I called Arnold the following day and questioned why. I was told his men had left Scarborough just before closing time (in those days there were no unlimited licensing hours) and had set off to tow the truck back to Bradford, but had quickly realised that they would not be back in time for opening at 5.30 p.m., being burdened by the extra weight and speed of the broken down truck, therefore they decided to abandon it and would collect it later since the truck was in a lay-by adjacent to a fairly large scrap yard.

As time went by I made almost weekly visits at one or other of my two sites, I spied that the truck was slowly disappearing in front of my eyes, firstly the doors went, then the wheels, then the actual tipper body. On each occasion I telephoned Arnold and questioned what the progress was, to be met by an almost standard reply of 'we'll get round to collecting it soon'. Arnold's modus-operandi on most issues was 'get round to it soon' and eventually the remains of the truck disappeared completely. I called Arnold again to tell him I had noticed this to be met with the response 'you wouldn't believe it, some bastard's nicked it', and 'we'll now have to claim on insurance, it was brand new you know.' Whether or not Arnold got his new truck I will never know, but I suspect a closer examination of the scrap yard would have given the answer to the fate of the old vehicle.

Whilst carrying out his various projects in Scarborough, Arnold would invariably move his crawler-mounted crane from one site to another on the road in the dead of night. Even in those days this was not allowed and the site of a very large crane complete with its extended jib grinding across the famous Valley Bridge in Scarborough on route to the Cambridge Hotel, must have been something to be believed. Arnold finished his two projects for RP & P behind schedule, to the further detriment to the Cambridge Hotel, where the client apparently became very 'arsy', to use Arnold's word, and threatened major deduction of damages and court action for non-completion.

At this point even the redoubtable Mr Marriott was worried and ordered that his men complete the demolition by whatever means necessary, and it was at this point that he hit the headlines in the local evening paper.

Apparently, his men, buoyed up by the promise of big overtime payments, first went out and spent their overtime money in the local hostelries and then decided they would finish the job, fortified by numerous pints of Tetley's Yorkshire bitter. Using the surrounding streetlights, they commenced work with the large concrete ball and chain only to succeed, one by one, in knocking out the lighting columns around the site. Anxious neighbours called the police and Arnold's biggest claim to fame was that they had convinced the North Yorkshire Constabulary that the building was in such a dangerous state it had to come down there and then, at which point additional police patrol cars were summoned and the demolition was finished courtesy of the headlights of four squad cars around the perimeter of the site. Arnold avoided the threat of damages from his client! At the end of those summer months, when the bad weather came in, the various occupiers of the shops adjoining the Balmoral site realised that much of the lead flashings on their roofs was missing.

Who is to say where, or who was responsible for this, but everyone had a good idea. Not unlike the time when contractors were building the M606 motorway link from the M62 trans-Pennine route into Bradford and a large earth moving machine went missing.

Word got around as to who might have been responsible. The police apparently were on the case and to this day the machine is allegedly buried underneath Bradford's wholesale fruit and veg market.

What a character!

Whilst involved in the Scarborough project I met and was involved in a rather curious piece of construction. The Balmoral had a six storey multi-storey car park, which was constructed by a company called British Lift Slab, a subsidiary of the large UK engineering company RM Douglas, based in Birmingham. The form of construction was unique, in that each of the floors was cast in situ on the ground and then literally lifted into place by large jacks placed on the tops of the various support columns. We had the unique situation where a very thin slab of concrete, the grade slab, was placed on the ground and finished with the appropriate brush finish to give a light ribbing effect. The first floor was then poured on top of it and finished in the same manner, thereby each floor provided the formwork for the subsequent floors and all six levels were poured on the ground and then lifted into place. The lifting process was unbelievable, at the rate of a few inches each hour, and hour-by-hour, day-by-day, week-by-week, the car park emerged as if by magic.

Progress was not good, as by now threat of industrial action against the Heath Government had materialised, and all areas of the country were suffering power cuts of four hours or so, Scarborough not being immune.

As the scheme was taking most of the capacity of the Scarborough Ready Mixed Concrete Works this made life very difficult. I visited site during one of the power outages to find plant standing idle, and was invited by the crew of a piling rig operated by Expanded Piling of Grimsby to descend the pile bore they had just completed and check the dimensions.

For the non-technical of you there are various ways of piling a site, depending on the ground conditions, for example in Holland where it is very sandy and unstable ground, concrete piles which are pre-cast are driven into the ground at small centres to give an overall stabilising effect, where as in clay conditions piles are often bored by what appears to be a giant corkscrew, known as an auger, which drills down into the ground and is then brought out to spread the excavated material over the surrounding area, before being reinserted to continue its task until the required depth is achieved. At this point a bell is bored out in order to anchor the bottom of the pile and it was this dimension I was invited to check.

As I have said earlier, all of this took place in the days before Health and Safety was a primary concern and I was inserted in to what could only be described as a wire mesh torpedo tube and lowered by a huge crane some fifteen metres below ground. Health and Safety at this point comprised of the ground crew talking to you at regular intervals to ensure that you had not been gassed by some earth generated methane, or other nasty. When I arrived at the bottom of the pile bore, I was invited to get out and measure the diameter of the 'bell mouth', this I did and found it was accurate, almost to the millimetre. At this point the wire cage disappeared and I was left with the company of a flashlight and loud laughter from somewhere in the distance, above my head.

After what seemed an eternity and just before the onset of panic, I was warned that the wire cage was descending and I sought refuge in it and started my ascent to the surface and safety – some hope! Approximately half way through the journey the cage came to a juddering halt and I was told that the crawler-mounted crane had run out of fuel, quickly followed by a rapid descent of about five metres or so caused, allegedly, by brake failure. Again after a break of probably no more than a minute, which seemed like a lifetime, my journey to the surface recommenced, this time uninterrupted, and I was greeted by four faces contorted with laughter and told how pale I looked. Initiation in all trades is always the same.

During the course of my time on the Scarborough projects I was to meet a young surveyor from Bovis, or Gilbert Ash Northern, as it became during the course of the contract, or later in the contract Ackroyd and Abbott, based at their Darlington offices. A young man by the name of Tony Cooper, who eventually left and set up his own construction and then development company and actually carried out work for Morrisons in my time there. These were all good days, with great experience and meeting some hard guys.

The three-day week and power cuts interrupted the way of life and reeked havoc with the construction programme and almost with me personally.

By now I had become aware that British Leyland, or was it still BMC, were to launch a limited edition Morris Marina, titled The Jubilee. This was to be a horrendous shade of canary yellow with a vinyl roof, a four-door saloon, but the real clincher for me was that it was powered by a 1.8 litre MGB GT engine.

I managed to order one from the local dealer, Cox of Keighley, and traded in my fifteen month old Ford Escort, which had served me well. The new car, registration OWT 7M, duly arrived in September 1973 and it was during the following winter and the three-day week that the Government introduced a voluntary fifty-mile per hour speed limit, in order to conserve fuel. Dashing to a meeting in Scarborough one day along the A64 duel carriageway, between York and Malton, I was clocked at 103 miles per hour, which was just about flat out for the car and certainly was not safe, for the brakes and the suspension did not match up to the power. In those days the only stretches of dual carriageway between Leeds and Scarborough were a section between Leeds and York and the section upon which I was caught, and in those days you had to navigate the centres of such towns as Tadcaster, York itself and Malton, which were a nightmare in the summer months and during race meetings.

I was duly stopped by the police and after pleading guilt but necessity, I was allowed off with a very, very severe warning as to the irresponsible consumption of the nation's scarce fuel resources.

The consequences of the three-day week led me to my first big meeting with a client. Ron Curry, the Senior Partner and John Burnley, my boss were unable to attend, when the client's new funders had called a meeting to discuss what was, by then, clearly a financial crisis. Frank Palmer, one of the Senior Partners at RP & P Leeds office was an expert on contract law and arbitration. In addition, he was a co-author of the Quantity Surveyors' bible, *The Standard Method of Measurement*, and was deputed to go to the meeting, with me as his back up. I hardly slept the two nights prior to our big trip to London and arrived at Leeds City Station loaded up with every file I could imagine we needed, to be met by the cigar smoking Frank, with a rolled copy of the *Yorkshire Post* and a document case in which he had a notebook.

We boarded the Yorkshire Pullman for King's Cross and in those days every table in first class was set for full English breakfast. Frank seemed to know everyone, either by name or by sight, and I eagerly spread out some key documents on the table. 'No need for that son,' said Frank, 'we'll have breakfast first'. This was all a big treat for the local boy but I could not do justice to the full English as my stomach was churning, and Frank seemed in no hurry at all to discuss the upcoming problems of the day. I believe we were almost at Stevenage, some thirty minutes from King's Cross, when he showed any interest at all in the problems and I hastily tried to advise him.

We attended our meeting and the architect in particular, a man rather inaptly named Robin Bird, was particularly nervous. There had been issues with the flow of information, but fortunately the Engineer had been majorly involved with a lot of the elements of the building and had 'bailed out' the architect.

The client was concerned as to whether or not he had grounds to determine the contract with Gilbert Ash, and Frank, or simply FP, as he was known in the practice, calmly sat back drawing on another cigar and proceeded to give his usual sage advice. The client's view was that he should not pay the upcoming Interim Certificate when it was due to the contractor and Frank was on the point of agreeing with this, until I advised that to do so could give the contractor grounds to determine the contract, which would not be good in terms of overall progress and getting someone else to start up in the middle of the three-day week. FP very quickly adjusted his footwork, gave the advice and we came away with compliments of the client in our ears to be followed a couple of days later by a very nice letter to Ron Curry, the Senior Bradford Partner.

By the end of 1974, I realised just what experience I was getting across a good cross-section of work types and client types, but I was very aware that I was in a queue of young and budding colleagues. By this time I had failed my final qualifying examination of the Royal Institution of Chartered Surveyors, on two occasions. The first I had put down to the fact that I was too busy to do the proper studying, but the second occasion had been a disappointment to me and I was now at a point where I was having a more active social life with a very good circle of friends and I wanted to be clear of the encumbrance of exams. Additionally, I felt that the lack of a professional qualification put me in a line for promotion behind the likes of my colleagues. Geoff Emmett was, or was about to be, appointed an Associate, Peter Hutchinson the same, Messrs Burnley and Wilson were now Partners and the young bloods of my era were qualified, in particular Steve Watkins, Steve Norman and Colin Swift. I saw professional practice and the promotion ladder as very much 'dead men's shoes' and saw myself a way down the line. This started to niggle at me and I shared my concerns with John Burnley.

Work continued through the end of 1974 and was generally good, I had had a number of girlfriends, social life in the office was great, I was following my beloved Bradford City, out on the tiles with my mates when girls were not involved, but I had a nagging doubt at the back of my mind. Had the examination 'yipps' struck again, and was I ever to make it? Was John Jackson's prophecy of the late 1960s to come true? Was I doomed to be one of the boiler room boys and not someone who was making a mark?

Clarity to all these issues came at the start of February 1975. I was finalising some negotiations with the contractor for the Morrison Head Office warehouse extension and was on site doing some measuring, when I received an approach from one of the warehouse operatives, who asked who I was, and upon notification, advised that I should go to the Head Office reception, as Ron Curry wanted to speak to me.

I duly appeared in front of the same redoubtable Stella Hartley, who had given me 'the treatment' during my earlier visit to Ken Blundell and was directed to Ron Curry's office, whereupon he proceeded to tell me that things had not worked out with the incumbent Estates Manager Alan Williamson, who had been in-post for approximately twelve months. The operations people, Ron's in-house client, were not happy and he was contemplating a change. Would I be interested in the position?

Ron knew that I was not qualified and that I was about to sit the Final exams for a third time and this was really make or break for me. I said I was concerned about ongoing professional training, should I join Morrisons and fail my exams, but I would be interested, but would like the weekend to think about it. I was also due two weeks holiday, which I was going to devote 100% to studying for my finals.

I was still living at home at this time and sat down to discuss the day's proposal with my parents. I saw immediately the flicker of disappointment across their faces. This was the son who had set this mind on a professional career with letters behind his name and was now contemplating joining the local grocer, but Mum quickly tempered this by what became a classic expression of 'Well, I suppose people will always have to eat.' Mum had grown up with the Morrisons presence in Bradford of a stall in Rawson market, where Ken's mother, Hilda had been a regular 'barker' and was not familiar with the new Morrison Supermarket concept.

I spent a lot of time over that weekend contemplating what I should do. I had not discussed terms with Ron, I was concerned about my studies and more concerned about my ongoing future if I was to fail, but in the end I decided I should take a leap, have faith that I would pass my exams and join something which may, or may not, be at the ground floor of future success.

The following Monday I returned to the office and gave Ron Curry my answer, together with my reservations, which brought a quite curt response in respect of my exams: 'Well you'd better make sure that you pass, then.' At that point I worked the remainder of the day, told my colleagues, packed my bags and went on two weeks holiday to study.

I was probably one of very few people in my arena of work to have been the subject of a transfer fee, whereby Rex Procter forewent its right to me working notice in exchange for a commitment from Morrisons that I would spend one day a week or so working on RP & P business, until my commitments had been cleared.

I had first met Ron Curry regarding my change of career on 21 February 1975, I went off on study leave and took my final exams on 3 March, and started at Morrisons the day after. There was no time for a leaving do, I just had to get my head sorted for the RICS and the future.

I left Rex Procter on a salary of £2,900 per annum to join Morrisons for £100 per year more, plus a company car, which turned out to be a Ford Capri. The 1.8 litre Marina went, the 1.6 litre Capri in its glorious puce purple colour came in, and I started my conversion to grocery.

CHAPTER 7

Bricks to Beans – The Conversion Begins

AFTER THE TRAUMAS OF THE previous three weeks or so, I sat my final RICS exams in Leeds on 3 March 1975 and felt surprisingly confident prior to and after the event. As opposed to my two previous failures which I had, perhaps selfishly, put down to hard work in the office and lack of study, I believed that the study break prior to the exam had done me a lot of good. I had put time in despite some girlfriend issues and genuinely came out of the examination hall feeling that I had done my best and could do no more.

The following day I reported to Ron Curry at 9.00 a.m. at Morrisons Head Quarters in Thornton Road, Bradford, Hilmore House, named after the Chairman's mother. Ron introduced me to the main key players on the Board and advised me that he had negotiated a seat in the Management dining room for me, where a three-course lunch was available at no cost. I then received my job description and a pep talk that my first aim should be to gain Board of Management status. This was the Junior Board made up largely of Heads of Department throughout the business, representing Personnel, IT, Manufacturing, Retailing, Produce, Property and so on. I was introduced to John Dowd the Personnel Director and his staff, who gave me a very brief induction and then Ron said he had the first project for me to work on and would introduce me to the Administration Manager, Rod Smaldon. Mr Smaldon wanted some of the open plan offices converted to cater for an expansion of his department and a new office creating for himself.

Hilmore House had been a very cheap building, having largely been made up of a pre-cast concrete frame structure, which was manufactured for a textile company in St Helens who had gone bust just before delivery was due. The manufacturers/installers, Leedsford Structures, who did a lot of Morrison store work, were looking to offload, and Ron had bought the frame at a very cheap price. The interior of the building had been fitted out just with simple timber frames and glazed windows on all floors, with corridors down the centre.

Ron walked me through the offices on the way and introduced me to more people, all of whom were extremely nice, and I remarked on it. Ron's retort was 'it will change when you meet Smaldon, he's an arrogant little bugger, but he has the ear of a few people'. Walking into Rod's office I was absolutely horrified: he sat behind his desk, smoking a cigar, feet on desk and never moved when Ron, a Main Board Director, entered the room. I wondered what my boss's reception and reaction would have been if one of his surveyors at RP & P had done the same. I think there may have been a broken window, with a body hurtling through it.

I duly took my instructions and organised the work. I had been told in no uncertain terms that my predecessor had achieved, quite rapidly, a reputation for non-delivery and that various people through the company, particularly Ken Blundell and his Operations team were thoroughly cheesed-off and I needed to put this right, quick time. My diary entry for the end of my first day reads 'an interesting day – is going to be hard – very big backlog of work to be shifted'.

At the start of my second week I was summoned to the garage to pick up my new car. Lined up were three identical specification Ford Capris, one all white, one light tan with a dark tan vinyl roof, one puce/purple. I selected the last on the basis that it was metallic paint which I had never had and it was simply different. In later years Lena, who had seen it before we started our relationship, described it as more akin to a brothel on wheels, but I didn't care, it was the company's responsibility to maintain it and on top of all that I got £25 each month for petrol money, a sum which I very quickly expended on business alone, let alone the active social life I was leading.

At this time I was seeing my old mate Keith Whawell who by now was living and working in Wakefield, going out for drinks with former workmates Dick Earnshaw and Bob Stephenson, seeing my mates at football, playing squash nearly every Saturday with Geoff Emmett from Rex Procter, together with the occasional Friday night drink, and at the same time I could be seen on a Friday at the rather

notorious Keighley Variety Club with others from RP & P, most
notably the late Stuart Humphries.

For some time previously I had been seeing Pam Parnell, a ward
sister at Bradford's second hospital St Luke's, situated not 200 metres
from RP & P's offices. Pam was a Scarborough girl whom I had met
at a party. At the time she was tipped to be the next matron at St
Luke's and we were of similar ages. On the occasions of her days off,
coinciding with my 'transfer fee' RP & P trips to Scarborough, I
would take her over to her parents and even on one occasion, was
invited to stay, although her mother quietly made it clear to me that
she had very good hearing in the night, if there was to be any
movement around the house. Eventually the relationship came to a
close in July of my first year at Morrisons.

The first six months of my time at Morrisons were a blur. I
regularly worked a six day, or even seven day week, punctuated by
one or two days each week being allocated to RP & P work, with
travels on successive days into Scarborough. I was really clocking up
the mileage and the hours, so much so that after a few weeks I
decided to keep diary entries for the number of hours I had worked
each day, and the first few weeks of these entries averaged at
something in the order of sixty six hours each week – add that to a
fairly active social life and I realised fairly quickly that I needed to
pace myself.

In May a letter arrived bearing the greatest possible news for my
career. My thoughts on leaving the examination hall back in March
had been justified and I had passed my final exams and would be
inducted into The Royal Institution of Chartered Surveyors – what
a major relief. A few months later I was to attend Leeds and sign the
RICS register, under the watchful gaze of John Smallwood. John was
Senior Partner of the Keighley estate agents Dacre, Son and Hartley
and indeed has written a book of his own about his career as a
surveyor and auctioneer in West Yorkshire, interesting reading. I was
so pleased, it was unbelievable and the relief was palpable, giving me
renewed vigour for my new job.

At this time the Morrison estate consisted of twelve stores around
Bradford, these being located in Bradford suburbs at Bolton Junction
(the site of an old Bradford City bus depot); Mayo Avenue in the
Bankfoot area, the scene of Sylvester Ramsden's chimney demolition

escapade; Park Avenue, in the middle of a large Bradford council estate and backing onto the old Bradford Park Avenue football ground and Yorkshire County cricket ground; Victoria shopping centre, which had initially been the old cinema, retained and let to a furniture retailer, with a new late 1960s build store on it; Westgate in the City Centre; Keighley, one of the most distant from Head Office; Sticker Lane on the Bradford ring road; Halifax, upon which I had worked during my Industrial Training period; Merrion Centre Leeds, where I had been spat on during the national building strike; Morley, to the south of Leeds; Bramley, another suburb, towards the Bradford boundary; and Yeadon, in the suburbs to the North of Leeds.

In addition to these stores there was a self-service supermarket at Vicar Lane in Leeds, which had been the forerunner of the Merrion Centre store and was under negotiation for disposal when I joined, together with the old Morrison market stall, in Bradford city centre. Gone were the discount self-service stores of Bradford city centre. The old Head Office and warehouse just off Manchester Road had been replaced with a brand new purpose-built facility in Thornton Road, which allowed the company to stock something in the order of 75% of the lines it sold and redistribute them to stores on its own transport fleet. The furthest distance from Head Office was probably no more than fifteen miles in a straight line, so when I tell you that I clocked up something in the order of 20,000 miles a year, you will conclude for yourself how hard I worked, or perhaps how active a social life I led.

There were no new stores planned for 1975, but Ron Curry was very busy working on plans for 1976 and of course, site acquisition, planning consent and tenders all have to be achieved before a single spade can be put in the ground. We had planned four new stores: at Mayo Avenue in Bradford, to replace Sylvester's laundry disaster, Rothwell and Hunslet to the south side of Leeds and Horsforth, to the north side of Leeds. In addition there was to be a new fruit and veg pack house to replace the facility we had within the Head Office warehouse, and a new wines and spirits and tobacco warehouse. Things were moving and the increase in floor area represented by these developments was a major step forward for a small company.

Clearly the onset of work load, particularly the backlog of alteration work within the stores and so on, required that I could not do this on my own and within two months of starting work Ron and I recruited our first technical member of staff, one Keith Atkinson, as a trainee building surveyor. Keith came to us from a local building contractor, J&J Obank, and as I left the company 34 years later he is still there, now in the role of Project Manager.

The developments which we had in place when I joined the company had attached to them in some instances a number of small shop units, duplicating the role as town centre, or local centre shopping developments. These were situated primarily at Girlington in Bradford, and Yeadon and Morley in Leeds, and drew a rental income of some £45,000 per annum. One of the key result areas in my original job description was to improve this situation.

My first formal meeting with my client, Ken Blundell and his Store Operations Team did not quite get off on the right foot. Being that I had been absent for two of my first four days on RP & P business, I decided that my first full week at Morrisons would see me 'making my mark', and I resolved that I would start going around the stores, since I had been introduced to Ken previously and nothing had been said about a Store Operations induction. I set off with happy heart to the Halifax store, picking this because I knew its construction and had been round it from the foundations to the finishing day and by doing so I thought it might impress the local general manager. I duly arrived and was engaged in some intense conversation about my predecessor and what was outstanding, when I was told that KB, as Ken Blundell was known, or KJB to others, was on the telephone. A rather gruff voice told me that I should not have gone to the store, he wanted to take me round all the stores himself, or with his two Regional Directors, Steve Butler and George Buttle, and that I should return to Head Office immediately. I did so with some trepidation, but was met with a genial 'I know you're trying, but let's do it properly.'

He proceeded then to take me to the nearest store, Victoria Shopping Centre, within walking distance of Head Office, and I learnt my first lesson.

As we were walking up and down the aisles, me a couple of paces ahead of him, a gruff voice from behind suddenly said 'Oi!'. I stopped, turned round and was met with KB pointing at some cardboard on the floor. He then followed by lecturing me that management, including management not involved with stores, should not walk past things like this, as they were a hazard to the public. This was followed by a lecture on what to do if I ever came across a pool of spilt cooking oil, or similar, which someone could potentially fall and break a limb upon. To this day I have never walked past anything again!

In those early days the Head Office warehouse, immediately adjoining the office block itself, was the scene, not just of storage for grocery items, but also included a cheese packing area, fresh food factory, bacon smoking (when it wasn't on fire) and some fruit and vegetable packing. All this could be accommodated because, of course, volumes and numbers of stores were quite small.

Within no more than three weeks of me starting within the Company we acquired our first automated packing line, which could be used to pack tomatoes and some fruits, but was principally involved with the packing of the former. The equipment was temperamental and regularly failed during the course of the normal working day, leaving output volumes way down on store order volumes. What to do?

There followed some three weeks of heavy engineering activity trying to resolve the problems and the packing volumes were made up by members of the Board and Senior Management staying behind every night for anything up to two hours packing product. If the elements had been properly costed I think that those would have been the most expensive tomatoes ever produced, but slowly and surely the problems were ironed out and ultimately, of course, the entire Morrison pre-packed fruit and veg operation is carried out within their own pack houses to a very high standard indeed.

Through the summer of 1975, my diary was a non-stop grind of outstanding RP & P work, principally involving trips to Scarborough or Darlington to the contractors, or my usual ten/twelve hour day at Morrisons, setting up new maintenance people, dealing with out-standing maintenance issues and increasingly assisting Ron Curry with the planning of the following year's developments. I took no holiday, not even Bank Holidays, as a break, even though in those days the stores were closed. The other foible of trading in those days was that all our stores operated a half-day closing, usually Tuesday or Wednesday afternoon, depending on which local authority the store came under. This was ideal for me, as much of the more major maintenance work including the creation of dirt and dust could be carried out on half-days and everything be put back for the following day's full trading.

Towards the end of 1975 things really started to bubble. We were invited to visit an old cotton mill at Failsworth near Oldham, operated by a company called Whelans Discount Stores. Dave Whelan had introduced some new features into this store, and we were also invited to look at refrigeration and display cabinets, although this, at the time, did not come under my remit. When we arrived at the four-storey, rather foreboding red-brick Lancashire cotton mill, I thought, my goodness me, what a mess. Little was I to know that some three years later I would be responsible for it, having acquired Whelan's in total.

At this time there was another major issue looming over the company, since the terrazzo floor at the Merrion Centre store in Leeds was failing. Not to put too fine a point on it the consultants acting for our landlords who had built the shell had not allowed sufficient floor loading in their design, despite having been given all the required details. The floor structure was flexing and the joints between the terrazzo tiles were failing and some tiles were cracking. The issue had been the subject of a court case by the company against the various consultants and the landlord and Morrisons had been successful, selecting to take as their award the replacement of the floor at third-party's costs, and this all needed planning, a major task for the company as we had decided to keep trading during the course of the work. Things were really hotting up and I decided I needed a holiday.

My old college mate John Jenkins had left Leeds for Jamaica the week before I left RP & P for Morrisons, and had gone to work as a Quantity Surveyor for the Jamaican Government based in Kingston, uprooting wife Margaret and three very young children. We had kept in touch during the course of the summer by letter (no email in those days) and out of the blue came an invitation from John and Margaret to take a two-week holiday as their guest at their house. By now I was unattached and very much single, tired out and in need of a rest, so I jumped at the thought, even though the trip to me appeared to be rather daunting.

On 5 November 1975, I left Leeds/Bradford and its short runway in a Vickers Viscount plane of British Midland Airways (now known as BMI), flew to Heathrow and then a British Airways 747 to Kingston.

John had indicated that my 'board and lodgings' would be covered if I gave a talk on my career to students at the Kingston Technical College, where he was 'moonlighting' from his Government post as a part-time lecturer. I duly agreed and gave the talk to some twenty students, who it had to be said had degrees of interest varying from wide-eyed, to very much closed-eyed.

John and Margaret had not changed at all, still living their rather bohemian lifestyle (at least to me) with a beaten up Triumph 1300 car, which managed to get round the island, and my two weekends were spent away from Kingston at Montego Bay and later on the coast.

I think my highlight however, was a site visit to Grange Hill, flying from Kingston in a Britton/Norman Islander aircraft, probably manufactured at Hull, and landing on a earth strip in the middle of nowhere, to be met by the site manager, George, who was an enormous guy with a Ford Lotus Cortina. He proceeded to whip us through the dense forest at breakneck speeds, until we slid to a halt in the middle of nowhere, with the announcement of 'beer-time'. We walked not five metres off the road into a darkened hut illuminated only by the whites of the eyes of the inhabitants, sank five Red Stripe beers and then continued.

We arrived at site, which was the construction of a new village Post Office for the Government, and John carried out his site inspection, prior to sitting down to do the monthly valuation. This brought to light one of the most amazing claims for delay I have ever come across. During our walk around the Post Office I turned a corner to find one of the site labourers asleep in a tin bath used for mixing plaster. George kicked the bath; the man woke up and went back to work. 'We'll deal with that later,' said George.

When the time came to agree the interim payment, George made a claim for an extension of time due to 'Act of God' which was allowed under the contract. My mate Jenkins questioned what this Act of God was, to be told that God had seen fit to take the men of the village away to Kingston to find work and when his men had arrived, they had been continually sexually harassed by the women of the village, leading to not much sleep at night and reduced output during the day for which he was claiming. I don't know to this day whether the claim was allowed or not!

My journey home was somewhat more exciting than the outgoing trip.

On arriving at Kingston airport for a 9.00 p.m. flight, we were advised that the incoming flight was delayed and after some time John, Margaret and the kids left me to go home since the plane had eventually arrived and we'd been told that there was some engine trouble on the way out which had been fixed. The plane was due to land on the way at Nassau in the Bahamas, which we duly did, a handful of passengers alighting and the same number loading. When it came to take off time, we got to the end of the runway on what was then a quite small airfield for a 747, the pilot revved the engine, and there was a loud bang followed by silence. After a five minute break the engines were started again, only for a repeat performance, by which time the locals on the plane were getting rather nervous.

When you're travelling abroad I have always felt happier to board a plane home and hear the sound of an English Captain's voice, and the guy from Kingston to Heathrow was no different. In a very calm manner he reassured everyone that there was just a minor problem with one of the engines, a fault that had occurred on the way out, but it would be fixed and we would be on our way. Shortly after a local mechanic with a step ladder came out, removed something from the engine cowling, scratched his head, banged his screwdriver and put the cowling back, at which point the Captain declared we were safe to proceed, unfortunately only as far as a repeat performance of the explosion in the engine.

At this point a number of people, quite naturally, had become very nervous and were making all sorts of comments such as, they should have flown Air Jamaica, they were frightened, they wanted a preacher, and so on. On the row behind me were four Methodist preachers on their way to an International conference in Switzerland and at the sound of this holy demand from the front, one of them calmly stood up. 'I's here brother.' The plane erupted in laughter, apart from a few, and we were ready to go on our way once more, until we were advised that the engine concerned was useless and that we could not fly across the Atlantic on three engines, but would fly to New York and get the problem fixed. This was followed shortly afterwards by an announcement that New York had become fog bound, and we duly arrived into JFK late morning, now twenty-four hours behind programme. We were put into a hotel, the offending engine was repaired, only to blow up completely in its test run, and we eventually made our way home via Air India to Heathrow, to be met by a baggage handlers' strike and further delays, getting me back to Yorkshire almost thirty hours behind schedule. A good experience, but not one I would wish to repeat.

My first year closed with me having apparently established for myself a decent reputation within Morrisons as a hard worker and someone who would get things done. We were slowly building a team between Ron and myself and we now had new surveyors coming on stream for maintenance and additional building work, but we were less than five in number and clearly regarded by some as a drain on the overheads.

CHAPTER 8

Sandcastles and Cricket

COMING FROM A HOME BACKGROUND where money was clearly tight in my young life, holidays were always quite modest, usually comprising a week at a Northern resort, with the rest of the long summer school holidays being spent with the odd day trip to the coast, or picnics on the nearby moorland of Baildon, or the local beauty spot of Shipley Glen.

When you're young it doesn't really matter, as time passes with seamless enjoyment and the memory, not just mine, but many people's, seems to be of summer holidays in endless sunshine, with warm temperatures.

My parents always tried their best and holidays up to the age of ten or so usually featured a coach ride from our West Yorkshire home to sample the delights of Morecambe, Cleveleys near Blackpool or, on one mammoth outing, a steam ship ride from Liverpool to the Isle of Man – heaven.

These early holidays gave me the opportunity to indulge my tiny mind with the fantasy of the ride on a West Yorkshire coach, or a smoke billowing, clinker throwing steam train from Shipley to the coastal resorts, followed by a week in a small, but always decent, guest house.

In those days the Northern seaside resorts, like many around our coast, were home to fairly local holidaymakers, indeed Morecambe achieved the nickname of Bradford-on-Sea at this time and I often marvelled at the splendour of the Midland Hotel, situated as it was, immediately adjoining the mainline railway station where hundreds and thousands of Bradfordians disgorged on day trips. Over the years The Midland was holiday home to many of the wealthy Bradford wool and textile people, as evidenced by the quality of cars parked outside. There seemed to me to be limitless displays of Rovers, Humbers and the odd Rolls Royce, as I gawped over the low boundary wall onto the immaculately manicured lawns.

The Midland, as with many places, was to decline and its Art-Deco frontage was to fall into disrepair over the years, only to be brought back in the mid first decade of the new century, but more of that later, as the wheel turns full circle!

I vividly remember one holiday at Cleveleys, when, having returned from the beach and dressed for dinner in my shirt, tie and blazer, we were standing outside in glorious sunshine, when there was a massive thunderclap, later to be confirmed as a new jet plane breaking the sound barrier over Morecambe Bay. This was followed by the most enormous rain storm which the 'experts' described as having been caused by disruption of the cloud system. At eight years old you'll believe anything.

Our trip to the Isle of Man was a major experience. Having taken the train to Liverpool we then joined the Isle of Man motor vessel *Manxman* for the four hour trip to Douglas, the main port. I had never experienced anything like it, a cooked meal served by waiters in the ship's restaurant and again endless sunshine. That particular holiday was punctuated by the loss of my spending money from a small leather wallet, perched, no doubt precariously, in my trouser pocket, as I hurled myself around the beach, keeping goal for Bradford City one evening after dinner. The purse was never found.

On those early holidays my grandmother accompanied us, which never bothered me, but clearly deprived my parents of what they considered was valuable time alone with me. It just didn't seem to matter to me and I always enjoyed the company of the four of us. I well remember on a cloudless day riding the Isle of Man tram and rail to the top of the Island's peak, Snaefell and thinking that we had probably climbed the equivalent of Everest, with the spectacular views across to Scotland and the whole of the Irish Sea.

Our holidays became a threesome when my grandmother started taking trips away with her friends and this led to pastures new, with trips on successive years to Boscombe, near Bournemouth. This was class compared to Morecambe, Blackpool and Bridlington and we stayed in a hotel where it was necessary to dress for dinner. We also had the added luxury of a two week holiday, which was fantastic, and the bonus of attending a Wednesday evening football match at the local club's Dean Court ground added spice if the home team were playing someone from the North, as Dad and I always cheered for the Northerners and indulged in some good-humoured banter with the locals.

Bournemouth was also a nice transport experience as they had trolley buses, just like the ones at home, the only exception being that these had three sets of wheels and I thought they were massive. Trips often took us to the local beauty spots of Christchurch, where the buses were turned on a turntable in the narrow streets to commence their journey back to Bournemouth. Bournemouth was a truly international location and indeed still is today with summer college camps for French students, the atmosphere was balmy with pinewoods and beautiful gardens, a very relaxing experience.

We would take odd day trips to the Isle of Wight to look at the various samples of varied coloured sands, and old Poole harbour to look at Brownsea Island, where Baden Powell started the Scout movement and had his early camps. This was wonderful and usually topped off every night by a cup of Horlicks in the local coffee bar, preceded by a round of putting, or a game of bowls.

At Bingley School I also had holiday breaks in groups. Being a member of the technical side of the school someone had the bright idea of extending our education by taking trips every other year to Scotland. There was a minimum age qualification for this, but I fell lucky in that I was able to go to the land of the Jocks on two occasions, in my third and fifth year. The purpose was to look at hydro-electric schemes and we based ourselves in Pitlochry in Perthshire.

The tours were undertaken, in my time, in coaches provided one year by Andertons of Keighley and the local firm Taylors of Bingley. We journeyed north mid-week during the Easter holidays to our base, from where we spent the first day, Thursday, visiting local power schemes around Pitlochry, such as the generation plant on Loch Tummel, taking in the environmental improvements of the day, such as the salmon ladder which would enable fish to take their journey from the sea to the spawning grounds uninterrupted by the barrier of the Power Station dam wall. We also visited a scheme under construction at Ben Cruachan, near Loch Awe, towards the west coast of Scotland. A real hike in a day.

Ben Cruachan was a fantastic piece of engineering, whereby a mountain loch was created artificially and the water dropped down through the mountainside and hidden generating plant, to discharge into Loch Awe. Off-peak electricity was then used to pump the water back up the mountain and I well remember our first visit, where we stood at the side of these massive earth moving dump trucks, with huge wheels that dwarfed us as fourteen year olds. We were allowed to take in the sights under supervision and all that was needed was a pair of stout walking boots. No Health and Safety issue in those days, just pure common sense and the care of our teachers and site staff.

On our second visit the scheme had progressed almost to completion and was opened shortly afterwards by Her Majesty the Queen, such was the importance of it.

These were happy days, punctuated by a free day on Saturday when, dependent on the fixture list, we could take the train into Perth and watch the first half of a St Johnstone home game and then leg it back to the railway station for the train back to our hotel. We always managed to blag free tickets on the main stand, on the basis that we were visiting supporters from Bradford, and the Directors of the Perth based club were always very kind to us. Ironically, the club later sold its ground to Asda and moved to a new stadium, out of town.

Our return home on the Sunday was punctuated by a ferry ride across the River Forth to Edinburgh, no road bridge in those days, lunch in the city, tea in Newcastle and then home. Absolutely wonderful, educational and friendship making, and supervised by teaching staff who really cared.

By now, of course, I was growing older and although remaining quite shy my trips to Scotland did generate a slight passing interest in members of the opposite sex. In Pitlochry, we were the boys from the big town and caused a stir when we hit the local coffee bars. Most Scottish towns of a smaller scale are very typical of each other, in that they often have a wide main street with a coffee bar where the local community collects. Our presence on these occasions gave rise to some friction with the local males, but it was very enjoyable banter.

Growing older, holidays with parents became something that I was not particularly looking forward to. I would spend summer school holidays biking with my mates around home and I think the last holiday I took with my parents was to Lyme Regis in Dorset when I had just passed my driving test. I'd previously indicated that I did not really want to go, but was persuaded to go with the bribe of being able to drive long distances. My father had never been particularly keen on driving and was a reluctant late passer of his driving test. I jumped at the chance, after all it was only for ten days or so, but blotted my copybook when as we approached the Avon Suspension Bridge in Bristol, when a loss of concentration caused me to run into the back of another car, fortunately no damage done, but pride dented. At that time we were the proud owners of a second-hand Austin A40, with its Italian body styling, a car which was later to pass into my ownership when it was really only fit for scrap, having regularly made the journey to Dad's place of work, which was still in Harrogate. After our last family holiday in Devon and Dorset I declared that I would not be going again, and thereafter my holidays were with the lads; but more of those in a later chapter.

CHAPTER 9

The Morrison Years 1976–79
Red Rose County, Exit Door and
Promotion

FOR THIS PART OF MY BOOK, I have had to think long and hard about the format. I believe that my basic problem is that I have too much information. My office is littered with Morrison Reports and Accounts, my personal diaries and my notebooks from virtually the day I joined this retail company.

For me, scanning the information page-by-page, the exercise becomes an interesting walk down memory lane, but for you, the reader, I would not wish to impose on you the day-by-day diary of Roger A. Owen, which would be tedious in the extreme, would lose many of you along the way and would condemn the book to oblivion, if it is not there already.

This chapter and the following, therefore, is a kaleidoscope of my career at Morrisons, the highlights, the lowlights, the successes and failures and an attempt to paint a picture of the development of one of the top four retail companies in the United Kingdom, from very humble beginnings to the day I retired and a little bit thereafter, for, as I am sure you can imagine, I did try to leave a legacy of something of a development programme for the ensuing two to three years in my wake. Abandonment was never a word in my vocabulary.

After the trials and tribulations of settling into my new job, 1975 finished on a good note, although I was not to know it at the time.

The Morrison Christmas bash led me to an introduction to the girl who was to be my future wife. Lena worked for the company in the IT Department, we talked through the beer and I arranged that after Christmas and early in the New Year, we would go out.

Research with Lena's boss, Chris Balaam, the IT Director, revealed a failed marriage and two young boys, but this did not deter me from the girl with the really quite charming smile, although I understand that she had reservations and was very keen to discover where I was going to take her, so she could advise her workmates just in case 'I go missing'. I did not realise that I had that sort of reputation. Nevertheless, our two or three dates together went quite well, although at that stage I think it was fair to say that there was no romance in the air, and then quite suddenly, without warning, Lena departed the Company.

1976 was something of a landmark year for the business, with the opening of four new stores adding over 35% to the company's sales area. This was accompanied by the opening of a new wines and spirits warehouse and a produce (fruit and vegetables, to you and me) pack house on the outskirts of Bradford, occupying one of Bradford's two former greyhound stadiums.

The new stores strengthened our presence in Leeds, with three of them being built in local centres during one of the hottest summers on record, which was itself to bring problems later on.

The produce pack house, located at Dudley Hill in Bradford, was a major step forward and, no doubt, a relief to some.

When I first joined the Company almost 12 months earlier, the produce packing, such as it was, was in a corner of the central warehouse, behind the Head Office in Thornton Road, Bradford. The new building took us way ahead of the game and produced volumes of pre-packed product, significantly improving product availability to the customer.

The long hot summer also saw me becoming increasingly involved with Haworth and District Round Table, which I was to join later that year. Geoff Emmett, with whom I had worked at Rex Procter, first invited me to one or two meetings, I then made guest appearances at football and cricket games and eventually was asked if I would join. This placed an added burden on my already expanding social life, as on two Mondays each month I would be at Round Table meetings.

Round Table in its day was a marvellous organisation, set up to help the community and those who were less fortunate, while at the same time having fun, and I recount some of the experiences later.

In March, shorn of my short term relationship with Lena, I went on holiday to Benidorm for a long weekend with Dick Earnshaw, one of my former Procter colleagues, and two others, and it was as a consequence of that that I became introduced to and eventually became a member of the famous, or maybe infamous, Bredbury Hall Country Club, near Stockport. It was only in the last twelve months that I discovered the Club was owned and run by one of the allegedly notorious criminals in the Manchester scene, featured in newspaper articles. None of this deterred me however from trips on a Monday night, whereby I would leave Round Table at 10.00 p.m., sprint across the M62 and meet up with one or two people I knew from the Manchester surveying scene, often arriving home to my parents, where I still lived, in the very early hours of the morning, necessitating an early evening most Tuesdays.

The weather through the summer '76 was most unseasonal and the construction of our four new stores suffered badly. The spring had been very wet, resulting in very treacherous ground conditions, but the summer was murderous, with contractors having difficulty getting roofing material properly in place and tarmac surfacing to set properly, and I was to become the victim of this early the following year.

When the weather eventually broke in autumn, we discovered that the damage inflicted by the weather was indeed grievous and the Hunslet development, a large scale district centre with a shopping mall as well as supermarket in South Leeds, literally leaked like a sieve.

My boss Ron Curry blamed the architect for bad detailing and I well remember a hilarious scene which ensued.

Early in '77, the Company held one of its few Management dinner dances at a hotel on the outskirts of Leeds. At this occasion it was customary for the Store Operations team, under the direction of Ken Blundell, their Main Board Director, to provide a cabaret. The particular theme for this year was the 'Merry Monks of Morrisons', in which all Store Managers were dressed as monks and Ken, who was Ken Morrison's brother-in-law, was dressed as Father Abbott. Unsuspecting victims had various choruses sung about them and then were invited into the middle of the dance floor, whereupon they were surrounded and dressed in appropriate gear, to mimic the particular verse of the ditty, which those merry monks were singing. In my case I was hauled onto the dance floor, surrounded by my colleagues, who were singing a very lively number about roof leaks and catching water in an Addis plastic bucket. The circle of garbed friends parted to reveal the Estates Manager in the centre of the dance floor dressed in a frog man's mask and flippers, with a snorkel and the appropriately branded plastic bucket in hand.

My one good mark of the evening was that I won the award for the best 'turn', much to Ron Curry's disgust, whose face I can picture now, set in thunder.

The following week, Ron called a meeting with the architects and explained to them, together with Ken Morrison, the folly of their ways with the design of the leaking roof. I was called in to give my opinion, as I was the poor soul who was doing the maintenance and had all the nasty telephone calls from store management to deal with. The architects, The John Brunton Partnership, were given a real talking to, but resisted the argument which Ron was putting forward, at which point he dispatched me back to my office to dress in the divers gear I had so brilliantly worn the previous Saturday evening. I can remember now flapping my way the 20 or 30 metres from my office to Ken's room, complete with flippers, and the best way I can describe it is a repeat of that very famous scene from the film *The Graduate* starring Dustin Hoffman and Anne Bancroft. Upon his graduation, Mr Hoffman's character Benjamin is presented with a scuba diving kit and the watching filmgoers see him walking towards his family swimming pool from inside his mask, with the in-out breathing of the snorkel as the only sound. I was like that as I flapped and padded my way into the Chairman's office, hearing nothing through the headgear, but seeing only my irate boss Ron prodding Peter Batty, the Senior Partner of our architects, in the chest and pointing in my direction.

Ron turned in my direction and I could but lip-read the words 'that's what his f****** colleagues think of him.' Personally I thought it was hilarious, the joke becoming even more funny when without my being consulted on the matter at all Ron described a circle with his finger and despatched me to pad back to my office without having uttered a word. The remedial works to the roof began the following day.

Ironic that in the following 25 years, all four of the stores were either extended and/or had petrol stations attached. The stores at Horsforth and Rothwell were ongoing as I retired, Rothwell having a replacement store which opened the day after I retired and

Horsforth being extended and refurbished during the summer of 2009.

The company's other diversion over this period of time was to significantly extend its non-food trading and range, launching the LifeStyle non-food range and introducing purpose designed departments and a specific and detached LifeStyle Store at the Merrion Shopping Centre in central Leeds. This was accompanied by a purpose operated LifeStyle warehouse in Bradford. We were starting to go places and 1977 saw us open our first new store outside of our West Yorkshire home, at Ripon, the princely distance of some 26 miles away from our base.

Early in 1978, a second large landmark to follow up our store expansion of 1976, arrived when we agreed to acquire the Wigan based Whelan's Discount Stores.

Many of you reading this will know of Dave Whelan as Chairman of Wigan Rugby League and Wigan Athletic Football Club, the former of which he has now relinquished to concentrate on his Premiership football side. Dave was born in Bradford and became a professional footballer with Blackburn Rovers, notoriously breaking his leg and effectively finishing his top line career in the FA Cup Final at Wembley.

As a footballer, he had started to develop market stalls around Blackburn and then went into the food retail business, developing a small but noted brand of six stores located in Wigan, Chorley, Preston, St Helens, Bolton and Failsworth, a suburb of Oldham. This was supplemented by a warehouse and Head Office in an old cotton mill in Wigan, and in addition Dave had acquired a site at Ince-in-Makerfield for which he had planning consent for a new store.

Unbeknown to someone at my level, the Board had been actively involved in discussions which Mr Whelan, who was also a close friend to Ken Morrison, for some months and in early 1978, decided that we should progress the acquisition, with one dissenter, my boss, Ron Curry, who voted against the deal.

In later times I could understand why, as Ron was clearly keen on developing our own estate with purpose-built modern stores. The image of acquiring an old cotton mill in Oldham, a retired saw mill in Chorley, a old steam locomotive engine shed in St Helens and run down small buildings in the centre of Wigan and Bolton, together with a modern, but split in half store at Preston, was not Ron's idea of how we should be going.

At least he had the courage of his convictions to vote against it and in later years Ken was always to say, you should never abstain when it came to a vote in the boardroom, even if it meant voting against something with which you did not agree.

Noting Ron's opposition to the scheme, I was pulled in together with Chris Balaam the IT Director and told that we were the kingpins to sort out any problems with the proposed acquisition, all of this taking place against my background of continuing involvement, on occasions, with Rex Procter, finalising the schemes in Scarborough, my active social life, including Round Table together with an ongoing commitment to developing the department, set against my boss who was opposed to the deal in hand.

This meant that Chris Balaam and myself spent days on end journeying across the M62 and then going our own ways to look at the validity of planning consents and examining the stores themselves, which were in a pretty sorry state.

We would spend all day in Lancashire, returning home early evening, whereupon I would sit down to write up a report of the day's events and take them to the house of John Dowd the Personnel Director, who was later to become Managing Director prior to his sad early death. John would then take my notes to Ken the following day and I would make telephone calls to the office to receive further instructions. You have to remember as the reader that there were no mobile calls in those days – how on earth did we manage!

One of the properties, a four-storey cotton mill at Failsworth, was a particular problem, in that it was leased by Whelan from a landlord by the name of Jersey Morning News, a company run by a very hard little Lancastrian by the name of Alfred Hatton. Alf made his money from stripping equipment from the dying cotton industry and exporting the looms etc. to China, where production costs were so much lower. He had then exported himself to Jersey, whereupon he bought a vehicle for his property investments. I quickly realised that Whelan's were in breach of a number of conditions of their lease, not least of which was the repairing obligations and I advised Ken that we were facing a bill of several tens, if not hundreds of thousands of pounds, even at 1978 prices, to put the property into decent repair and comply with our obligations. This story eventually got back to Dave Whelan, who was none too pleased and during a visit to the Whelan's Head Office at Poolstock in Wigan, Dave apparently asked who the stranger was with David Greenwood, his Accountant and Company Secretary. I got to know the answer fairly quickly as Dave's voice boomed down the office 'well you can tell him to f*** off now and never to come back into this office again, he is costing me a fortune'.

All was well that ended well and on 10 April 1978 Morrisons became the owners of Whelan's discount stores and set about a rather punishing but short term programme of rebranding the stores, widened our geographic representation and taking on a company which had sales of some £10 million per annum, a figure we quickly doubled.

Over the subsequent years all the stores were replaced, having got our foothold in Lancashire, and Ron Curry's opposition to the deal evaporated, as he took control of the development of the former Whelan's site at Ince to a purpose-built store which was subsequently expanded and refurbished by myself.

The days after the Whelan acquisition were in some ways amusing, but in practice, frustrating. The Morrison fleet was despatched to run across the M62 from our central warehouse in Bradford. The fleet at that time comprised some twelve or fifteen rigid box wagons of various vintage and these were regularly seen on the hard shoulder of the M62, surrounded by a pool of oil or gushes of steam, and this quickly led us to our first articulated vehicles, two Rolls Royce engined ERF tractor units, which went like the wind. We were on our way once again.

Equally we were on our way further North. The success of our Ripon store the previous year had given way to Teesside, as it is now called, when we were approached by the Darlington Indoor Bowls Club, known locally as the team who always played away. That was not a reference to what the players got up to themselves! It was rather their inability to have home fixtures due to lack of appropriate facilities. More later.

I was chasing backwards and forwards to Lancashire, dealing with various extensions to the Whelan's estate, completing extensions to the central food warehouse and opening the LifeStyle warehouse in September of that year. I was exhausted, but my load was lightened a little, when Ron walked into my office. At this time the old purple Capri had served its time, failed its MOT and been relegated to use by the Personnel Manager, Pat Norman, who had been dealing with the integration of Whelan's staff in Lancashire, trips which it was felt were unsafe to take in her ageing Company Mini.

As a diversion, Pat herself, now in her late eighties, was an interesting character. She was a semi-professional/professional dancer who toured the clubs of West Yorkshire with her husband and who, perhaps more famously, is the mother of Chris Norman, the former lead singer of that well known Bradford based group Smokie, still doing the rounds of Eastern Europe, where they are idolised, as is Chris himself, appearing on many German and Eastern European television shows, and in the case of the group itself, appearing in the Presidential Palace in front of Putin himself, not too long ago. End of diversion.

The ceaseless travelling, long hours and long days had been taking their toll on me for some time. I suddenly developed a problem with my eyes, which manifested itself in a series of cysts in the eyelids which had to be surgically removed. I was run-down and found that my life outside Morrisons was contracting somewhat. I was still working a six day week, at least during the summer when I would meet up with Ken Blundell and his Senior Management team of Steve Butler and George Buttle for lunch in one of the stores on a Saturday. In exchange for a free lunch I would discuss ongoing projects, projects to be brought forward and maintenance issues.

The one bright spark of this time was when Ron came to see me one evening in my office, as he was about to leave for home. At this time I was driving Pat Norman's old Mini as an interim issue, or any other spare car I could get my hands on. Ron came in and smiled at me and threw a set of car keys on the desk with a typically gruff 'It's in the car park.' When I raised my eyebrows questioningly, his further response was 'If you look out of my window you'll see it.' I duly did and noted an ice blue Ford Cortina. There then followed a discussion that this was no ordinary Cortina, it was the only one that Keith Naylor, Ken Morrison's other brother-in-law in the business, could get his hands on. A 2 litre, GL, with all mod cons, effectively an interim between Board of Management and the rest and not to be bragged about as 'this car is going to cause trouble when they all find out about it'. I went outside to look at my new possession, AUM 120S, a lovely machine, but before I could even leave the building to go home, I was set upon by three colleagues asking how on earth I had managed to pull this one.

The car was lovely and Lena remarked, when we met up again the following year, just what a lovely car it was and how sorry she was to see it go in due course.

The new car did lift my spirits but did not reduce my fatigue, and I happened to mention this to my former partner at Rex Procter, John Burnley, during a conversation. John was responsible for the Morrison account at RP & P and said that if I was so unhappy perhaps I should consider my position. This was not something which had crossed my mind particularly, but I said that I really did not feel appreciated within the Morrison organisation and that I felt I deserved more reward for flogging myself to a standstill. John was very sympathetic and a few days later, called me to say that if I was interested, he would arrange a meeting with a certain Kevin McCabe, whom I had been indirectly involved with in one of my Scarborough schemes as a Quantity Surveyor. We duly met at a hotel in York in the beginning of July and I then further met Kevin at his offices at Scarborough in the middle of July, following which I was offered and accepted a position with County Properties. There was no immediate panic about this, as I was to go away on holiday in August, to France, my one and only trip to that country for any period of time.

Prior to my holiday however I interviewed and appointed as my second Senior Maintenance Surveyor one George Robert Monkman. Bob was to become my right-hand on maintenance, progressing to Senior Maintenance Surveyor before his retirement due to ill health and sad early passing.

By some piece of bad planning Ron and I had arranged our holidays so that they overlapped and my resignation came as a bolt out of the blue to him, and very unhappy he was.

These were agonising days for me and I am sure that anyone who has been in a similar position can sympathise. I did not really want to go, I had considered my time at Morrisons over the three and a half years to have been very successful. I think I had the respect of

most people, from the Board down and I believe that I had
demonstrated, quite successfully, my commitment to the company
and at the same time had the feeling that Ron and I together were
building a good team. We had problems of one or two setbacks with
staff, but those had been dealt with and we were now assembling a
team of youngsters, mixed in the experience of my two maintenance
men, Bob Monkman and Wilson Wrigglesworth. The Whelan
acquisition was turning out well and really I had everything to play
for, but I really did not feel I was being appreciated.

Ron had given me the target when I joined the company,
replicated in my job description, of achieving Board of Management
status. I looked around me and without wishing to appear arrogant I
believed I was better than some that occupied that elevated position,
but there was no sign of promotion coming my way.

Kevin McCabe had painted a very good picture and with some
justification, for he went on to develop County Properties and its
subsidiaries into the Scarborough Property Group, subsequently he
has become Chairman of Sheffield United Football Club, significantly well-off and perhaps, in hindsight, I was mistaken not to join him,
but I don't really think so.

Ron's parting shot to me before he left for holiday was 'the
Chairman wants to see you'. I was ready to depart myself, I was going
with five others to France and I had a long drive ahead of me to the
ferry at Portsmouth. At the same time we had a big scheme which
had been costed, to convert the old cotton mill of Whelan's at
Failsworth, and I needed to get this through the Board and advise the
architects.

I went to see Ken on the morning of my departure, with some
trepidation. We went through the scheme and all the costs. I
answered all the questions, and there were many, for we were not
over endowed with money.

At the end of the conversation, it was agreed that the project would
proceed and that Ken would advise the Board accordingly, as Ron
would still be on holiday.

Ken could be and was quite steely on occasions and looking over
the top of his glasses said 'Now then son, I understand you're going
to leave us.' I replied that was my intention, and there then followed
a very emotional ten minute conversation, which concluded with

Ken saying, and I still remember to this day, 'Well if it's any consolation, neither I, Ron or the rest of the Board want you to go. I want you to go away and think about it.' I advised Ken that I had accepted the job and indeed Kevin McCabe had in his possession my personal car radio for fitting into the new company car, things were so far advanced. At this point Ken made an observation, which he was to repeat to me once in my later career on the Main Board and which I have repeated to many people in their careers: 'remember one thing son, all mistakes are rectifiable, it's just the cost that varies.' He suggested that I should use my holidays to think about my position, and to cut a very long story short, I agonised over the next two weeks, came back, told Ron I was withdrawing my notice, which was gleefully accepted, but not so gleefully by Kevin McCabe, and life continued.

My reward for this was to be advised that Ron was going to staff up the department to take the pressure off me, we were moving out of Hilmore House to some offices in Horsforth, and that my actions had been a very serious wake up call, which had been heeded. To his credit Ron delivered on his promise and in the autumn, we moved to our new home in Horsforth, which we were to occupy for the next six years.

In February 1979, I was appointed to the Board of Management. The first goal in my Job Description had been achieved, now for the bumpy, difficult road to the rest.

CHAPTER 10

Consolidation in Many Ways 1979–84

AFTER THE HEAVY WORKLOAD OF converting the former Whelan stores the previous year, 1979 promised to be a little calmer, or so I thought, but retail is a very fluid business and stability, at least in terms of workload, is never easy to achieve.

Having got over my flirtation with the 'departure lounge' in late summer of the previous year, I had settled down and convinced myself that my future lay with 'the big M'.

The former Whelan estate, even given its very diverse make up of former industrial and railway premises and small shops, was really beginning to pay off and the Lancastrians were showing a fondness for our offer. Ron Curry, despite having voted against the acquisition at Board level, threw himself into the programme by taking direct control of the conversion of a unit in the Preston Guild Centre. This store had almost been the stumbling block on the deal. Trading on two levels, with a public walkway running through part of the food sales area and disappearing into a tunnel which then re-emerged in the centre of the rather iconic, but very 60s/70s, concrete bus station, it was difficult.

Above our store were about twelve storeys of offices, much of which was given over to British Leyland, the car, bus and truck manufacturer, and in turn their staff monopolised the adjoining multi-storey car park which was the only means of our car-borne shoppers using our store. Not a good start and we were very unhappy.

Ron, after much argument, managed to convince the Borough Council that we should floor over part of the tunnel walkway, thereby allowing our customers to shop around the whole store, rather than buying their beans, checking out and then going to the other side to buy soup. No one in their right mind should have really entered into such a deal but there it was and here we were to rectify it.

Having carried out what was really a quite difficult scheme in his usual minute detail and manner, Ron decided that our opening late in 1978 should be something of a jamboree. As a consequence this store was the last we opened with a 'celebrity'. The actor Patrick Mower, now of Emmerdale fame, turned up in a white suit, chatted most of our checkout operators up to some degree, and then did the honours (with the scissors on the tape, not elsewhere!). In addition to the celebrity status, the store opening also achieved some notoriety, as the following day quite a few of the guests were struck down with food poisoning. The Borough Council had insisted that we have our celebration lunch within the Guild Centre itself, the home to many famous snooker tournaments and other events, and that they would do the catering. Ron agreed to this on the basis that we would do the bar and enlisted the help of our own catering controller, Geoff Sanderson, who prepared the welcome drinks tray of champagne cocktails – what a disaster. Ron had warned me and my Chief Maintenance Surveyor, Bob Monkman, that we could have one drink but no more, as these were 'dynamite', and so it turned out. The food became secondary and I well remember the Mayor of Preston, in that year a lady Councillor, rising to give her congratulatory speech to the Company on its investment and so on, as they do. Her hat was skewed to one side, almost obscuring one eye and she delivered her speech with one hand firmly on the table and swaying from side to side. Absolutely hilarious, but unfortunately twenty-four hours later at least two of our guests were hospitalised. I was mightily relived it wasn't us doing the catering.

The early months of 1979 saw the Company face some fairly serious challenges. First of all there was bad weather, and although much is made now on news bulletins when the slightest fall of snow occurs, 1979 was worse than anything we experienced over the winter of 2009/10. My beloved football team did not play a home game until 3 March that year, such were the freezing conditions and deep snow, and all this was added to at store level.

By now I had introduced a snow clearing scheme whereby local contractors were employed together with their JCB machines to clear snow. In a moment of over eagerness I had the idea that the Company should put out on local radio in Bradford the 'Morrison weather forecast', which took the form of declaring all of the car parks were clear and the stores were open for business. We were immediately reported to the appropriate Standards Agency by one of our competitors, as one car park in particular had not been cleared, and I received a firm but not too serious ticking off for misrepresentation.

On top of the snow came a national road haulage strike. Our drivers were unionised, but they were well treated, with benefits such as subsidised canteens and a newly introduced profit-sharing scheme, and as a consequence they continued to work at least for a few days, until they became the subject of various rather unseemly threats, which resulted in their joining the strike. Ken told the Union that the strike was against the conditions of the profit-share payments and that the drivers would not be receiving anything that particular year, and ultimately was true to his word.

The Unions, in all that, made one concession. Provided we did not use HGV transport, we could continue to distribute to the stores as, clearly, food was an issue for the nation. This saw a good week of absolute teamwork, which to my mind epitomised the Morrisons of those days. Management took to manning trucks in the central warehouse, clerical staff were utilised for the spare half hour here or there and company cars were drafted in, to become the haulage fleet.

This was not as hard as it perhaps sounded. Apart from the former Whelan's stores, most of our units were still located within a fifteen mile radius of the Head Office and over the five or six days that the transport situation was in limbo, we managed to deliver more product by car than we did on our own transport fleet, prior to the strike. This was a true tribute to the efforts and determination of everyone involved, although it did result in a number of cars being pulled in by the police for rather obvious overloading.

In spring 1979 Ken and the Morrison family suffered a very sad blow, when Keith Naylor, one of Ken's two brothers-in-laws, died.

When I joined the Company Keith Naylor was working on the buying side on the limited non-food product range and later moved to head up the central Purchasing Department. Indeed, it was he who had been responsible for buying my brilliant Ford Cortina 2.0 GL the previous year. He was a nice guy who possessed a very dry sense of humour, a total opposite to Ken's other brother-in-law, Ken Blundell, who ran the stores with an iron hand in a velvet glove.

Having completed the rather tricky conversion of the Whelan store at Preston, Ron Curry turned his attention to the former

Whelan's site at Ince-in-Makerfield. The site had come with the Whelan deal and with the benefit of planning consent for a new store. The site was situated out of the centre of Ince and we were very dubious about its long-term success, so it was built along the lines of something that could be converted to a distribution depot, if all else failed. Crinkly tin, as we often referred to the cladding material, was not really our style, or at least had not been for a good ten years, but crinkly tin it was. The store ultimately was successful and I was delighted in my time to undertake a major programme of extension and rebuild, adding at the same time a petrol filling station, and the store trades well. Having had a brush with the Transport Unions earlier in the year Ron was then faced with a brush with the Construction Unions towards the completion of the store, which was built for us by Leeds based contractors Manston.

Much of the labour force came from West Lancashire and Merseyside, the latter of which, shall we say, has a certain reputation for its industrial relations and militancy. As we came towards the end of the job the contractor, Manston, was approached by various people working on the site who indicated that completion and severance bonuses should be paid. The approach was declined and every morning for the last two weeks of the project the contractor arrived on site to discover that the previous two days brick laying had been pushed over and the walls concerned were simply piles of rubble. Various messages were received to the effect that this would continue and ultimately the bonuses were paid and the job finished. At that time Morrisons had an unofficial embargo on building or opening stores anywhere near Merseyside, although things have changed dramatically in the twenty years since.

Through the previous year and 1979 I became more heavily involved directly with Ken. When I joined the Company, Morrisons had a very small area of its Head Office allocated to the production and packing of bacon and cheese products, but the facilities became wholly inadequate for the volume of business and it was decided that we should invest in a large scale fresh food factory, which became known as 'Farmer's Boy Limited' and operated then and now under that banner. Having proclaimed himself busy on other areas Ron Curry divested the Project Management of this ground-breaking scheme to me. Ken became involved when his two specialist meat and factory people, Ronnie Holdsworth and Ray Hayhurst, both decided, for whatever reason, that they would take retirement and disappear and a new factory manager was brought in.

This was an exciting time for me, being involved in a ground-breaking experience and I had weekly meetings with our architects, which were preceded by lengthy meetings with Ken himself, taking place in late afternoon, at my department's offices in Horsforth. Ken would attend from 4 p.m. and we would finish at whatever time, before he drove off to his home in Otley. The scheme, whilst large and covering over 80,000 square feet, was after all construction, and Ken took on the task of sourcing the equipment, which was to provide us with a major platform going forward in the production of fresh food, cutting out, as Morrisons often did, the 'middle-man' and thereby increasing margin, or reducing prices. Either way we were going to be competitive and we were going to make money.

Throughout that time Ron was busying himself with another ground-breaking and retail based scheme at Darlington. Up to this point the furthest north we had ventured was Ripon in North Yorkshire, but County Durham, as it was then, was another stepping stone away from our base.

We had been approached some two years earlier by representatives of the Darlington Indoor Bowls Club (as I mentioned earlier), on the basis that if we were to build a new facility this would constitute a good element of what was then called 'Planning Gain', which would overcome the hurdle of the site not being allocated for retail purposes, and the Company jumped at this approach. There then followed several months of very hard work and the reader must put themselves in the position of a world with no email and very little computing power, a world where everything actually had to be done manually.

The consequence of this was that yours truly spent days either sitting in a cold car checking the numbers of buses and timings of these vehicles past the proposed site, to validate our claims that the site was accessible to public transport. At one bus every minute, on average, I think it was.

I also enlisted the help of one of the founder members of the Bowls Club, Joe Burrows, when I 'borrowed' his daughter for several covert shopping trips, in order to establish the comparative cost of a shopping basket in our competitors, compared to ourselves. Not the scientific research of today with a standard shopping basket of some thirty items, but one which we made up ourselves and then necessitated actual physical purchases. The Burrows family dined out on us for some time.

After a public enquiry and many demonstrations outside the Town Hall in our favour, planning consent was granted and throughout 1979 and into the spring of 1980 Ron busied himself with the development. Perfectionist as he was Ron wanted the indoor bowls facility to be the best in the country, if not the world, and set about achieving an absolutely flat floor surface. Ron's definition of this was that there was no plus or minus tolerance, everything had to be dead level, and consequently when, some weeks after our own store opening in March of 1980, the bowls club opened, I saw the pride on his face when the first 'woods' were delivered and those in the know pronounced this the best green they had played on. Unfortunately for Ron the time spent on the scheme appeared to do little for his marriage and within the next period of time he had divorced and formed a relationship with his former secretary, Caroline, whom he subsequently married and, it has to be said, became a better and happier person.

Our own store opening at Darlington caused something of a stir, with hundreds of people arriving over an hour before the opening time, in freezing cold March conditions. Darlington became our top store and retained its position for sometime thereafter, and in its own way gave us the confidence to go forward with other units in the North East, pushing the boundaries of our expanding empire.

On a personal front, my relationship with Lena was becoming more and more settled and solid, but I know that she was concerned that some degree of permanency should come into our relationship. Lena's first thoughts over the years, after her own marriage breakdown, had been at all times for the two boys. I had had quite some exposure to Glen and Jason. I liked them, they were always immaculately behaved, despite the inevitable sibling rivalry, and I well remember Lena delivering, not quite an ultimatum, that for the good of the boys we either ought to make things permanent, or draw a line in the sand, a statement which hit home really hard with me, and at Christmas time of 1980 we became engaged and set a date of July 1981 for our wedding. We took my parents for dinner to make the announcement and I think it fair to say that they were quite shocked. They had not met Lena previously, though they did know about her, but the sudden revelation of marriage and the greater revelation that there was an instant family of two hit home with them. To be fair, they entered into the impending roles of grandparents with great enthusiasm, quickly taking to the boys and embracing them into the family. The boys in turn responded brilliantly to this new leg of their family and became very attached, as Lena and I witnessed when my father died.

Over more recent times and especially as my mother is in frail health at the time of writing this book, both of them have continued to make contact at any time Lena and I are on holiday and have taken to driving whatever it needs to visit my mother in her residential care home, as a mark of respect and reassurance. Two superb beacons.

In early 1979, I had been 'rewarded' for my loyalty of the previous year, when I had decided to stay with the company. This reward took the form of promotion the Company's Board of Management, in the role of Building and Services Director, and I was now responsible for the Company's refrigeration and maintenance on top of the general portfolio issues, the role having been passed to me by Ken Blundell, who by this time had ceased to be responsible for the retail elements of the business, this having been passed to Ken Morrison's protégé, Steve Butler.

In late 1979 therefore, I was also rewarded by the appropriate uplift in company car. I don't mean to sound ungrateful and I wasn't – but the car was a disaster!

First and foremost at that time the available models were either the Triumph 2000, or the Rover equivalent. Ron badgered me for some weeks into taking an automatic car, the first I had ever had. His sales pitch was that with the mileage I was covering I would arrive at my destinations fresher if I didn't have to worry about changing gear. Ultimately I had delivered a burgundy coloured Rover SD 1, which was commonly used by various police forces at the time, although mine was the 2.6 litre engine and not the 3.5 litre.

Over the next period I had something in the order of six accidents in the car, none of which were my fault, but, I discovered later, were largely the fault of the car itself in that burgundy is one of the most difficult colours to recognise and people simply kept driving into me!

Apart from one occasion when driving through Pool-in-Wharfedale, a small village between Harrogate and Bradford, returning from a Bradford City game in Hartlepool with colleagues Martin Ackroyd, who was later to become Finance Director and Phil Robinson, plus another guest, I hit a taxi which was turning across me.

The vehicle concerned was a Lada, yes a Lada, which was much maligned in those days. I hit the vehicle square on its rear axle and the Rover collapsed in pieces on the road. The offending taxi driver was able to drive his car some distance down the next street in one piece, although he did get a three-month ban thereafter.

On getting my car back and visiting our ill-fated Harrogate Conference site about which I comment elsewhere, the rather large fan unwound itself from its mounting and embedded itself in the radiator, bringing to a halt that particular journey, which ended in a local village garage.

Upon repair of the radiator and fan I had driven no more than a mile when the gearbox failed and I completed the journey in bottom gear. Ultimately the Board decided that Rovers as a group were costing far too much on maintenance, even taking my own inflated costs, and scrapped the fleet completely in favour of something more reliable – good old British Leyland!

The car was to let me down on one further occasion when, taking Lena and boys to Blackpool Illuminations. It overheated in the middle of Blackpool promenade and I embarrassingly had to wait on the roadside whilst things cooled off, with the sibling rivalry as to who could sit in the middle of the back seat and see through the windscreen, bubbling along all the time. I have not been a fan of Rovers or anything connected with Leyland ever since and I was not sorry to see their demise.

The Main Board decided that the maintenance costs of those cars were so high that they simply had to go. My particular vehicle was disposed of very cheaply, to one of the warehouse lads, who ironically and very sadly found the same colour problems as me. His car was hit by one of Morrisons' own delivery vehicles within the first two weeks of ownership, resulting in the car being a write-off, its charmed life eventually coming to an end in a Bradford scrapyard.

Through the later months of 1980 and the early part of the following year, I decided to learn to drive a Heavy Goods Vehicle and started taking lessons with a one-man driving school at Crosshills, near Keighley, quite conveniently situated near the Test Centre. I had developed a weird notion that, as now we were getting bigger and bringing more and more articulated vehicles into our fleet, we were getting more and more problems with the sizes of our service yards and manoeuvring. I thought I could drive one of these vehicles and we could do the experimenting ourselves within the Property Department, rather than tying up a driver as had been practised previously. After all, I was partly a King of the Road, having passed and obtained my bus driver's licence, years previously.

Unfortunately, things did not go the same way as with the single decker in the early 1970s. My mind was far too occupied with work and when it came to the test day, I was absolutely dreadful and failed. The examiner, a kindly individual, told me quite clearly that he thought and expected that I would pass on a second outing, but by now my mind had turned to my impending marriage, and the pressures of work were dictating I be elsewhere. The dream evaporated!

After one year of marriage and living in the wilds above Bradford, we moved home to be nearer to the boys' schools, and were to remain there as they both passed through the majority of their secondary education at an excellent establishment which was to see them both into University. Lena, who had never been particularly interested in driving, had herself passed her driving test at the first attempt and now had what was euphemistically described in our family as the 'perfume burner'. This was a second-hand Fiat 500, but did have a small sized racing steering wheel, a convertible roof and a fire extinguisher! The boys, or at least Jason, thought it was great, but Glen always instructed his mother to collect him from school, 'around the corner'.

Through the early 1980s, upon reflection, we didn't really seem to do much, and Ken's statement to the Shareholders on more than one occasion noted that there were a number of schemes awaiting planning consent. What we did however, and did very well, were extensions to existing stores, and in the early 1980s this saw such schemes at our earlier locations such as Halifax, Girlington, in Bradford and Keighley, before we again picked up the baton of development.

During this time, the Company changed its name to Wm Morrison Supermarkets Plc and in October of 1981, the Company finally opened the much-troubled Harrogate Conference Centre store, of which, more later.

Having acquired Whelan's Discount Stores five years earlier, in 1983, we went on the acquisition trail again, buying three 'Mainstop' stores from the International Group, at Gainsborough, Eccles, in Manchester, and Southport, which were all upgraded, and we sold one of our first disposals, a previously converted bowling alley at Park Avenue, in Bradford, to the West Yorkshire Co-op.

In the summers of those early years, the Company had banded itself together to organise a Company Sports Day, which was held at the Horsfall Playing Fields in Bradford and comprised the finals of various regionalised heats of football, rounders and athletics, together with side shows and other events, notably a celebrity football match, of Store Managers versus Head Office.

In 1982, stung, I think, by some criticism from his colleagues, Ron Curry decided that the Property Department, or as it was more normally known, the Estates Department, would feature. The chosen sport was Tug-of-War.

Ron, with his attention to detail, went into this in a big way and having sat in conference with him for some time we decided that we would have to use everything in our power to obtain a victory, including cheating, if it came to it! Consequently, I was despatched to smooth talk the groundsman at Horsfall Playing Fields into loaning us every Tug-of War rope, on the pretext of needing it to practise with several teams. This of course was not true, but it stopped anyone else getting some practice.

By this time we were ensconced in our offices at Horsforth in the leafy suburbs of Leeds and Ron decided we should spend some lunchtimes practising, in order for him to select the team for the big day. Imagine the scene: a team of grown men trying to pull over a 100-year-old oak tree in the local park while being called all the names under the sun by the local youth, who happen to be on half-term holiday. This training extended to after-work events. Ron decided that we should pull a moving opponent rather than a rather mature tree. By this time I was driving a loan car, a Vauxhall Cavalier, and it was decided that the team would pull the car uphill on a grass mound adjoining the Leeds Bradford airport, after work. I was not well, suffering from a heavy bout of flu and, as you do, felt like death, but stick to it we had to. The rope was fastened around the car and the team instructed to pull. I was advised to make it as hard as I could for them and was only too pleased to sit in the warmth of the car, with my foot on the brake.

Ron, not realising what was going on, felt that the lads were not really committed to the task in hand and decided that he would give them a lesson in technique, joining the back of the team. At this point I woke from my semi-slumber and on instruction to pull, took my foot off the brake and the car moved forward very smoothly, with the pulling warriors ending up in a muddy heap on the floor. I can see Ron's face now as he marched down the hill towards me, having been sat upon by at least six members of the team, in some glee. Walking towards me with his face set, I sat calmly in the car until he had drawn level, calmly wound down the window, to be regaled with an 'I suppose you think that is funny . . .' whereupon Ron declared practice closed for the evening.

Our final training session took place with a proper Tug-of-War team, from the Greyhound Pub, in Tong, to the south side of Bradford. This was class stuff. The team here had a well trodden path with a rope and pulley system over a very large tree, and their training consisted of pulling a 50 gallon oil drum filled with concrete up and down the pulley. When the Morrison boys were advised it was their turn, they hardly made an impression on this massive opponent at all, and we came back to the original concept, of 'if you can't win, cheat'. There then followed a 30 minute lesson on how to cheat, based on the fact that we would not have a professional referee on the day.

Tug-of-War is about physics and mechanics. Quite simply if you are against a team of opponents who are heavier and stronger than you, you simply adopt the technical term of 'lying on the rope', which is to say, the entire team, on the command of pull, drop to as near to horizontal as possible, with heels wedged into the ground. This way the entire team becomes almost a wedge, which it is impossible to pull over. The idea then is to let your opponents tire themselves out trying to pull you, and as their pulling gets more ragged and the gaps between the pulls get longer, you pull back when the rope is at its slackest. Off we went to the main event.

On a sunny and warm Sunday afternoon, the Estates Department's finest took the field, and using the well-honed technique of cheating, we managed to get to the final, against the brutes of the Farmer's Boy Fresh Food Factory. These were butchers, pie-makers, bacon slicers and so on. Big Lads, who took one look at us, smiled and got their hands on the trophy. Imagine the expression when on the first pull our guys dropped to the floor as though they had been shot and remained there for fully five minutes with the opposition becoming more and more cross. When the time came the midgets of the Estates Department pulled the giants over. Unfortunately, enthusiasm got the better and the equalising pull was not too far away. By this time we had been 'rumbled', and lost in the deciding pull, but it was a great day, and a great few weeks of getting everyone together.

1983 saw the opening also of a major extension at our Keighley store, site of demolition contractor Arnold Marriott's finest hours, recorded elsewhere and our first in-store bakery, whilst at the end of the year we ventured further afield into Heywood, a suburb of Rochdale, with a new build store, which was subsequently re-developed and leased to the Irish retailer, Dunnes for one of their textile and clothing outlets, whilst we occupied a brand new store on an adjacent site.

Throughout 1983, indeed from early 1982, and into April 1984, the Company was very concerned with the development of its largest project to date, the redevelopment of Grantham town centre.

Grantham was known in its time as the most boring town in the country, but it did have one claim to fame in that it was the birthplace of one Margaret Thatcher, whose family were also in retail. The site had been won at tender by the Midlands steelwork and contractors, Conder, but they had been unable to put the scheme together in retail terms and we were brought in to take over. The development comprised some 30 shop units, a redeveloped library, multi-storey car park, superstore for ourselves and a brand new bus station, all constructed on a very tight site. The development saw shop units let to Mothercare and other National chains and true to form, Ron Curry was at his most meticulous best, spending weeks deliberating the type of light fittings for the main shopping mall. Ron took charge of the main development himself, together with Project Manager Steve Price, and I looked after the fit out of the Morrison store, but inevitably got dragged in to the rest of the development. Site meetings were a nightmare, as my former Rex Procter colleague Steve Watkins often remarked.

Ron and wife Caroline would journey down the night before the site meetings, have dinner with the very amiable Russell Cann, the Chief Executive of the Local Authority, and then Ron would arrive fresh at the site meeting the following morning whilst the rest of us had driven the 100 miles or so down the A1. Site meetings were often preceded by a lavish spread of bacon or sausage sandwiches and most of the day would be taken up with minute detail, Ron often leaving the site meeting around 4.30 p.m. to journey home, at which point the real meeting started, often finishing as late as 7 p.m., whereupon, Steve Watkins and myself together with others would go for a pint and then drive back north, Steve probably taking half the time it took me.

The shopping mall at Grantham has been revamped on a couple of occasions in the intervening years from its opening in April 1984, but we have always been at pains to retain the feature clock, which so many generations of Grantham people have now had the pleasure of seeing in action. Ron designed the clock in conjunction with the specialist firm of Hayward Horological and it is designed on the basis of the ideas of Isaac Newton, another famous Granthamian. The clock takes the form of a face with roman numerals, set in an apple tree with a lion asleep under the tree. When the quarter hours come up the lion's tall flicks, the bell chimes, the lion momentarily opens its eyes and then falls asleep. On the hour, the lion's tail strikes every chime and the so called vibration shakes loose an apple from the tree, which drops in accordance with Newton's Laws of Gravity to the ground. A super piece of engineering, which unfortunately came unstuck on the night before the development opened.

We were in a major rush to get the work finished, not helped by much of the shop fitting work which was going on for the incoming tenants. Ron wanted a big bash to celebrate, quite rightly, one of the major triumphs of his Morrison career and we duly invited well over a hundred guests to take part in the buffet and booze-up, which was held in the central shopping mall. Ron meticulously timed all the speeches, so that the event would finish one minute before 9 p.m. The clock was turned off, to be turned on again by Chief

Maintenance Surveyor Bob Monkman, just before the clock struck. Imagine then the grief, when the clock struck 10 p.m. and the time was actually 9 p.m., although I think that most of our guests, by then, were so 'delighted' by our hospitality that they couldn't count in any event.

The store opened the following day and was a success, but has always suffered from a rather small car park, a very inhibiting factor when you are trying to grow sales. Nevertheless, it's one to be proud of, although as I recount later, Ken was not too happy, for a number of reasons.

CHAPTER 11

Other Travels

M Y CHILDHOOD TRAVELS ARE chronicled in chapter 8 and during my late teens I was delighted to take three holidays abroad with my great mate Keith Whawell. These were in the days, the very early days, of cheap package holidays and took us to exotic locations, such as Lloret de Mar, Arenel in Majorca and Porec in the former Yugoslavia.

Out first trip to the Costas was memorable. Flying out of Leeds/Bradford in a British Midland Viscount, we proceeded over the next two weeks to do everything wrong as virgin tourists. I managed to get horribly sunburnt by falling asleep on the beach, almost necessitating hospital treatment. Thereafter I spent several hours trying to sleep on the cold ceramic tile floor of the bedroom, such was the heat of my body. Our first night memorably saw us mistakenly overdoing the information I had been given by Stuart Burkinshaw, a friend who was the son of my family's painter and decorator. Stuart was a year ahead of me in academic life and advised me that booze was cheap in Lloret and that the rum and cokes were great. To a Tetley's bitter drinker this seemed like heaven on earth, especially when we found that rum and cokes were the equivalent of the English two shillings, or 10p. Having downed several of these in no time at all Keith and I thought that this was child's play until the alcohol hit home and we staggered back to our hotel, getting half way back to the room before we realised we hadn't collected the key. I volunteered and on returning to the balcony of the floor I thought we inhabited, could not find my mate who had wandered off down another flight of stairs and proceeded to empty most of the contents of his stomach down the stairwell. British abroad!

Having learnt that very early lesson, topped up with my sunburn episode, we very quickly became seasoned tourists and engaged in moderation. It seemed that the whole of the holiday featured nights of one of other of us not feeling on top form! We learnt much before our next adventure abroad to Majorca the following year.

Around 1970 came our hairiest moment when we decided on a trip to the now former Yugoslav resort of Porec, flying from Luton through the military airbase of Pula with one of the earliest charter airlines, an outfit by the name of Court Line whose feature was that each aircraft was painted a different colour in pastel shades.

Shortly before we undertook our venture, a group of British tourists had been arrested at Pula Airport, allegedly for spying, and this unnerved Keith and me a little, not to mention the observations from our protective parents. Before we left British shores however the matter got cleared up and the tourists' protestations that they were plane spotting at the military base seemed to be accepted.

We had a nice two weeks in this communist country where everything was cheap, the weather was nice and the resort featured an open-air disco, which was extremely good. The highlight of our trip was to be a day out in Venice, just across the Lagoon from our resort and accessed by means of a two hour or so Hydrofoil ride. This was quite spectacular, skimming across the water at something like 35 mph and seeing the towers and domes of Venice appearing over the horizon.

We took a trip around St Mark's Square and then into the back streets, where refreshments were considerably cheaper, even though they were not accompanied by the stringed orchestras of the St Mark's cafes, returning to our speedy transport with happy hearts, having had a really good day. Then things started to take a turn.

Our travel courier was a very smart, southern Irish lady, probably fifteen years or so older than us, with a short skirt and nice legs – need I say more!

As we pulled out of Venice, she approached us with a bag, to say that as she made the trip regularly, she was always buying Duty Free cigarettes for the rest of the tour crew and hotel staff, but the Customs people at Porec were very aware and consequently would we be good enough to carry her bag when we disembarked the Hydrofoil. There was much nodding and winking and Keith and I melted like butter.

On our arrival back to our homeport, she told us not to approach her at all but to simply leave the bag on the seat of the coach when we arrived back at the hotel. Something then started to feel wrong and very surreptitiously Keith and I opened the bag, to discover not cigarettes, but various rolls of film, tapes and other items, which were clearly not recently purchased. Were we in the middle of a spy ring?

For two honest Yorkshire boys the strain of dismounting the Hydrofoil and making our way to the coach without simply blurting out to the watching soldiers, that we thought we were carrying something 'iffy' was almost too much, but the thought of a dirty Yugoslav prison overnight, drove us forward. All of this was partly in our own minds but we had to question why we had not been told the truth about the cargo we were carrying, and resolved that we would question our host at some appropriate time. Unfortunately, the opportunity never presented itself, as we were leaving two days later and a note on our operator's board advised us that the lady concerned had been involved in a rather serious accident and would not be seeing us off at the airport – more suspicions were raised.

As we departed Yugoslavia and just as we passed through the barrier that would not allow us to turn back, we saw our hostess appearing at the back of the departure hall, with two black eyes and what suspiciously looked like a broken nose and various other bruisings. Keith nudged me to draw attention and we received a very weakly mouthed 'thank you', before we were whisked back to the UK on our charter flight. Was this a close shave, or was it make-believe? I'll never know but nowadays when I check in at airports and I am asked if anyone has given me anything to carry on the plane that answer is always no, because I will never, ever do anything like that again.

For a number of years, post full-time employment, I never took proper holidays. In 1980, Lena and I had a week in Newquay and then spent our honeymoon in Jersey, before involving the two boys in holidays, firstly to Torquay and then we took the big step of going abroad, with holidays in locations such as Tenerife, Minorca, Ibiza and so on, until we reached a point that the boys no longer wanted to come with us.

The watershed of travel for Lena and myself arrived in September 1993, as we were flying back into Manchester, from a trip to the Canary Islands. Circling Manchester while we waited for a thunderstorm to pass through, Lena turned to me and said that she had concluded that if I was to continue working at the pace I had been all our married life, then there was going to come a situation where

I may become ill, or simply 'conk-out' and die. Therefore she had decided that it was time for some resolution and that her resolution was, that from 1994 I would start to take my full entitlement of holiday and that we would go away three times each year. That way, she said, 'you can work as hard as you like, for the rest of the time', but at least she was happy in the knowledge that I was getting some rest and we would have time together.

I think in similar circumstances, most men have the same reaction, which is to nod, agree, and then rely on the lady in your life forgetting about it – not this one!

From the spring of 1994, therefore, we embarked on a really nice period of varied breaks, although some of it did become quite routine. For several years the pattern was to take ten, or eleven nights in March in the Canary Islands, starting with Gran Canaria and then moving to Lanzarote, where we stayed six or seven times at the hotel, Melia Salinas. Lanzarote in March can be variable, but generally the weather is such that you get a nice dose of winter sun. The hotel in our first two of three years was excellent, but as with a number of large chains, it became rather tired and despite two years of complaint, very little was done to refurbish.

During our visits there we met a lovely couple, Marlene and John Alexander from Humberside, whom we have not seen now for several years, but whom we keep in touch with. I know that they have visited the Salinas a couple of times after we finally 'kicked it into touch' and report that there is now much work done and the hotel is back to something of its former glory. I am pleased, because it really was nice.

Our summer holiday, two weeks in June, was determined to be a long haul. Neither of us had gone particularly long distances, but falling in with Lena's wishes, I was more than happy to join in. Our first such venture was carefully planned with the excellent Jack Doyle, of Classic Travel in Shipley. Jack has now retired, but handed us on to another equally keen, attentive and good agent in Hanson Travel, in Pudsey, between Bradford and Leeds.

Lena had always said she had wanted to go to Hawaii, being a huge Elvis Presley fan, so we duly embarked on a flight which took us from Manchester, through Chicago, to Las Vegas for two nights and then on to Hawaii via Los Angeles. We had a two island, twelve night stop, firstly in Honolulu and then to Maui. On our first night, drinking gin and tonic on the bar terrace, we heard and then saw a school of dolphins playing in the sea, just off the hotel beach. Heaven.

We returned to Hawaii, but different locations some years later, to find, somewhat to our dismay, just how commercially developed things had become. There is much beauty, but there is also an element of Vegas in some of the resorts. Hawaii is particularly attractive to Americans, as they can go 'abroad' without needing a passport and, of course, the United States is so varied in climate and attractions that I believe only 25% of all Americans possess a passport. I would recommend Hawaii just for the experience, but look at more than one location.

Honolulu is a big city, with all that brings, especially when the fleet's in! You could be in New York, Chicago, Manchester, or even Leeds by the sea, but the one thing that struck me very hard about Honolulu was our visit to Pearl Harbor. This has now been designated a National Park/Monument and has a very good visitors' centre, where the Park Wardens show films of the original attack by the Japanese, which brought America into the Second World War. This is followed by a boat trip to the USS *Arizona*, sunk in the deep waters of the natural harbour and still leaking fuel oil, all these years on. This is a National War Grave and the solemnitude of the whole experience is superbly recreated by the calmness of the surroundings. The Americans, I believe, are very good at this sort of thing and the Vietnam and Korean war memorials in Washington DC also bring home the horrors of war in a graphic way, each different, but each combining the same message, indeed, the message of the park wardens at Pearl Harbor to the youngsters in our group was 'you must never let this happen again'.

Our second visit was to Bali in Indonesia with a four-day stopover in Hong Kong and the hair-raising landing at Kai Tak Airport. They say you can see people shaving as you fly, amongst the tower blocks. This is not quite true, but nevertheless, it's extremely scary. The hustle-and–bustle of Hong Kong, pre–return to the Chinese, was to be seen to be believed. The sights, smells and sounds of a city that never appears to stop were amazing, matched only by the curiousness of the heavy downpours and high humidity of a June day.

Touring the harbour on a traditional junk reminded me of that very successful Yorkshire business man, Paul Sykes who, in conjunction with another of his fellow county men, Eddie Healey, was responsible for the development of the Meadowhall Shopping Centre, at Sheffield.

Paul is a very down-to-earth Yorkshire guy, who started life breaking old buses for a living; a section of his family's business is still involved in this. Sitting on board the junk as we went through the various moored boats, which form housing for many of the Chinese-Hong Kong inhabitants, I was reminded that Paul once told me that most of the junks in Hong Kong are powered by bus engines from his yard in Barnsley, which, perhaps, accounted for most junk drivers not sounding their horns to avoid collision, but simply shouting 'Ay up, see thee' – only joking.

Bali was fantastic, with its very peaceful people, and we took a tour with our guide in traditional dress, witnessing again the sights, sounds and smells of the various herbs and the terraced paddies of the hill areas. Simply wonderful, and it's a great sadness that the terrorists have seen fit to attack tourists while they are enjoying the same sights and sounds as we did.

Lena and I, together with younger son Jason and his then girlfriend Helen returned to Hong Kong just before the colony was returned to Chinese rule, this time landing at the brand new airport miles out of the city and marvelling at the engineering feat, not only of the airport itself, but of the connecting roads and railways back into Hong Kong City.

The purpose of our visit was to meet up with elder son Glen and be introduced to the girl who is now his wife, another Helen, as they paused on the Robin Knox-Johnston 'clipper' round the world yacht race. Glen had taken himself off on this adventure, which lasted some ten months, following his return from working in Germany. Helen, a London based solicitor, was taking time out from a chaotic business life of mergers and acquisitions and was sailing on another boat. The six of us had a hilarious first meeting when we went for a meal and got outrageously the 'worse for wear'. Later in the week, we were to meet Helen's parents, David and Elizabeth, and the riot act was well and truly read, about avoiding a repeat performance. That trip was to see the start of a relationship, between Glen and Helen, which led to marriage and now two super grandchildren, Emma and Jack.

Other long-haul holidays have seen us visit Bermuda on no less than three occasions, staying on the first two at the famous Elbow Beach Hotel, originally owned by the family responsible for Littlewoods Pools. Bermuda is fantastic, it is not large, there are no hire cars and therefore transport has to be via a hired scooter, or taxi, or the beautifully coloured pink and blue buses of the Bermuda Transport Authority, which possess a significant number of female drivers, all highly dressed with the longest false nails I have ever seen for someone in that kind of job.

Bermuda is very colonial, where the Bobbies on the street still wear pointed hats, with Bermuda shorts, and it is simply a superb place to visit, seeing the sights of the old English Naval dockyard, the caves inland, and watching the locals playing cricket. The sweet onions are something else.

We have also taken holidays in St Lucia, Barbados, Bahamas and Tobago in the Caribbean, but I have to say that perhaps my first ever visit in the 70s to Jamaica has rather coloured my judgement on these places. I listened to people raving on about the Islands and the resorts and yet when I speak to people face-to-face, I find that very few actually enjoyed their holidays there and I do not believe this is an area of the world we shall visit again.

Two years after I joined the Board at Morrisons, I was invited by our Refrigeration Contractors, George Barker, based in Bradford, to attend the Food Marketing Institute annual exhibitions and seminars in Chicago and I was lucky enough to visit the city on business on three separate occasions.

Chicago is a fantastic city, in terms of its architecture, its shops and its lakeside parks and museums, all built on reclaimed land. Chicago suffered a great fire, not unlike London, and in typical American style the rubble was simply pushed into the lake and the city rebuilt with some of the highest buildings of their time, Sears Tower and Hancock Tower being two of them. Chicago also has the attraction, if that is the right word, of a tremendous variation in climate, which can occur in two consecutive days. I've been there when the temperature, with wind chill, has been $-20°C$ and the following day has been $+20°C$. The architecture is stunning, including not just the high-rise tower blocks, but also medium-rise, or even low-rise, such as the Wrigley Building, the Head Quarters of the famous chewing gum company.

I have been fortunate to go back to Chicago on a number of occasions not associated with business, either with my family, or with our friends Christine and Michael Taylor. In the last ten years, the four of us have taken to having a long weekend away on the East Coast of the United States, having spent weekends in New York, Chicago, Boston, Washington and more recently Charleston and Savannah.

One particular long weekend in Chicago with Michael and Christine gave us the opportunity to attempt a fairly major 'scam' on Lena, who has always been an avid Elvis Presley fan. Unbeknown to Lena, we organised that having spent Friday and Saturday sightseeing around the city and the mandatory shopping trips, we would take a trip to Memphis to visit Graceland and the associated tourist sites.

For two or three weeks prior to our visit, I played the game of having been invited to one of Morrisons' suppliers to experience a home barbecue lunch, but that lunch would be approximately a ninety minute flight away from Chicago. This was met with all sorts of protestations from my wife along the lines of 'it isn't fair to Christine and Michael, three hours flying for a barbecue rib', and so on. We were able to keep up the pretext until early evening of the Saturday, when I said that I had to be in the hotel lobby to pick up some flight tickets, waiting until Lena took her shower before exiting the room, only to be caught by my suspicious wife, taking the flight tickets out of my bag to supposedly bring back into the room in triumph! The cat was out of the bag and we had to tell her about the following day's events.

Our trip to Graceland was excellent, even for me as a not very devoted fan, in fact, not devoted at all. The flight down from Chicago to Memphis with ten of us on a 737 was quite good as we were able to listen to the pilot almost land us on the wrong runway, into the path of an outgoing aircraft. We then had a variety of taxi drivers ranging from people we were convinced were Vietnam Vets on speed to someone who was almost certainly a member of the Ku Klux Klan, who berated the state of the local population. Graceland was something else, with all the stage costumes, and the house still largely as it had been in the family days, and a really enjoyable experience. The Americans do this thing very well, almost always equipping you with a Walkman running commentary and signage of when to switch the tape on and off. The major disappointment for me however were the Presley family graves, which were decorated with cheap and tacky plastic flowers. All that money coming in from tourists and they couldn't afford fresh flowers every day!

From the museum we took another taxi ride into town, which in the old quarters is really run down. They say that Memphis is the law capital of the United States and indeed the really gripping film *The Firm* was based on a law practice in Memphis, as I recall. The original book of the same makes super holiday reading. We visited the Peabody Hotel for lunch. This is supposedly one of the great hotels of the world, and its biggest feature is an ornamental fountain in the middle of the bar area. Every hour a clock chimes, a mechanical drawbridge of small proportions is lowered and a group of ducks waddle their way through the hotel foyer, over the drawbridge and into the fountain, to leave shortly afterwards. This was a wonderful sight, accompanied by many smart black American ladies in their cocktail dresses and shoulder length gloves, and all at 2 p.m. on a Sunday.

Our ride back to the airport was one of the most hilarious thirty minutes I have spent. On leaving the hotel, we spied a sparkling clean taxi and headed for it, immediately to realise that there was something awry, and something more major, which told us something about the Memphis economy. We asked the driver if he would take us to the airport, he told us it would be something in the order of fifteen dollars (£12) and then proceeded to ask us if we had the money.

Lena closed the rear door to find the handle came off in her hand, but said nothing and we set off on our ride back to the airport. The taxi driver was uncommunicative. Trying to break the silence Christine remarked on how quiet the centre of Memphis was, to be replied in a southern drawl 'Weeeeell sometimes it is, and sometimes it isn't'. As we crested a rise and drove down towards the mighty Mississippi, Michael asked if the river often flooded and the reply came 'Weeeell sometimes it does and sometimes it doesn't'. As we drove along the river Michael again asked about the variation in climate in this central area and whether or not they got snow, 'Weeeeell,' came the predictable answer, 'sometimes we do and sometimes we don't.' By this time we were on the freeway heading to the airport and the taxi's gear box developed a mind of its own,

11. Students union ID for final year, October 1971

12. Jethro Tull meets the Bay City Roller, me and Andy Sedgwick in our final year, complete with tie dye t-shirt

13. *The original Girlington Supermarket*

14. The 'new' Victoria supermarket, 1969–70

15. *Keighley, 1968*

16. The original Mayo Avenue, Bradford store, on conversion from a laundry, with Sylvester Ramsden's famous chimney, yet to be felled on the cornflakes!
(Picture courtesy of Bradford Industrial Museum)

17. *Two great guys! Ken Morrison, left, presents Ron Curry with his retirement gift, May 1987*

18. *Ron's legacy – a full spec Trinity House lighthouse, at Preston's Riversway, July 1987*

19. *The Morrisons Petrol station at Preston*

20. *The interior of the Preston store*

automatically changing down without any warning, and with me in the front I soon developed a fairly severe case of whiplash as we sped along, jogging between gears. Our arrival at the airport couldn't come fast enough.

On mounting the ramp to the departure doors the taxi suddenly decided that it had had enough and we staggered up the slope, with the driver exclaiming in a very loud voice 'Don't you give up on me now!' Three rather scared voices from the back said 'No we won't.' We dismounted in a heap on the pavement in fits of laughter, but having discovered during the drive that our taxi driver had previously been a long-distance lorry driver we had visions of the man being a knife wielding Alfred Hitchcock type killer. I am sure we were all wrong.

On arrival back in Chicago we had dinner at the famous Chicago Chop House, which is a big tourist attraction and noted for its enormous steaks. By this time, unfortunately, we were all rather tired by the day's events and the staff simply could not believe that we had travelled to Memphis and back in the day. There then followed a debate with our waitress as to various Elvis Presley films, and in particular, who played Elvis' mother in one particular screenplay.

No-one knew the answer but before we knew where we were, in typical American service industry fashion, the whole restaurant was involved in the quiz, with bar tenders ringing their partners and so on. Shortly before we left, after a rather truncated meal caused by our fatigue, the answer came that it was Shelley Winters, and the final throw of the dice came as we walked through the door into the cool evening for our taxi, to be greeted by the very burly doorman, whispering 'It was Shelley Winters' – a hilarious end to a wonderful day.

I am not intending this chapter to be a travel documentary, but one tip I would give is always take a bus tour of the city you are visiting. It can be fantastically amusing and also gives a useful insight and identification of specific locations that you might like to go back to.

Further afield in the States, interruptions to journeys have seen us spend time in San Francisco, which I found fascinating, not just from a transport point of view, with its trolley buses, trams and normal modes of bus transport.

We visited Boston, during what was called the Big Dig, where a whole freeway was sunk under the city into land which had formally been landfill. There is a very interesting documentary film, which sometimes features on the Geographic Channel, about the forming of this roadway, an enormous feat of engineering.

Our one and only trip to Boston took place just over a month after the tragedy of 9/11. The tourist trade was well down and the hotel staff and restaurants that we visited could not believe that we had not cancelled our trip. The Americans, I have found, are always extremely jumpy about issues such as 9/11, or any other major events, and it is hardly a wonder to me that young children are often patients of psychologists and psychiatrists. For such a big nation it is amazing so many people seem to suffer such massive insecurity complexes.

Go to Boston we did, however, flying out with Aer Lingus from Dublin, as we had flown with them previously to the States. The year in question had also seen large countrywide outbreaks of foot and mouth disease in the UK, which had caused some of the international rugby matches to be called off, and we left on the weekend of one of these rearranged games in Dublin. Boarding the Aer Lingus 767, we were told by the crew that 'The video's broke' and that unfortunately Paddy who usually fixed these things was on day-off at the rugby and there would be no point trying to contact him, as 'he'd surely be pissed by now'. It was eleven thirty in the morning! The crew were fantastic and provided the girls with some freebie perfumes as consolation to missing the big film. I was very sorry to see Aer Lingus in difficulties not too long afterwards and they are now a shadow of their former selves.

By and large I find the Americans very welcoming, very interested in the fact that you are a native of the United Kingdom and always keen to find out something of their own heritage. I have met people who tell me that their relatives come from Peterhead in Northern Scotland, name them and then ask if I know them at all, me who lives some 300 miles away. The American's take on the UK is fascinating and their service is, by and large, second to none.

As I now enter retirement phase, we are continuing to look at long-haul holidays but one closer to home, which we shall not drop, is a trip we started back in 1994, in September each year, to Cyprus.

In our first year Lena, despite recommendations from Ken Morrison and his brother-in-law the late Ken Blundell, decided on the Four Seasons Hotel in Limassol, and we have been back, without fail, every September since. How boring, you might say.

When we first visited the hotel was less than two years old and unlike most other hotels it has been refurbished on three occasions since then. This is not the 'run it into the ground' philosophy, which applies to so many hotels, particularly those in the United Kingdom, but it is refreshed every so often, with the result that over 70% of its customers are repeat. In addition to this we have made friends with local restaurateurs and even taxi drivers, who we see every year.

Cyprus is a fascinating island and although I have never been to the Turkish side, I find the history almost overwhelming in some of the areas. Driving up into the mountains is an experience itself, not just because of the roads with their nightmare bends and steep drops, but the forests, the changing climate and the history of the independence struggles and the terrorists who fought long and hard for their beliefs. Mountainsides dotted with monasteries set in olive groves or vineyards are simply tremendous, and the island is so relaxing, although of course it does have its moments, with resorts such as Ayia Napa.

Our house in Spain has somewhat altered our holiday plans and in 2009, for the very first time in midsummer, we did not go long haul but spent three weeks at our house, which is located in the pleasant but small fishing village of Caleta de Velez, some forty minutes drive from Malaga Airport, on the less populated side, away from Marbella and all that those resorts bring. I think our long-haul time is now beyond us for summer holidays and we shall spend an increasing time in Spain, and who knows my wife's view that she is a better golfer than me, having never played myself, may be put to the test!

During 2009 after my retirement I think we did too much travelling and this, allied to my own inefficiency and domestic issues with my mother, have delayed the writing of this book somewhat from my original programme.

Other than our routine visits to our house and Cyprus in my first year of retirement we also managed a short break of four days in Dubai, which we had never visited before. Determined to 'see the sights' we booked dinner at the Burj Hotel on the top floor. I had been warned that afternoon tea checked in at £75 per head and that dinner would be considerably more, but we decided that as part of our retirement gift to ourselves we would 'do it' just for the experience. I am not sure that a couple of drinks, a bottle of wine a two course dinner and a coffee are entirely worth £600 and we shall not be visiting again.

One variety note involved the presentation to me of the retirement gift of a trip on the Orient Express, which was undertaken in April 2009. Lena and I flew out to Venice and stayed overnight at the Cipriani Hotel which is in itself part of the Orient Express group. We had stayed there for a mini break a couple of years earlier and really enjoyed it as the hotel faces directly towards St Mark's Square, but is separated from the hustle and bustle by the main canal.

My two trips to Venice in the last three or four years are somewhat different to the rather undercover spy story I have told earlier of my visit in the late 60s with Keith Whawell. The ride in to the hotel from the airport is quite spectacular in a high-speed water taxi, bouncing along over the wash of the other boats which speed backwards and forwards across the Lagoon.

On our first visit we found the Cipriani in need of some care and attention, despite the famous Michael Winner always raving about it in his *Sunday Times* columns. However our visit at the start of our train journey home found the hotel having undergone significant refurbishment and it was really so nice that we wished we had stayed longer than one night. Met from the taxi on the jetty by the excellent Roberto and the hotel's Assistant Manager really does add a little gloss to things. Roberto, on our earlier trip, had arranged for us to go to one of the famous glass blowing factories on the island of Murano within the Lagoon where we, surprisingly for us, actually purchased some glassware and had it shipped back to the UK; it really is lovely.

Roberto with his usual efficiency organised a water taxi to take us to the railway station the following morning, and I would seriously recommend a trip on the Orient Express for a present or special occasion. We had decided to enter into the theme of things by taking formal evening dress. We left Venice in a rather juddering and slow fashion, but soon found out what this train is all about, it is quality from end to end, all be it belonging to a different era. For travellers expecting en-suite bathrooms and the like, forget it, there is one toilet at the end of each nine-berth carriage and a very small corner hand basin in each cabin. Our attendant was brilliant and the whole thing is so well organised with two sittings for each meal, lunch on two days and dinner on the first night. You can have the choice of sitting on a table for two or joining others, and we did the latter for lunch on both days, meeting some interesting people.

Unfortunately, the Simplon Tunnel was closed for our trip, so we never actually went through Switzerland, but diverted from Innsbruck north to Munich and then west to Strasbourg, to join the originally planned route. From lunch in the dining car we seemed to go immediately to afternoon tea in the cabin, and found ourselves changing whilst on the platform at Innsbruck, awaiting a locomotive swap. As we departed for our pre-dinner drink our attendant advised that he would clear the cabin and make the beds, and we returned to find a very warm glowing room, with bunk beds neatly laid out and surprisingly comfortable, managing something in the order of five hours sleep before we rolled into France, where we hit the only real problem of our journey.

I have never liked the French particularly, stemming back to 1978, when six of us went on holiday to a rented cottage near Ille de Oleron on the Atlantic coast to the South of Brittany. This was around the time of my near departure from Morrisons. The weather was great, but it was during the usual Paris holiday season, when the city closes down for a month and everyone goes to their homes on the coast. Visiting a nudist beach, we realised that we would all have to join in, and duly stripped off. The French, I find, are very arrogant about themselves when there is not always a cause to be so, and on this particular beach were two extremely arrogant French guys, who spent most of the day standing in the sun posing. Being from Yorkshire you don't always get the message about street credibility and off we plunged into the freezing Atlantic to come out again as we were born, but having suffered the effects of the cold water, if you get my drift. As we walked back up the beach these two French men nudged each other, gave knowing glances and sniggered. I have never forgiven them!

So it was the case as the Orient Express pulled into Paris that true French organisation took over and they discovered that they did not have a locomotive to pull us back out of the station the way we had come, so as to continue our journey to Calais. We waited two hours in that station, before being hauled some ten miles out of the city into a godforsaken goods yard in the middle of nowhere, whilst the locomotive was swapped from one end to another and we continued our journey. The Orient Express company builds so much slack into their timetables, having always to give way to regular rail traffic, that we finished up arriving back at Waterloo only ten minutes behind schedule. The journey up to London from Folkestone was on a British Pullman, with yet another meal, but this time pulled by a rather ordinary diesel freight locomotive, although it was said that this locomotive usually pulls the royal train.

A fantastic experience, brilliantly organised and executed and, as I have said, something I would recommend as a once-in-a-lifetime trip to anyone, but hopefully not to become the anorak types we met during the journey, who were on their tenth, or twelfth trip. A bit like taking locomotive numbers!

One of our last travel aims, however, will involve long haul. Tennis has always been a favourite and Lena is a significant fan. We have been lucky to visit Wimbledon on several of occasions as corporate guests and during our discussions in my run up to retirement we agreed that visiting the Grand Slam Tournaments in Australia, Paris, Wimbledon and New York would be a nice thing to do, sprinkled in with some of the Masters Tournaments, in places like Germany, Italy and the Middle East, so that is our next aim.

The occasional travel by private charter plane on business did whet my appetite and in 2006, to celebrate our silver wedding anniversary, we decided to take out, effectively, a second mortgage and had a family trip, by private plane, to Florence. The group comprised of Lena and myself, my mother, Glen and Jason, daughter-in-law Helen and at that time, our one grandchild Emma. To be able to arrive at our local airport, climb aboard a sleek jet and be in the air within fifteen minutes of arrival is absolutely great, but clearly not something for every day means.

Our time in Florence was superb in lovely weather, punctuated by a heavy thunderstorm at 4 p.m. each day, but to have our family around us on this special occasion was super. Unfortunately, by this time, my mother was ailing somewhat and could not fully join in, but the spirit of the event was fantastic and in the autumn of 2010, instead of our usual jaunt to the east coast of America, we shall be repeating the experience with our friends Christine and Michael Taylor. This time the trip will be to Monte Carlo and Michael and I, as nerdy anoraks, are very much looking forward to the flight deck experience and the helicopter ride into the Principality.

Travel is a great thing; to see the way of life of others and to experience their cultures is wonderful, and if nothing else makes you realise just how lucky you are to be in a position to do it.

CHAPTER 12

On Market Street 1985–87

Although the previous year had been a success, with sales increasing 25%, to in excess of £330 million, and rental income, on my side of the business, pushing close to £1 million per annum, Ken was not a happy bunny.

At the opening of the Grantham Complex the previous April, his clear irritation with some unfortunate circumstances surrounding Store Operations Director, Steve Butler, had spilled over to a thinly veiled criticism of the ambience of stores internally and, although I was not party to it, it was clear he had had a 'go' at Ron Curry about this.

1985 had us scheduled to open two new large stores at Killingworth, in North Tyneside and Rotherham, in South Yorkshire. Each of these developments were challenging in their own ways.

Killingworth was a new township, established to accommodate the slum clearance and overspill of the nearby city of Newcastle, but like many 1960s developments it had been carried out by the Development Corporation very much at a cost, with a mixture of multi-storey flats and low rise developments in extremely cheap materials which very quickly showed their age and manifested significant basic defects, giving rise to damp and the like. Killingworth very quickly went downmarket and became almost ghetto-like in its appearance.

The local authority had wanted to kick-start redevelopment of the area with a new, large, supermarket and then work outwards from the centre with regeneration. The local authority, North Tyneside Council, appointed Dysart Developments, the husband and wife team of Jack and Caroline Fawcett, to carry out the scheme. Jack was a man of the North East and well connected. The pair of them had carried out a significant amount of work for Asda, but in this case it appeared that Asda were not interested in the site and the Fawcetts turned to us.

I well remember our first meeting with them and the local authority. They picked me up from our potato packing plant, at

Flaxby, adjacent to the A1 trunk road at Knaresborough, and proceeded North at a speed which hardly ever dipped below the 'ton', including screaming across the Tyne Bridge at a speed which, I swear, was touching 60 mph, with Caroline at the wheel.

Not knowing these two, I was rather on edge about them and the meeting and very concerned that we were going to be late. Jack sensed this and drawing on his umpteenth cigarette calmly turned to me and said, 'don't worry, they'll wait for us, this is a big deal for the area.' Needless to say the scheme proceeded and I found out very early on just how rough Killingworth was.

The 1960s shopping centre had incorporated a very large Woolworths hypermarket type development, which were known as Woolcos and which had sprouted in numerous areas of the country. There were new road systems around the site and a bridge link from the shopping centre across one of the main roads directly into the adjoining multi-storey blocks of flats. The whole thing was in terminal decline and the local authority had taken to housing recently discharged inmates of Durham Jail and others into the crumbling flats.

At our first site meeting, I was horrified to see one of the locals hot-footing it out of the shopping centre to the flats carrying a large television and being pursued by a security guard, who was rapidly catching him up. The fugitive, half-way across the elevated walkway to safety, realised that he was being caught, calmly put the television down on the bridge deck and flattened the pursuing security guard, with a perfectly executed right hook. Following on from which, the fugitive calmly picked up the television and made good his escape. What were we coming to!

The Rotherham development was a very similar size, but a totally different proposition. John Glaisher operated a local store at Wickersley, a suburb on the south side of Rotherham, and had approached Ken Morrison previously as to whether or not we wanted to acquire his business. The business consisted of one store and a small one at that and we had initially rejected the notion, but when Mr Glaisher came back with the business, plus a large land holding upon which, he was convinced, planning permission could be granted for a large store, then we were interested and the deal went through.

The store at Bramley, Rotherham, sat on top of some planned mining works to excavate one of two large scale coal seams running underground and the design for the store broke up the large area into six smaller portions, each one hinged to accommodate the 'ripple effect' of coal being extracted beneath and subsequent ground movement. As a consequence the external skin of the building marked a complete change in Morrisons' approach to design. Gone was the well-favoured local facing brick or stone and in came plastic coated metal panels, each one of which was capable of moving within certain tolerances, and the main tolerance was to be taken up the six major hinges which ran through the building from floor to roof level. There was a cost penalty for this, the irony of which was not lost on me when following the miners' strike the previous year the coal industry was slowly but consistently closed down. The coal never was extracted from beneath us and the marvellous design was never called to justify itself. The store was subsequently extended, the site developed, which generated significant income for the Company and is now a major shopping focal point at Junction 1 of the M18 motorway.

Ken's rather pointed comments about the business not moving forward, made the previous year, had hit home hard, and not just on the property side. Work was carried out and we decided to go electronic with bar scanning checkouts and everything that came with it, including better stock control and so on.

The installation of EPOS, or Electronic Point Of Sale, was entrusted to the Administration Manager, Rod Smaldon, of whom I have spoken right at the start of my Morrisons career, and his Admin Manager, Linda Padgett, and they, in fairness, became the lynchpin of the installation in our first two stores for 1985; indeed, EPOS became less known as a point of sale and more to stand for Either Padgett Or Smaldon.

On my side of things Ken's irritation with the interiors of our stores manifested itself with an instruction from Ron Curry to improve the area of the rear of the check-outs, that it to say the public circulation area once they have paid for goods. I looked at all sorts of schemes to get us away from a simple flat ceiling and eventually at both the Killingworth and Rotherham sites, I settled on a very glitzy metal strip ceiling, formed to the shape of a vault. The mirror effect gave the impression of greater space and the lighting, which shone up into the areas, gave a very good reflection. This method of stylising stores in this area continued for many years until, rather perversely, costs indicated we should go back once more to a flat ceiling. Everything goes round in circles and nothing is new!

In March of 1985, while both stores had commenced work on site, came the major conversations and meeting which were to change, in my opinion, the whole course of the Company, for the future and to the current day. 'Market Street' was conceived.

Enter Francis Robert Emmott. Bob had been a Store Manager when I had joined the Company, but had progressed and by this time was Produce Director on the Company's Board of Management, along with myself and others. Bob was short in stature, but huge in enthusiasm. Aggressive, bad tempered, loud and argumentative, but an excellent retailer. Over his career, including joining the Main Board on the same day as myself in February 1987, Bob would upset many, but gain the respect of even more, including me.

In my time up to March 1985, a telephone call from Bob was usually to question why some maintenance had not been carried out or to explore the possibilities of further extensions to the produce pack house in Bradford, which was his responsibility and which was seemingly in a permanent state of under-capacity, in terms of floor area, to the volume of product which was being turned out. The place literally bulged at the seams.

In March Bob walked into my office and proceeded to repeat the various carping criticisms which had been uttered by Ken the previous year, at the same time announcing, 'You and me are going to do something about it.' I explained that I was already charged by Ron Curry to deal with the areas behind the checkouts, which brought a comment to the effect of, 'that's alright, but I am talking about an overhaul of the retail business. I have had an idea and you and I are going to see the boss'.

'What's the idea and when are we going to see him?' I asked.

'The idea is in my head and we are going to see him now,' was the answer!

I explained to Bob that I didn't usually go anywhere, not least of all the Chairman's office, without some idea of what we were going to discuss. Bob's answer was to take a piece of scrap paper and draw a series of angled lines, which he said represented the face of some new counter service departments he was intending to introduce.

'We are going to be the butcher, the baker and the candlestick maker,' he said, 'and you're coming with me, because you're going to build it.'

I protested to Bob that I felt we would last no more than five minutes, or get the sack, or both, but he was undeterred. Bob was a determined little fighter and was not going to let this go in a hurry.

We lasted five minutes, with Bob first of all blustering and then getting cross when the Chairman started questioning the motives and everything else. Upon being thrown out rather 'on our ear' I set off to walk back to my office, with Bob behind me effing and blinding all the way down the corridor. My reaction was that 'that was that', but Bob was having none of it and indeed rather perversely thought Ken was interested. I thought Ken showed more interest in what he was having for lunch than Bob's earth shattering proposal.

Undeterred he was, however, and Bob went away and got some drawings which showed that we could duplicate our pre-packed food offer by incorporating counter service for fish, delicatessen, bread, cakes and so on and that this would become known as the 'Market Concept'.

A few days later we returned to Ken's office and this time got a grudging acceptance of the proposal and a further acceptance that it could be incorporated into the new stores at Killingworth and Rotherham. I feel to this day that Ken's consent was forthcoming because we were only opening two stores in 1985 and that way the damage couldn't be too great if we had got it wrong.

Weeks of frenetic activity followed with Bob monopolising my Project Manager Vic Sephton for both schemes, and the drawing and construction team of Allan Nuttall, the Midlands based shop fitters.

No costs or budgets were prepared for this work, we simply ploughed on and did it. So here we were with two new concept stores with a new electronic point of sale installation requiring new skills, additional staff to man the new departments and additional training resources to teach people the dying arts of the High Street, namely fish filleting, in-store butchery and bakery.

These trades have now been salvaged for the industry and Morrisons, over the last fifteen or twenty years, have been a prime supporter of college courses to train these previously vanishing/ diminishing skills.

Norwest Holst and Wimpey, the contractors for Killingworth and Rotherham, found the accommodation of these extra works difficult to swallow, and indeed when we opened the Killingworth store on 22 October 1985, they had been working until 5 p.m. the previous day, finishing work off. It did not make for a very happy birthday for me and although I did not attend in the North East, the criticisms from Ron Curry rang in my ears for days after.

One week later we opened the Rotherham store in a more comfortable manner, at least until Edna Morrison, Ken's wife, pulled Bob Emmott and myself to one side and took us on a tour of the Market concept, our new baby. Edna, who was a great lady and one possessing significant retail knowledge, pointed out to us that if we were housewives responsible for cleaning the store, we would not have put in such stupid details as brass bar rails around the front of the various counters. We had gone over the top, but over the years following the scheme, Bob's initial idea was developed, refined, taken apart, re-developed and so on and so on, to the point that Market Street, as it became known, is the brand leader for Morrisons.

When I started to write this book, I spoke with Bob, who now lives a quieter life somewhere near Gatwick Airport.

Bob joined the Main Board of Morrisons in February 1987, on the same day as myself, and progressed through the ranks of that Board, until a point where for one reason or another his relationship with Ken became less successful and he departed. Bob's subsequent career led him to similar fresh food roles as the one he had occupied at Morrisons with, firstly, Sainsburys, then Asda and for a short time Somerfield.

I called him at the start of this writing epic and explained to him that I was going to feature Market Street in one of the chapters. We had a few laughs about the exploits over those frenetic months of early 1985 and a further frenetic twenty-four hours in 1993, which I shall recount later.

Bob Emmott and in my view, Bob Emmott alone, deserves the credit for catapulting Morrisons along the route to where it is today, at least on the fresh food front. I do not believe that Bob ever fully got the credit he deserved, but interestingly around the turn of the decade in 1990, when Market Street was more established and developed, Morrisons were awarded 'Retailer of the Year' in two successive years, and I believe that Bob's efforts, ideas and pure inspiration had much to do with this.

In 2005, the company was establishing itself with a full quota of Non-Executive Directors and in September of that year, I spent the full day with one of my colleagues, Susan Murray, trying to explain the property side of things. We visited an established store at her home town of Banbury, a store almost completed, in construction terms, in Gloucester, and a small acquired Safeway store at Ross-on-Wye, which was to be the subject of future extensions. During our journey between points in the car Susan raised with me the issue of Market Street and I explained to her the story as I have just unfolded it to you.

Susan expressed surprised and said that she had thought it was all Ken's idea, and had found my story interesting and revealing.

Ken's tactic on all things such as this was always to say that it was a team effort. When we won awards, it was a 'team effort', when we got good results it was a 'team effort', but in with all this Ken never, ever went out of his way to contradict the view of the public and the City that 'never mind what Ken says, we all know it's him.' Well in this case it wasn't and in many other cases too it wasn't, and whilst Ken never went out of the way to actively claim credit – because he couldn't – he also never went out of the way to disclaim praise – which he could have. This in my view led to problems in the Company at the time of Ken's succession in that the City and many others formed the view that Morrisons was a 'one-man-band'. It never was and its performance since Ken's retirement has, in my view, very clearly demonstrated that.

After the major activity of 1985, albeit producing two stores, but two stores of a vastly different image to what had gone before, 1986 was something of an anti-climax, with only one store, in Dukinfield in Greater Manchester, opening. This was a small version, which was subsequently extended, but incorporated the Market Street concept. Such was the interest created by only three stores with this image that we had a visit to Greater Manchester, by Senior Executives of the Dutch retailer, Albert Heijn, who Ron Curry had known for some years and they left for the Netherland's mighty impressed.

During this time we introduced a new focus of refurbishing and extending existing stores and almost constant updating and expansion of our central facilities for fresh food production, produce packing and distribution.

Ken Blundell, who had been Store Operations Director at the start of my career with the Company, he of the fearsome response, stepped down from his then current role of Company Secretary, to concentrate on development and help Ron Curry with site finding and development leads. Ken had been doing this for some four years during the property and development divisions' sojourn to Horsforth, which had lasted from 1978 to 1984.

Ken Blundell's work within the property function also brought him into contact with a touch of project management when the rest of our team were busy, and it was on one of these projects that our on/off contact with the ace demolition man Arnold Marriott was renewed.

Ken had always had a soft spot for the store at Keighley, which was originally built and opened in 1968. The store overtraded, traded on two levels and was really too small for the emerging market. Goods had to be unloaded from the street outside the main warehouse door and this often gave rise to conflict with our neighbours who were almost all involved with the remnants of the wool textile industry, being engineers of one description or another.

I came to develop a certain fondness for the Keighley store, becoming accustomed to meeting Ken for our regular Saturday morning discussions there. Keighley was located some three miles away from Ken's house and it was well known that this was always his first call on a Saturday morning, for a cup of tea and some light refreshment. Indeed the Keighley store was where I served my own apprenticeship on stocktaking and the management service of Christmas lunch to the staff.

Through the early 80s we had set about acquiring land around the store, demolishing the property and forming better facilities, and Ken took this as his opportunity at project management, although I think I did assist in a few ways!

We came to a point, eventually, when we decided that we should go for broke and ultimately end up with a large store, effectively rebuilding the 1960s version while at the same time trading, and Keighley was to see three or four major exercises of this nature to get the property to the state and condition it represents today.

Keighley, as I have probably recalled elsewhere, was very much a frontier town in the days of the Industrial Revolution. The Irish immigrants journeyed down from Scotland and found Keighley as one of the first industrialised towns in which to settle. There was much slum development and indeed adjoining our store was a tenement block which would have graced the darkest slums of Glasgow in its time. We needed to get this down, but got wind that the Local Authority was going to list it, as an example of the Industrial Revolution in Britain. The notion was utterly ridiculous, as the building was derelict and even in today's trend of converting old mill buildings to luxury flats would never have fit that bill. Enter, Arnold Marriott.

By now Arnold had decanted his Bradford operation to Pencaitland, on the exposed corner of Scotland, the Southern entrance to the Firth of Forth. There was one road in and one road out. Arnold never revealed the reason for his sudden move from Bradford, but did confide in Steve Watkins of RP & P fame that the one road gave him an opportunity to 'leave by the other exit, if I see a blue light coming my way'. I think Arnold overplayed his hand somewhat.

Upon hearing the discussion of the tenement building, Ron Curry decided that he would renew his acquaintance with Arnold and take control of this rather tricky demolition. Arnold was contacted and a meeting arranged for the following evening at a public house in Riddlesden on the outskirts of Keighley. Ron said he felt that we should go incognito, which for the benefit of this exercise meant that we should both take our wives, and Caroline and Lena duly accompanied us, arriving at the pub just before 7 p.m.

Arnold, his usual chirpy self, was sitting in the tap room accompanied by his 'minder', a man a Scottish descent, dressed in a full length Crombie overcoat, who filled the door entrance to the tap room.

Negotiations began, to be disrupted after about five minutes with the Scots 'minder' telling the locals who were assembling for their nightly game of dominoes, that the tap room was hosting a 'private function, now get lost'. Arnold had us over a barrel and he knew it, but we managed to chip away some of his asking price and it was agreed that the work would take place early the following Sunday morning. Arnold gleefully responded, 'I knew you would agree, now come and see the equipment.' We were escorted to a plant yard quite near the Keighley store, where stood a brand new machine with a telescopic arm and a hydraulic grab mechanism. These were new to the market in those days, although they are now used for pulling down a lot of high-rise buildings, the 'nibbler' on the end of the telescopic arm being particularly useful. Both Ron and I noted that the machine was brand new, there was not even any mud on the tyres, but we also noted that the owner's name had been obscured by masking tape. Ron, being particularly 'undercover', said he thought that this was a good idea as it would prevent the press asking questions about the demolition contractor. Arnold, more down to earth, replied that the masking tape had been used because the owner did not actually realise that Arnold had the machine! Oh dear.

The following day we duly filed notice of our intention to demolish with the Council, and at 10 a.m. the following Sunday morning I received a call from Arnold, which was simply to the effect 'It's down', whereupon he hung up. What he didn't tell me was that in felling the building, which had taken all of fifteen minutes, he had also severed a mains electric cable, which led to trouble.

Bradford Council denied any knowledge of receiving the notice of intended demolition and prosecuted Arnold, for which he was fined, although it has to be said the amount of the fine subsequently became a variation on the contract price and the Keighley scheme was able to proceed to what it is today.

I never felt that we did anything wrong, as indeed it was never our intention to do anything wrong anywhere. I believe that the Council were somewhat dilatory, it being a Friday afternoon when they received the notice.

With hindsight, 1986 was very much a year of preparing for change, the change which was to come in the early part of 1987. The slacker pace of new store development and the more 'routine' work of numerous existing location extensions and refurbishments had become quite routine and was being well handled and I found that my attentions were being drawn elsewhere, either deliberately by others, or just by force of circumstance.

Early in the year, together with selected other parties, notably our electrical and suspended ceiling contractors, I made my first ever private charter flight to Liege, in Belgium, to visit a lighting manufacturing company who had pioneered a new system of lighting, which was in use on most of the road networks in Belgium.

The system relied on lengths of highly polished duct work, which diminished in their sectional size over the length and relied upon two lamps only, one at each length of the duct, and thereafter reflected light to discharge downwards. The benefit of this was lower running cost, less lamps to replace and so on. I decided after two trips that the system was not for use in our stores, but could be beneficial for the planned centre distribution depot which was to be built at Wakefield, and duly commissioned it.

The two trips I made to Liege were fascinating to me. The opportunity to take the front seat of a small aircraft and listen to the air traffic 'buzz' was a great experience and one I came to enjoy over the following years.

My third trip to Liege was made in the company of Bob Emmott, Store Operations Director, Steve Butler, and Security Director, Trevor Bryan, and in a more sedate manner, by car, in the spring of 1986. In addition to a visit to the lighting factory, we also took in a visit to the chicken production factory of Albert Heijn, at Eindhoven, a produce packing machinery manufacturer, and my first encounter with our Dutch Agents, Bos Brothers, at De Lier, near the Hook of Holland, a relationship which I was to renew in the early part of the next Millennium.

At the end of March 1986, I found myself in a rather unique office position for the first time since joining Morrisons. My secretary of almost ten years, Susan Everett, left the company. Sue had been with me since the department's move to its Horsforth satellite office in late 1978, and like her ultimate successor Glynis Wilkinson, had been loyal and steadfast. But since our move back to Bradford, some two years earlier, Sue had been involved in a couple of road accidents and had decided that the time was now right for retirement. Shortly after she left me she and her husband Charles adopted first one and then a second daughter and she settled down to the life of motherhood, for which she had obviously yearned.

In May of the same year, I was invited to follow the footsteps of two or three of my staff and take a visit to the factory of Besam, the automatic door-gear people, in Sweden. Ron Curry was not too keen on this, seeing it as a 'jolly', and even suggested that I should take holiday to accommodate the trip. Ken thought otherwise. Some years earlier I had visited a building exhibition in Germany to look at automatic door equipment and we had eventually settled on a little known manufacturer, but quickly changed to Besam, who are the world leader in this field and with whom we developed some unique solutions for one-off situations.

Our trip spanned some four days, taking in two nights in Copenhagen and a middle night near the factory, which was located quite close to Malmo in Southern Sweden. The journey coincided with the suspected spread of atomic radiation, as a consequence of the Chernobyl Power Plant disaster a week earlier and caused three or four of the original party to drop out. I thought there was not much danger, although I was not much reassured by Ron Curry, on my return, when he advised me that he thought he had seen an atomic cloud passing over the Yorkshire Dales. I laughed this off at the time, until some twelve months later farmers in North Yorkshire were reporting problems with that season's lambing!

The trip was fascinating and reassured me that Morrisons were ahead of at least two of our competitors in terms of our demands and requirements for automatic door gear.

In late September my final trip of the year took place. *Supermarketing*, a trade publication, ran an annual Manager of the Year award through the industry and our Southport Store Manager John Tame was one of the winners and recipients of a study trip to the States, which took in several days around Washington DC, followed by two or three days around Orlando in Florida. Each award winner was to be accompanied by a Head Office Executive, and the circumstances conspired that no one from the Board was able to go and that I was nominated.

Ron Curry gave me a very stern talking to and said that he required a full report, with photographs, to be tabled to the Board within five days of our return, and this was duly produced by myself and John.

John Tame had joined the Company in 1983 as a consequence of Morrisons acquiring three stores from the International Group, located at Southport, Gainsborough in Lincolnshire and Eccles in Greater Manchester. The stores were not great and Southport was ultimately one location which we were glad to dispose of, following the acquisition of Safeway in 2004. The Eccles store was replaced by a new build unit, which we acquired as a site from Safeway, prior to us acquiring the company as a whole. John was, and remains, a smashing bloke, whose company I enjoyed over our week away, although the start was somewhat hairy.

In those days there was no Visa Waiver and you had to have the proper form in your passport. I had checked and had been told that this was unnecessary, only to find on my arrival in London the evening before our flight that I needed one. Arrangements were made with the US Embassy in Grosvenor Square and I presented myself as the doors opened, returning to the Heathrow hotel with an hour or so to spare before our flight departed.

The trip was fascinating and took in a visit to the Food Marketing Institute in Washington, whose exhibitions I was later to attend on three occasions in Chicago. The differences between the US and European trading are quite marked, the financial performance of the companies concerned being significantly different, but I was struck particularly by the Publix stores, which are very regional around the South and in particular in Florida, and I have visited two or three of their stores, even since my retirement. They very much remind me of Morrisons, being focused on food sales.

The second part of our trip to America was based in Florida and we arrived in Orlando late Saturday afternoon, with the prospect of a day off, the following day, to visit Disney World. John Tame had been to the self same amusement park only two weeks previously on his holidays and was our excellent guide for the day, which finished with the tumultuous ride on Space Mountain, a ride which left me with blistered fingers, I held on to the protection rails so hard.

A great trip and a report following it that was well received by the Board.

Coming up to the end of 1986 and to the start of what was to be my 'historic' year, I felt fairly good about things. The Company was going forward, but I did have growing doubts as to the succession of Ron Curry, the path for which is revealed in the next chapter.

CHAPTER 13

The Big Reward and Meeting 'God'
1987–90

THE YEAR STARTED MUCH AS the previous one had ended: we were due to open three new stores in the course of the year: at Bishop Auckland, Preston and in our home city, where we had planned a huge, 22 acre development of retail for ourselves featuring our largest store, some non-food retail sheds and a small industrial park with an enterprise centre. We were also well into planning our opening programme and our site acquisition programme for the following year, which was shaping up quite nicely.

One major area of uncertainty hung over the Property and Development Division, which was the succession plan for Ron Curry. Ron was approaching his 58th birthday, due on 1 May, the same day as my wife's, and had previously announced that he was going to retire at that time, but had given no indication whatsoever as to the succession process. Late the previous year Ron and Caroline had invited me, Peter Roberts my Board of Management colleague, and Russell Walker the Estates Manager, to his house for supper. We had not really known at that time but this was clearly part of Ron's selection process for his successor, but he had not said so. Peter and I, being the next senior members of the Department, had taken it upon ourselves to decide that there was probably not going to be a clear Board appointment. The Morrison philosophy at this time and for some years after was to always to promote from within, to allow for seamless succession and continuity of strategy and mindset.

Ron's situation became increasingly debated between the two of us and we had sat down on several occasions and come to a loose working plan as to how we would operate.

The first six weeks of the year went, as most six weeks had done for me up to that point, in extensive travel and meeting planners for the following year's stores, getting teams together and my routine

133

day-to-day events such as monthly insurance meetings with our brokers and so on, all of which changed dramatically, on Thursday 19 February.

Peter Roberts and I had been to an early afternoon meeting with Bolton Council regarding a planned new store, adjoining the town centre. We had been awarded the scheme, in competition with others, based, as it usually was, on a financial bid and architectural design, and the store would replace one of the former Whelan units in an adjoining street.

We left the meeting round about 3 o'clock in the afternoon, with Peter setting off to go and look at other things west of the Pennines and me planning to return to the office. As I was leaving, one of the Planning Department secretaries pulled me to one side and advised me that I was to call the office immediately. On doing so I was told by Glynis Wilkinson, the girl who was to become my loyal, faithful and really quite brilliant PA, that I was to return to the office, not to go anywhere else and immediately upon my return I was to see Ron Curry. No time to take the coat off, or anything else. I questioned Glynis as to the purpose of this call, but got nowhere and, as was my usual custom with anything to do with a demand from Ron, feared the worse. There was a Board Meeting that day and I assumed that something had come up which Ron had been unable to answer, probably felt I should have told him about but had not, and retribution was possibly at hand.

I drove back across the M62, oblivious to what was to happen, but gained something more of an impression when, upon getting out of my car I was met by Glynis, standing on the corner of the office block in a cold northerly wind dressed in just her office attire, quite clearly freezing. It transpired that she had been looking through the window waiting for me, remember no mobile telephones and therefore no ready checks on progress.

A second chance to quiz the PA who, through chattering teeth, told me that it was a very important summons, but nothing to be worried about. Further questioning produced a stonewall.

Upon arriving at Ron's office, he slowly rose from behind his desk and walked round the side and stuck out his hand. Seeing the quizzical look on my face, he simply remarked 'Congratulations, you're on the Board, Ken wants to see you now.' Before I had chance to ask anything further, he was ushering me out of the office and telling me to return once my next duty was fulfilled.

I walked passed a beaming Glynis, deposited my coat in my own room and walked the same walk that I had done ten years earlier, in frogman's mask and flippers, to Ken's office.

Upon arrival, Ken advised me that several changes had been made on the Board that day. The biggest of all, and a major shock, was that Managing Director, Bob Stott, had resigned, apparently following a difference of strategic opinion, though shortly after it emerged that Bob was joining Cleckheaton-based Hillards Stores.

The Board had decided that rather than new appointments leaking out of the ship, two birds would be killed with one stone, and in addition to my appointment as Property Director, there would also be Board appointments for my fellow Board of Management Directors, Martin Ackroyd as Finance Director and Company Secretary, and Bob Emmott as Fresh Food Director. Martin had been Company Secretary for some time, working under the previous Finance Director, Howard Watkinson before the latter's departure, and had effectively been carrying out the Finance role for some time.

Ken passed me a few warm words, advised me that the other two already knew their 'fate', and left me to get on.

I returned to Ron, with all sorts of scrambled thoughts passing through my head, the prime of which was, how would Peter Roberts, my fellow Board of Management Director until today, react, as I was sure Peter had ambitions for the top job. Peter was a few years younger than me, but had made a mark on the development side of the department. Glynis, who had known about the appointment almost from the minute it was made, was ecstatic. As I have recalled elsewhere, I had known Glynis from school A-Level age and had been party to selecting her as Ron's PA and Office Manager some six months earlier, as the utter stand-out candidate for the position.

Ron said he would talk things through with Peter Roberts that night on the phone, but felt that we could expect that Peter's remaining term with the Company would be relatively short, and so it ultimately proved. There was no difficulty between us as far as I was concerned when Peter returned to the office, having taken the following day off, but clearly he was promptly on the lookout for new employment, and left fairly speedily, indeed before I had taken up the position of Property Director totally on 1 May 1987. He has subsequently done very well. Peter has had a succession of positions of power with various Development Companies and, I suspect, has made quite a financial success of life, and good luck to him. Our paths did cross on a number of occasions, either at corporate social events or on site acquisition matters, and whatever his whereabouts today I am sure he is still doing well.

After the initial 'talking to' by Ron and a lecture in the fact that time was short between now and his departure and 'I have much to tell you', I telephoned Lena and introduced myself as the new Property Director.

Celebrations were very low key, after all I would not take the 'chair' until 1 May, and prior to then I had an important issue of a significant court appearance to overcome, so I celebrated with a couple of quick pints with Glynis, cancelled the evening meal at home and went to one of Jason's favourite steak pubs in Bradford. By this time Glen was away at University in Nottingham. And that, simply, was that.

The following week Bob Stott gave a private dinner for a few colleagues and I was fortunate to be invited. Bob wished me well and of course our paths were to come together some years later on his return from his sojourn, firstly at Hillards and then with Geest, the banana people, based in Lincolnshire.

The next two weeks were a blur as I was inundated with letters of congratulation on my appointment, and telephone calls of sage advice from many whom I respected, such as the noted Bradford Planning Solicitor, Roger Suddards. Then come 9 March I was off to London for an appearance in the Royal Courts of Justice on The Strand, a period which was to span the next three weeks or so.

Our court appearance arose from the Company's part in the rather ill-fated development of the so-called Harrogate Conference Complex.

Morrisons had sought representation in this North Yorkshire spa town for some years, it being a natural progression from our West Yorkshire roots, and we thought we could do well. Harrogate, although dressing itself as a spa town and holiday resort, a role which it fulfils with some accomplishment, also has its seedier side, with drug problems and deprived families.

In the spring of 1976, we had been approached by a Scottish developer John 'Jock' Maxwell, who had been appointed by the Council to carry out construction on the new Conference Centre, including retail, exhibition halls and a hotel, on a rather cramped site in the centre of Harrogate. Harrogate was one of the first locations in the country to host exhibitions, trade fairs and the like, a role it usually fulfilled from a rather decrepit exhibition hall and temporary tented accommodation, but it was at the forefront in its time. More recently, however, Harrogate had been losing out to purpose-built exhibition and conference centres, such as Birmingham NEC, Brighton and their like, and the Borough Council had seen its attraction ebbing away, together with the trade which came with it.

Mr Maxwell had convinced the Borough Council to go with him, and after to-ing and fro-ing on the very outline and undetailed scheme Morrisons signed an agreement in July 1976 to take the retail space. We were the prime tenants and institution finance depended on us to bring together a scheme which had been on the books since 1971.

Things did not go well. Maxwell failed to obtain the necessary finance, defaulted on various payments to contractors and consultants, and twelve months on from the original signing the Council terminated its agreement with him and assumed the developer's role. By this time, Laing Construction had been appointed for the project and I well remember attending the site with Ken Morrison and John Dowd, together with then Finance Director Howard Watkinson, to the sod cutting ceremony. As I recall Ron Curry was on holiday.

Sir Kirby Laing and the Mayor of Harrogate performed the duty by putting the bucket of a JCB digger through some concrete on the site, Sir Kirby wearing a broad smile and Ken Morrison, rather dryly, commenting 'he knows more than we do'. Laing's, at that time, had something of a reputation for making most of their profits on the back of contractual claims, and so it proved. The building was not designed properly, over-ran by a significant period and the original plan, that Morrisons would take occupation of the superstore in May 1978 for shop-fitting and opening, did not materialise, the store being handed over and opened almost three years late. In and amongst this, we had refused to accept the shell of the building, on one noted occasion because the floor was so out of level that it required major remedial work.

Another interesting, but certainly not welcome, aside of this scheme revolved around the design of the building. Despite its genteel image as a spa town Harrogate is, in fact, quite isolated and exposed in terms of weather and we were anxious that the original design, for which we would be responsible under a repairing lease, properly dealt with our own aspirations.

Morrisons had always specified a weather struck or bucket handled joint to its brickwork. Not for us a deep recess, and it was to our horror that we discovered the architect for the Conference Centre has specified just the latter. We did not accept this, we had certainly not asked for it, but the architect would not budge. This was his monument.

We argued that the deeply recessed joints would become a haven for moss and other growth. In the winter months, wind driven snow would nestle in the deep joints, the resultant thawing water would remain and if followed by keen frosts this water would work on the brickwork, expanding and contracting and eventually blowing the face off the brick. In some instances we discovered that the recesses were so deep that water could eventually track its way across the cavity ties to the inner leaf of block work and the resultant damp would eventually work its way through and blow the plaster off the internal wall of our store, necessitating extensive repairs. Ron and I were not having any of this.

The legal documentation between ourselves and the Borough Council allowed for arbitration in the event of a failure to agree, and so we duly went to arbitration and won our point. The Borough Council and their design team were horrified and refused to accept the decision, ultimately coming to an agreement with us that the deeply recessed brickwork would remain, but the Council would absolve Morrison of its repairing liabilities for the external walls, the cavity, the internal block work, the plaster and the decoration on it all. In effect, we were absolved any liability and cost for looking after the outside skin of our own building. Visitors to Harrogate today will observe a Conference Centre with brickwork shrouded in moss in its sheltered areas and the judgement of the arbitrator thoroughly vindicated.

The Harrogate arbitration gave rise to one of Ron Curry's proudest moments, when he stood up in front of the arbitrator and proclaimed that Harrogate was the first place in England that the snow from Siberia would hit, as it was the next highest point. A story I have recounted to many people, whether it be actually true or not, but Ron was usually accurate with his facts with circumstances like this.

The final account to the Borough Council for this fiasco was some £36 million against an initial contract value £6 million. The Director of Technical Services Bob Mayo was wrongly slated for his part in the role and one or two others got away scot free. A so-called independent report produced by two architects Anthony Selman and George Palmer attempted, wrongly, to paint Morrisons as one of bad boys in the scheme, being 'very experienced negotiators', the inference being that we had run rings around the Borough Council.

The delays and associated costs which we had incurred meant someone had to pay. I well remember Ron reading the report on the debacle, a copy of which I still have in my possession, with Ron's pencilled comments in the margin on almost every page. He was very much in favour of suing the report writers for defamation, but in the end we settled on suing the Borough Council for just over £2 million, which in 1987 terms was rather a lot of money, and I was charged with making sure we won the case.

Our side of the case was to be conducted by one Sean Spencer QC, a member of a rather eminent Chamber in Leeds, who had acted for us in other issues to do with the Conference Centre, most notably the arbitration when we failed to agree the type of pointing to the brickwork.

My appearance in London brought me in front of 'God', the same Donald Keating QC, who had written the various books on contract upon which my final year thesis at college, had been based.

Unfortunately for the Borough council, they had compounded their errors on the Conference Centre, by appointing the wrong barrister to present their case. Not to say that Donald Keating, or Sir Donald, as he later became before his death, was an incompetent barrister, far from it. He was the king of the building contract, but this case was not necessarily about a building contract, it was a complex web which required the judge to determine over twenty answers to different questions, and the sum total of the claim to be awarded would depend on a complex equation, which put simply, I can only describe as the answer to problem one, multiplied by the answer to problem fifteen, divided by the answer to problem nineteen, equals £X . . . and so on, through the whole issue.

Sean Spencer, who is now a circuit judge or recorder in the North East was simply superb. His grasp of the issues, along with the rest of the team which we had assembled, was just brilliant and he was very amply aided, in particular by Grant Thornton, the accountants.

The case was so complex that we even had to give evidence and agree a notional review of the rent which would have accrued after the first five years of the lease and, of course, accrued five years after the issue of the real lease, when the market, and therefore rental value had changed. Other issues had been introduced, such as the automatic doors, now common to most retail shops, which were not a feature at the time the store should have been complete, and we had to agree, through the court, the costs of these doors at the original completion date, compared to what we had actually paid. On top of all this, of course, came the addition of percentages for professional fees and so on. The whole thing was an accountants' and surveyors' nightmare.

Our team came together however, under Sean and our instructing solicitor John Hall, of Gordon's in Bradford, who the Company used totally for every issue of its business for many years. At my side was my former colleague at Rex Procter and Partners, Steve Watkins, by now a Partner running the Morrison Account and of course, qualified like me on the back of the writings of Donald Keating. When it became our turn to give evidence and be cross-examined by the great man, I, who cannot speak for Steve, was shaking like a bowl of jelly, but as I have said the Borough Council had picked the wrong man and I was able to answer his questions with some ease.

We won through, the judge found in our favour and we ended up with an agreed settlement, rather than having to go back to Court. I believe to this day that the Borough Council could have settled with us before the Court hearing, but had to go through the process in order to justify themselves to the District Auditor and the electorate of Harrogate, who were paying off the debt for the Conference Centre for many years afterwards.

During our time in London we built a team: the solicitor, myself, the barrister and our advisors, who came and went depending on when they were required to appear in court. Most of us, barrister excluded, took to eating in Covent Garden every night at a restaurant called 'Penny's Place'. As conservative Yorkshiremen we knew what we liked and we liked what we knew, so it became easy for us to make a decision.

On one particular night and buoyed up by several glasses of wine, we noticed a rather furtive couple dining in the corner and in animated conversation, with hands held across the table. On the back of a dare, we drew a heart on a table napkin and sent it across with the words 'for goodness sake, ask her to marry you', the couple left shortly afterwards, but as they passed the young lady concerned said 'I would, but he already is', upon which John Hall quickly pulled out his business card and announced himself as an expert on divorce hearings!

One of the waiters, who had got to know us quite well, upon hearing this, told us that his own marriage was in difficulties and fuelled by a few more glasses of wine, we took it upon ourselves to call his wife in Brighton and try and effect a reconciliation. She was absolutely staggered to receive the call and promised that she would make the trip to London the following day to see him. What became of that, only they know.

Armed with our victory in the London courts, I became buoyed with a new confidence. Ken and Ron had started monthly Property Board Meetings, in order to save excessive time at the normal Board Meetings, and I attended these together with Ron. In April Peter Roberts left and I started to nurture his Deputy, Chris Evenson, who I was later that year to promote to the Board of Management and who was to remain as my Deputy for my entire period, up to my retirement.

After a rather grand dinner at Ron's favourite restaurant at the end of April, he left following the Board Meeting on the last day of that month, and I was 'It'. Lena also retired and left the Company the same day, to avoid any future conflict of interest.

In mid June I was responsible for the opening of my very first store as Property Director at Bishop Auckland. In those days, as in the past, we had a 'bun fight' the previous evening in the store, to which we invited the Local Authority and others, and everything went well to finish off the site on an old railway goods yard where I had become marooned on my site visit. The morning after the store opening the

Board and wives drove the relatively short distance to Newcastle, walking over the site of the old Vickers Armstrong Gun Works next to the Tyne. Thereafter, my thoughts concentrated on the next opening in July at Preston.

The docklands area of Preston, like many in the UK, were worn out and unused and became the grounds of a massive regeneration scheme, of which we were the first. Ron had started the store off and, like everything in those days we were looking for a theme, when Ron hit upon the idea of a lighthouse attached to the store entrance. This was to be no ordinary lighthouse, this was to be a Trinity House Lighthouse, and so I spent one Sunday afternoon visiting a similar scheme on the Great Orme at Llandudno, and ultimately the Morrisons' version appeared to standard Trinity House specifications on Preston docks. From this we fired lasers on the first Christmas of trading. Preston Riversway, as it is now known, became a significant regeneration project, with quality flats and apartments in the old warehouses, new built residential area, non-food units and so on, complete with a marina. A super location and our top store for many years.

In October, the largest store in our home city was opened at the Five Lane Ends site, formerly occupied by the famous Bradford car builder Jowett, and thereafter International Harvester, the American based tractor manufacturer.

There had been a problem with obtaining planning consent for the site, which Ken had dealt with personally, making it his crusade to put something back in his home city. Ken hit upon the novel idea of an Enterprise Trust, which would help business start-up. The idea was that an eighteen week course would give you, as an unemployed person, a grounding in Marketing, Finance, Product Development and so on, and having finished the course you could launch off into business, whatever that was, with the opportunity to retail out of the front of your unit, or just manufacture in some smaller units around the back and expand your business with a mix of industrial sheds of different sizes, and eventually become so successful that you would have to move off the site.

Whilst all this was going on, the Trust would provide central facilities for typing, telephone answering and so on, in order to keep your overheads to a minimum. This successful formula was repeated on a larger scale at Darlington in 1995, with just the same success.

We opened our store in a fanfare in mid October and with a sales area of over 70,000 sq ft, it was the largest we had ever operated, blighted only by a fire after a few days trading, which caused us to close for three days and thereafter reopen.And so came to an end my first part year on the Board.

I was now getting invitations to industry dinners which I had not previously received, and spent happy times at the Grosvenor House Hotel in London at the RICS Quantity Surveyors dinner, or the Institute of Refrigeration dinner. I was involved in City Institutions visits to the Company, but the calendar year came to an end with my first disciplinary issue of any serious nature.

I was persuaded by Glynis Wilkinson and Chris Evenson, against my better judgement, to have a Christmas function at a Bradford hotel, and this duly took place, only to find that members of our fresh food production subsidiary, Farmers Boy, were also present and another party. There was also a certain element of baiting going along between two members of my staff, regarding a female colleague, which all led to a very bitter evening.

Upon arriving at breakfast the following morning, there was somewhat stunned silence between various people around the table and it was not until later in the day that I discovered that there had been a significant brawl and hospitalisation, at least to the casualty department for my PA's husband, who was trying to calm things down. That put a stop to that, at least for twelve months, and eventually these events faded away.

The following year saw the opening of seven new stores including the replacement of two former Whelan's units in Lancashire and most in particular the opening of our new grocery warehouse at the popularly known Junction 41 industrial site in Wakefield. A site of over 200 acres which Ken Morrison had acquired from the receivers of the previous developers and which saw us, over a period of time, sell off parcels of land, develop infrastructure and generally make a significant surplus on our purchase price. The site was subsequently enhanced by the construction of non-food, frozen food, vehicle maintenance and fresh food units, but the largest jewel in the crown in our development strategy was the fact that in conjunction with Wakefield Council, we were able to entice Coca Cola to construct one of their largest European production units on the site.

The story for 1988 had largely been settled, prior to Ron's retirement the previous, but had needed much work to finish it off and I was delighted that my first full year in charge would give us such an opening programme. The two former Whelan stores to be replaced were both single shop units in high-street locations in Wigan, which was replaced by a brand new town centre development, and Bolton, where we were able to dispose of the old store to Iceland Frozen Foods.

Other store openings were at Heckmondwike, in West Yorkshire, near to our Bradford base, the very difficult Blackburn site which I have recounted elsewhere, Carlisle, a northern outpost, Stamford, a new southern outpost, and Newark, a town centre location.

All of these brought their own difficulties, but the significant increase in floor area started to move us forward with purpose.

In the spring of that year we were appointed by North East developers Dysart to be involved in a regeneration site at Seaburn, right next to the North Sea, in Sunderland. Jack and Caroline Fawcett and their company had been the promoters of our site at Killingworth New Town in Tyneside, which had opened some two years earlier.

Jack, unfortunately, passed away in November 2006 and I was privileged to be invited to speak at his memorial function the following summer. Jack, the kind, quiet, unassuming man from County Durham and his wife the outgoing Marketing Executive, were in the box seat and after negotiation, agreed terms with us. I duly attended a sod cutting ceremony and press conference, which was held at the adjoining Swallow Hotel, and as we marched up the beachside footpath, I saw a rather elderly gentleman wading into the North Sea, complete with trunks and bathing cap. I remarked to Jack that this looked rather foolhardy, given the January day, to which his response was 'it'll be no warmer in August than it is now'.

Our development programme went very well that year, including the completion of schemes which Ron Curry had been involved in at the start and which had been left to me to complete.

The new regional distribution centre at Wakefield made a massive difference to the Company. The growth in volume and range of product offered had become a major problem to us and the old warehouse, adjoining the Head Office building, had reduced from supplying 50% of our goods, to somewhere around 20%, or less. The new warehouse took us back to 90% of goods supplied on our own transport, which of course, improved our buying terms and the control of delivery to stores.

During this time Ron Curry remained on the Board as an Non-Executive Director together with his sparring partner Ken Blundell, the same Ken who had run the stores in his day and who I had appeared in front of as a very nervous young Quantity Surveyor back in the 1970s.

One amusing incident which occurred arose from Ken's son Chris, who was involved, at the time, with the Company's non-food catalogue and who had been invited by EMI records to visit their studios in Slough, as I recall.

After Ron's retirement, he took up all sorts of hobbies, reverting to his favourite powerful motorbikes, incorporated ballroom dancing and reintroduced himself to music, where jazz was a particular favourite. Ken Morrison announced at a Board Meeting, that the invitation had come to visit EMI and suggested that Ron and Ken 'who have nothing else to do but attend Board Meetings', should go and enjoy the day out with breakfast on the train, lunch at EMI and dinner on the way back. After some protesting Ron agreed and spent the next week, or so swotting up on music.

I have the story from the mouths of both the gentlemen concerned and it is for you, the reader, to decide the hilarity, or otherwise of it.

At the time of their visit, there was a light drama series featured on ITV, called *The Beiderbecke Affair*, which featured James Bolam and Barbara Flynn in the key roles. Beiderbecke, of course, was a jazz musician and the story goes that on arrival at EMI studios my two colleagues were met by the boss. Ron asked him what projects were on, the boss replied that he had been advised of Ron's interest in jazz, and the feature LP being produced was a compilation called *The Biederbecke Tapes*. Ron allegedly looked the man straight in the eye and said, 'I don't know why you're bothering with that, he was crap'. Ron's criticism was allowed to pass, but Ken Blundell recounted the story to me.

After a Board Meeting early in the new year of, I think, 1989 I tackled Ron on the subject. I had read in the previous day's paper that *The Beiderbecke Tapes* was number four in the LP charts at the

time. Ron, obviously not remembering whether he had told me of
the visit or not, was surprised when I announced that I had noted the
achievement. Ron, obviously being proved wrong, and not wanting
to be so, thought for a split second and then uttered the classic 'well
that just goes to show how thick the British public are.' I had
different sides of the story from two people, but it was absolutely
priceless. Ron was someone who researched his subject, knew his
subject and very often was right, but on this occasion was undone,
by the great British public.

Our penultimate store opening of 1988 was at Stamford, Lena's
favourite store, and the first which had been carried out by architects
Jackson Calvert, where Senior Partner, Terry Scott is still a close
friend, having carried out many more stores for us since then.
Stamford became one of the top stores for some time after it's
opening, but we did have something of a downside shortly after
opening, when we discovered that there had been a major leak from
the petrol station. Stamford's fresh water supplies were drawn from
boreholes and the leak had first been noticed when fumes had started
to permeate the adjoining hospital's drainage system, causing a fairly
major evacuation and regional alert. Fortunately, it was the Contractors' fault rather than an operational one, but a very hairy
forty-eight hours.

Perhaps the most curious development that year was the store in
the centre of Blackburn, an East Lancashire mill town of humble
proportions, where our Lancashire acquisition, Dave Whelan, had
plied his trade as a fullback for the town football team.

Ron had acquired the site of a brewery adjoining the town centre
railway station and had put to work our favourite demolition
contractor, Arnold Marriott. Some weeks into the contract we
received a rather agitated telephone call to say that Arnold had
discovered some bones. There was a full scale police alert and
exploratory digging revealed more bones of a human nature and then
more, and then some more and then more still, and eventually we
realised that we were excavating the site of a plague burial ground.
The mass grave had skeletons, some of which were still in their
sack–cloth clothing, and all of this on an uncharted site. Ron decided
that we could not leave the bones stacked up in the old Ribble Bus
inspector's office of the adjoining, now redundant, bus station, but

that they should have a proper burial and deputed my then colleague, Peter Roberts, 'you bought the site', to attend the funeral.

Arnold Marriott did us proud that day. On a typical East Lancashire day with thick drizzle, which had provided the humidity for the Lancashire cotton industry, over the years, Arnold turned out his best tipper wagon full of bones. Peter walked behind the Senior Clergy from Blackburn Cathedral and in front of the wagon along the drive of Blackburn Cemetery, where the bones where rather less ceremoniously tipped into a common grave. The weather was what the Scots would call 'dreicht' and Peter returned to the office cursing and wet through.

The scheme was a nightmare to build, being on different levels with a multi-storey car park and semi-underground petrol station. The store also brought my first contact with Mark Gunter as Store Manager. Mark was ultimately to become my colleague as Store Operations Director on the Main Board. Unfortunately the store never, in my opinion, fulfilled its true potential, but you can't win them all.

The following year's store openings in Guiseley, a nice suburb of Leeds, Seaburn, where the sea bather had disappeared, and Stoke, on the site of the former Garden Festival, were all tremendous successes and remain so to the present day. The final year of the decade saw us open a further four stores at Coalville in Leicestershire, Wellington in Shropshire, Pontefract, and Rochdale, nearer home.

By this time Ron Curry was on his last months as a Non-Executive Director and Rex Procter had carried out some work in Coalville.

I remember taking the site proposal to the Board for approval, which was voted through and subsequently constructed. Ron pulled me to one side afterwards and in no uncertain terms asked me if I was desperate for sites. I said not, upon which his reply was 'you must be, if you are considering Coalville.' The site was constructed on the pithead of an old colliery (miners never took coal out from beneath their own feet) and became extremely successful, being added to with some non-food retail units and later an office block.

The Rochdale site was rather unique, in that it was formally the home of Rochdale Hornets Rugby League Club, our first foray into buying sporting facilities. The rugby league club moved off and now share with the football club in the town at their Spotland ground.

The Pontefract site started a relationship with West Yorkshire based Developer and Contractor Paul Caddick, more recently know for his part in ownership of the Headingley Sports Complex which features the Yorkshire County Cricket Ground and the home of Leeds Rhino's Rugby League team and Leeds Tykes Rugby Union team. Paul was and remains a no-nonsense engineer by profession and negotiated the construction contract of the store as part of our site acquisition process at Pontefract, his home turf.

Being used to engineering type contracts, where the Contractor usually gets paid for every conceivable cost, including clean handker-chiefs if he has a cold, Paul was not used to coming up against some fairly competent Quantity Surveyors and a determined client, and I remember well his observations to me some years later.

Paul apparently kept some key letters from his career path in the safe of his office, rather than in letter files. He claimed to me once that he had three such letters, two of which were from me. I don't remember the content, but I do remember one of them starting with the words, 'I like to start the week with a laugh and your letter dated . . . certainly provided me with that.' Needless to say, the matter about which he was complaining, or had written about, was dropped.

The Coalville store preview provided my Chief Maintenance Surveyor Graham Carter with a particular problem. Shortly before the guests started arriving I rather unfortunately split my trousers. Ken Morrison was not able to be present on this occasion due, as I recall, to the illness of his wife Edna, so it was left to me to conduct the evening's events. How do you do that with a gaping split in your rear? Graham was dispatched to find a needle and cotton and Lena pulled me into an office to disrobe and have the repairs carried out. Again stores in relatively new locations for us, all went very well.

As my first year on the Board moved into my second and third, I found that I was increasingly becoming involved in what could be entitled, 'Main Board' activities. In addition to attending Corporate/ Commercial dinners, I was also expected to speak at our own internal conferences for Managers, represent the Company at Industry meetings, on issues such as refrigerant gases and ozone depletion and take on an increasing corporate role.

In May 1989, I made my second visit to America on business. My first visit had been some three years earlier, but this time I was to visit the Food Marketing Institute's Annual Exhibition and Conference in Chicago, the first time I had visited the 'windy city', subsequent visits to which are mentioned elsewhere.

I well remember flying from Manchester on 6 May 1989 in temperatures which were unseasonally warm, at around 20°C and landing in Chicago in snow flurries and −20°C, with the wind chill. I was hosted on my trip by Bradford based refrigeration contractors and cabinet manufacturers George Barker, and had an extremely hectic, but rewarding, three days. The FMI, as it is known, conference has now moved to Las Vegas, which I think loses some of its appeal, but to me the two large halls of the exhibition and the numerous classrooms were almost magical. Here you could do anything, from inspecting the latest refrigeration display cabinets to stuffing yourself with new product pizza, all day long. Much of the American market, of course, in the areas that I was interested in, are geared to air-conditioned stores, which the United Kingdom does not operate, by and large, but one interesting event took place.

Towards the end of the previous year in 1988, Morrisons had decommissioned and evacuated all its CFC based refrigerant gases from its installations, the first UK retailer to do so. Whilst that sounds grand, given the number of stores that we operated at that time it was not such a great problem as for our competitors, who were much larger. Nevertheless it represented a milestone achievement and set us on a road of environmental awareness, which still exists today. The Company's commitment to reducing its carbon footprint by a greater amount than most of its competitors and also its position as the only food retailer to be awarded the Carbon Trust Standard for managing and cutting that particular element within its business use are huge plusses.

One of the seminars I attended featured a spokesmen for the US Government of the day, who was pontificating about ozone depletion and all the rest of it. Halfway through even I, as a non-technical person, realised that the Government Representative was not particularly switched on, and I remarked on this to the late Graham Mitchell, Sales Director of George Barker, our cabinet suppliers. Two rather burly individuals sitting in front obviously overheard and turned to face me. Expecting some confrontation from some rather irate Americans I did take a step back in my seat, as it were, only to hear the dulcet Australian tones proclaiming, 'Too right mate, this is bullshit.'

Not to dwell too long, when question time came the American Representative was shredded by our Antipodean colleagues to the point that time was called on the debate, and the consensus view of us Commonwealth dwellers was that the Americans would do little or nothing to cut carbon. How surprising therefore that in the intervening years nothing has happened with America, and as I write this book I have just seen the close of the Copenhagen Summit, in late 2009, where President Obama has clearly brokered a deal with the emerging industrial nations, in particular China, which will smokescreen any attempts to genuinely cut carbon emissions and assist global warming being reduced. Nothing changes!

The following year, 1990, I conducted my second or third repeat visit to the European equivalent of FMI, which is Euroshop, held in Dusseldorf every three years. If FMI was big, this is larger still, occupying some fifteen exhibition halls of the Dusseldorf Messe and featuring everything from fashion mannequins to the latest refrigeration cabinets, shopping trolleys, lighting, checkout tills and so on and so on – but no pizza, unlike the Americans. I continued to visit Euroshop right up to February 2008 and have some very happy memories.

The old town of Dusseldorf is really very nice but the accommodation has been varied, the most interesting of which has been several visits bunked down on one of the very large Rhine cruiser boats, moored right next to the Old Town and its restaurants. This is a fascinating experience. The vessels are really quite palatial with all facilities on board if you wish them, the down side being that usually when we have attended, there has been a heavy weekend of snow preceding our visit high up in the Alps, which has then turned to rain, or melted with increase in temperature. The upshot is that the Rhine floods, causing very strong currents, and therefore during the night your sleep is often interrupted by the heavy boats going upstream to Basle from Rotterdam at full power, making hardly any headway against the currents. Coming downstream the window of your berth can regularly be tapped upon by loose branches, logs, or even dead cattle as they float past towards the sea, many hundreds of miles away.

My most amusing and yet most frightening visit to Dusseldorf occurred in an earlier visit and involved the whole 'team' from George Barker, and my own Manager. Having had a good night out in Dusseldorf, we were unfortunately staying at Leverkusen, some miles distant, as all the hotels and accommodation were full. Sampling the nightlife, Barker's Engineering Director, Roy Prentice and myself were left in a nightclub with a rather big bill. Roy proclaimed that he didn't have any money and that he suspected that his wallet had been stolen. We mused on this for some time and Roy was obviously embarrassed, with me as the client. I decided that the most diplomatic solution was to take a leak, while Roy sorted out the dilemma.

Once in the Gents I was looking at the prospect of escaping through a window and other eventualities, as the men on the door looked a bit 'heavy'. The small combo playing in between the turns of the 'exotic dancers' struck up a big jazz number, which was completed to rapturous applause and at this point I thought I ought to make a return to the stage, as it were. To my surprise I discovered that the amazing pianist had been no less than Roy Prentice himself, which at least guaranteed us some goodwill, and we overcame the problem of the money. The following morning Roy announced that he had left his wallet in his bedroom at the hotel! Other visits have been equally entertaining in other ways and Dusseldorf is a lovely city, at least on the tourist side of things, which I would recommend. There are some lovely restaurants in the Old Town, or Alt Stadt, none less than the famous Zum Schiff Schin, 'The Ship Inn', which does fantastic steaks and ham and pork off the bone.

Euroshop was, and remains, a very educational visit, and is aided by the fact that taking place only every three years, you usually have something new to see there.

CHAPTER 14

This 'Sporting' Life and 'The Knights'

I HAVE NEVER BEEN, OR ASPIRED to be, a great sporting character, athlete, or anything else – nothing beyond the occasional player and armchair, or terrace, watcher. I have recounted elsewhere my early sporting days at school and these continued, all be it at my convenience, in later life. I never aspired to be, or had the ability to be a top line amateur at anything, although most sports interested me and I have played many in my time, generally to a very average standard.

Like most kids growing up I was influenced in my sporting interest by my father whose own sporting affinity equally lay with his own upbringing and working life. Coming from Lancashire, he influenced me to be more interested in the red rose when it came to cricket, than the white 'daisy' as he often referred to Yorkshire Cricket's emblem, an apology for a rose, he always described it.

My father's other sporting influence, being born and brought up in St Helens, was the town's Rugby League team, but when he moved to Yorkshire with Pilkington Brothers and his family he had an affinity with Doncaster Rovers, who at that time, played at quite a good level.

My first attendances at professional football were shared between the two Bradford professional teams, City and Park Avenue, and at the age of five my parents decided that it would be suitable for me to go and watch some games. I eagerly awaited my father's appearance at the bottom of our street on his return from Saturday morning work in Harrogate, whereupon we would rush off to either Valley Parade, the home of City, or Park Avenue, of the football team of the same name.

In those days Park Avenue played in the old Division Two, whereas City were in the old Division Three (North) and the former, generally speaking, had significantly higher crowds than the Bantams. This gave me the added bonus of being taken into the Main Stand to watch the green and whites, as my Dad was somewhat concerned about the crowds and the crushing on the terracing. Our journey to watch the green and whites was rather longer and necessitated a journey into the Chester Street bus station of West Yorkshire Road Car Company, my long time favourite, followed by a walk of about a mile to the ground. The Park Avenue ground was unique with a number of others at that time in that one side of it was a first class cricket ground, often played on by Yorkshire County Cricket Club, the other side being the football ground.

We usually took our seats in the main stand, my father having sometimes persuaded the kindly gate man that I was too young to be paid for, so that I was often lifted over for nothing. There we sat in the main stand with a flask of cocoa, watching good quality football. This unfortunately was not to last for Park Avenue as they slowly drifted down the leagues and some fourteen or fifteen years after my visit they became the first football league club to voted out of the league, having failed to gain re-election, finishing at the bottom of the old Division Four and losing their place to Cambridge United. They never regained it, although in current times they are now back on the pyramid of promotions to the football league. I fear this may be some time coming, if ever.

Our journey to Valley Parade to watch the claret and amber of Bradford City was much shorter and often taken on the blue trolley bus of Bradford City Transport. Unique for these times was the fact that we often shared the same bus with the Manager Peter Jackson, his twin sons Peter and David who played as part time professionals, and centre-half Jim Lawler who lodged locally, along with the fans.

The Valley Parade ground was nowhere near as posh as that of what was to become our rivals in terms of my sporting affections. Valley Parade was located on the slope of one of the many hills and valleys of the city, with terraced houses and cobbled streets, rundown terracing and a stand on one side of the ground which was perched precariously on unstable ground, above a large drop.

The crowds were not quite as large here and my parents, clearly watching the pennies, decided that visits to Valley Parade should take place on the terracing rather than the comfort of the main stand. I was usually perched on a concrete buttress at the rear of what was known as the Midland Road Stand.

What made me firm up my allegiance? One day my father said to me that I would have to decide which team I wanted to support as we could not keep going to a match every weekend and I chose what was to become my lifelong favourites and heroes, the Bantams of Valley Parade, Bradford City AFC. Why did I choose them?

Quite simply they had the better Brass Band, which played before and at half time in each game. Whereas Bradford Park Avenue utilised the services of the Victoria Silver Band the Bantams had the Division One players of Hammonds Sauce Works. In those days works bands were quite famous, there were colliery bands such as Frickley, Grimethorpe, mills bands such as Black Dyke, engineering bands such as Foden Works and others such as Hammonds Sauce. Hammonds was a local delicacy, manufactured in my home town of Shipley and the band, whilst not quite being first division, were exceptionally good, often winning their class in competitions and performing regularly as local venues and the seaside during the summer. What swung it for me was that they had a bass drummer who when the big circle was strapped to his chest could hardly see above it. He would march round the ground at the back of the band, beating time but, goaded by his many friends in the crowd would often perform party tricks with his sticks or do a mock dance, when the conductor was clearly not watching. I thought that this was brilliant and looked forward to my fortnightly visits which were to become my life on the football front to the current day, but more of that later.

In those days and prior to Secondary School, I was very keen on goalkeeping and therefore it followed that my heroes were such as Geoff Smith, but others caught the eye, Bobby Webb, a dashing right-winger, and the cultured play of the Jackson twins, Peter, an accountant, now deceased and David, who I was to meet in later professional life as an architect.

Standing on the Midland Road ceased in 1959, when I passed my eleven plus and was rewarded with a season ticket for one season, and we took our seats, my dad and me, in the main stand. This coincided with the introduction of brand new floodlighting in the ground, which meant that there were more reserve team fixtures mid-week and we no longer had the problem of regular ball washing on quagmire days with the original forty-watt-bulb-type floodlights.

I have many memories of Valley Parade, I recount some of the more recent, sad and nice ones later in the book, but the early years that stood out for me were clearly cup runs and promotions.

As with most grounds then, Valley Parade had usually lost most of its grass by the end of November/early December and often resembled a quagmire. This was a great leveller for cup runs and one of our most noted came in 1959/60 when, having made it to the third round we drew First Division Everton at home. The Toffees arrived at Valley Parade with their famous sweet throwing ladies dressed in crinoline dresses dispensing Everton mints and the like to the crowd. Their side was sprinkled with Internationals such as Bobby Collins, Jimmy Gabriel, Alex Young and many more, but were seen off by the rampant home team, the consequence of which gained us another home draw in the fourth round against Bournemouth.

The day of the match arrived and by this time my mother was ensconced in her sweet shop in the opposite side of town. Heavy snow started to fall mid morning and my dad was convinced that the game would be off. Several phone calls to the club assured us that this was not the case and we duly set off down the steep Wakefield Road to the ground, arriving to find the four inches or so of snow had been rolled, the lines had been cleared and the match took place amid flurries of snow, sheets of slush and the result of further victory for the Bantams. We were on a roll!

The next round saw us drawn against another First Division team, Burnley, but again at home. A full house in excess of 25,000 saw us go to a two nil lead on another quagmire pitch, only for the Claret and Blues to equalise in the tenth minute, yes ten minutes, of injury time, of which there was no precedent, and to this day many hardened Bantams fans, including me, feel we had been robbed. The draw for the fifth round saw us at home again, if we could beat the mighty Burnley, we would be playing their neighbours Blackburn and be one step away from a semi-final place, unbelievable. We did not go to the replay where City were beaten 5-0 in front of a crowd in excess of 50,000, with traffic jams allegedly starting three miles out of Bradford on the night for the trek through Keighley and Colne to Turf Moor, and so ended my first dream of glory.

There have been many other notables along the way and much more disappointment, I think the most comparable to the exploits I have just recounted were in 1976, when we were drawn away in the fourth round to Norwich City, managed by John Bond, whose son

Kevin is now Assistant Manager at Tottenham Hotspur. Norwich had beaten fellow members of our Division Rochdale in the previous round, but only after a replay, and the arrogant Mr Bond had declared that teams like Norwich, who were in the First Division at that time, should not have to play such lowly opposition and had more than one declaration of what his team would do to us.

Just before the match was scheduled to take place the Valley Parade boys were struck down by flu and the League had no alternative but to agree to a postponement as Bradford only had about three fit players. This further infuriated Mr Bond, who really lost it when a few days later the entire Bradford City first team played a reserve game as a means of checking their fitness, won the match easily, but were then declared unfit to play a cup match which would have been more demanding. John Bond fumed further, and I along with my new Morrison colleagues such as Martin Ackroyd, who was to go on to join me on the company's Board of Management and Main Board as Finance Director, trekked all the way down to Norwich to see our boys gain a glorious 2-1 victory. As I recall John Bond did not last too much longer in his job.

In the next round we were drawn at home against Southampton, but I missed the game having departed for a weekend break in Benidorm with Dick Earnshaw one of my former Rex Procter colleagues and two others, but we lost 1-0 to one of the most unusual goals of its time, often repeated on television, where one of the strikers, Peter Osgood, flicked the ball up and Jim McCalliog cracked it into the net on the volley.

In between that the Bantams' cup exploits gave rise, allegedly, to one of the famous football songs of all time.

In the late sixties, we were drawn at home to the famous Tottenham Hotspur, managed by Bill Nicholson and littered with International stars, such as Gilzean, Greaves, England, the upcoming Steve Perryman, Knowles, Kinnear and so it went on. Spurs had something of a reputation of drawing away cup games against lower Division opponents, to benefit those opponents with the gate money of replays at White Hart Lane, and this was to be no exception.

Drawing 2-2 on a treacherous, icy pitch with minutes to go City were awarded a corner, the resultant header being spectacularly cleared off the line by full-back Cyril Knowles and giving rise to one of the most famous songs 'nice one Cyril, nice one son'. We lost the resultant replay, by five goals.

Much of the rest of my time following the Bantams has been in the lower Divisions, apart from our rise through the Leagues in the late 90s to amazingly find ourselves in the Premiership for two seasons at the beginning of the new Millennium, unfortunately followed by two administrations and relatively quick demotions back to where it all started in the old Division Four, now known as League Two. I finish my story of the Bantams later.

On the cricket front, my dad's Lancastrian influence was significant and I was brought up to admire and support the red rose, particularly in the early years when the greats of Bob Barber, Geoff Pullar, Brian Statham, Peter Lever and many others were playing. Lancashire were to become first undisputed kings of the limited over game, and I remember visiting Old Trafford to see a rather crucial game against Yorkshire with my mate Keith Whawell, when Lancashire fielded a team including the names of Lloyd, Engineer, Barry Wood and others and reigned quite supreme for a few seasons in that type of cricket.

Yorkshire cricket did not hold the same attraction to me although, of course, they were regularly champions in the County game with names such as Illingworth, Trueman, Binks, Close, even before the appearance of Boycott, possible the best of them all. Dad took me to two County matches, one at Headingley and one at Bradford Park Avenue, in my time. Park Avenue had by far the better atmosphere, as it was smaller in capacity and the crowd were much closer to the players, and individuals such as Freddie Trueman were such great entertainers and had a fantastic rapport with their supporters. But the game never really held the same fascination for me. I know that my mate Keith Whawell still goes to County matches as frequently as he can, but I never felt that attraction.

On the playing front, because I was much more interested in watching, I never entered the realms of Saturday football, as I always wanted to be somewhere else. My old school mates Steve Knight, Michael Donoghue and Steve Exley in particular were local League players for many years, but I preferred to be on the terraces. My competitive, if that is the right word, career started relatively late when at Rex Procter I was invited to play for the Leeds office league team, which was run by the practice and which appeared every

Sunday morning on a ground in the shadow of Leeds United's Elland Road. We were pitted against other Quantity Surveying firms, architects, North Eastern Gas and others and played around West Yorkshire, and it was here that I transformed myself back into a goalkeeper, where I had started at the age of ten or eleven. RP & P were moderately successful, usually finishing in the top five but never threatening to win anything in a spectacular style. We had some good players and some, like me, who were a bit average, but Sunday mornings were quite enjoyable, particularly in the pub afterwards, and if nothing else the football strengthened the bond between those in the Leeds and Bradford Offices of my then employer.

On the cricket front I have played more than I have watched, other than on the television, and after my early failed exploits as a schoolboy junior in the Bradford League I played several times during my career with Rex Procter and in the early days of Morrisons.

John Burnley, my Partner and tutor at RP & P, was a very good all-round sportsman, particularly at soccer and cricket, playing regularly on Saturdays at both. During my time at RP & P he invited me to join the Yorkshire Electricity Board club, who played in the Bradford Amateur Council League, on some quite dubious pitches. Sad to say my Bradford League form continued at this level, not scoring many runs, but being quite a good fielder, taking several catches throughout the season, but giving up, once the club folded, when the ground was sold for residential development purposes.

Around 1974/5 I was invited by one of my other Procter colleagues Mike Bowmer to join Idle Upper Chapel, who played in the Bradford Sunday School League, and I duly went along and played for two full seasons with the second team, again on some dubious pitches. I eventually stopped playing when six day working in my early Morrisons time had to take precedent over the red ball and willow. Idle went on to join the second most senior Bradford League, the Central League, and were very successful for several years before folding. Whilst at Idle I took a fairly bad injury to my knee whilst collecting a ball on the run, twisting and tearing a ligament in my knee, which necessitated, not surgery, but several weeks of stabilisation and remedial work. This did not stop me spending a full week of my holidays in 1974 reseeding the whole of the square and levelling up years of neglect, an effort which at least brought me 'Clubman of the Year' award at the annual dinner.

Sporting engagement in more recent times was largely limited to football at Morrisons in the various competitions between stores and Head Office in the early days, which led up to a football final on the company sports day, though I was never successful enough to reach the final game. And cricket I played, amazingly, for the MCC. No, not the one based at Lord's in London but the one based at Hilmore House in Bradford. Morrisons Cricket Club was founded in the early days of my career there by Trevor Bryan, the Company's Security Controller at the time, who first arranged matches against other local companies, generally ones that we knew, and then persuaded the company to donate some funds for equipment. The team ran for over twenty years on a very enjoyable basis, featuring mostly staff from the Head Office, and in its time some fairly good players.

Trevor Bryan himself had played Bradford League cricket and was joined by Keith Hutchinson, a main Board Director, now sadly deceased, who had played Yorkshire League cricket, and Bob Stott, who as a Main Board Director was first in charge of trading, left for a while and then came back to eventually become Chief Executive, a first rate left-arm fast-bowler playing for years in the Bradford Central League. There were others, who had not necessarily played League cricket but who were no mean performers. Martin Ackroyd, for example, in his pomp could hurl down a fairly mean ball and there were others who followed this, Russell Walker, my own Estates Manager, Chris Balaam, the IT Director, and players who came and went as they left the Company, such as Andrew Sanderson, who had played in the Huddersfield League to a good standard. We thoroughly enjoyed our twenty or so years together and once Trevor Bryan retired the mantle was taken on by Accountant Trevor Kershaw for two or three years, but as we all got older and the company got much larger, there was not the same interest from the younger ones and the organisation was gradually dismantled and disbanded.

We had a pretty good record over the years, although Ken Morrison used to joke that we only ever got fixtures against people we owed money to and therefore they 'knew their place'. This was not entirely true but certainly in the first season I well remember that after five good wins we suffered our first defeat, and the intensity of the feelings amongst those playing was shown in a furious dressing room bust up between Martin Ackroyd and Mick Robson, who at that time was one of the buyers. We had to learn the meaning of 'it's only a game'.

At the end of each season we had a dinner and awards night, which featured the hard core of the team and partners. These were generally excellent events and brilliantly supported right the way across the spectrum of the Company's strata. Main Board Directors such as Bob Stott, Keith Hutchinson and John Dowd were more than happy to join in with the Board of Management Directors such as myself, Martin Ackroyd and Trevor Bryan and the lads 'on the shop floor' as it were. Each year two people out of the team were delegated to run the awards themselves, trophies were presented and the awards became the focus of a mini cabaret for those doing them, often on a themed version which was riotously funny and very much enjoyed, with the following year eagerly awaited. Happy days, when, just like when you were a kid, the sun always seemed to shine on a Wednesday evening.

Over my time I have played most other ball games other than golf, although in retirement I look forward to playing a few rounds near our home in Spain with Lena, who has played for a short time with Caroline, the widow of my former boss Ron Curry.

My other sporting activities of a physical nature largely centred around walking and for many years, ten in succession, I took part with friends in tackling the Yorkshire three peaks of Pen-y-ghent, Whernside and Ingleborough, a twenty-five mile walk or thereabouts with ascents and descents of some 7,000 feet, from memory. I ought to know as the aches and pains represented every one of those single feet climbed, or descended, in weather conditions which varied from sunstroke to blizzard and frostbite.

My last walk across these famous hills in the Yorkshire Dales near Settle came in 1984 when, as Chairman of Haworth and District Round Table I got heavily sponsored in our aim to buy a new minibus for a local Children's Home. That to me was pressure as I was not fit, but had something in the order of 75% of the sponsorship riding on my back that day. I managed to do it, staggered up the drive when I got home and declared, at least in my own mind, that I would never walk all three again, a promise to myself that I have found no problem at all keeping; but, nevertheless, they were spectacular days in spectacular scenery.

Sport has, and continues to give me much enjoyment, I have enjoyed travelling the miles watching my beloved Bradford City, enjoyed the other end of the scale, to some extent, watching Keighley Rugby League for a few years with Geoff Emmett, a former colleague at Rex Procter, and very much enjoyed as a child watching St Helens Rugby League team in its absolute pomp, with my dad and uncles. In those days St Helens used to reach the then Championship Playoffs, now called the Grand Final, and often in those days the Final would be between Saints and one of the other teams of the day, Wigan, Leeds, Wakefield Trinity, Castleford and so on, and being a Yorkshire/Lancashire clash the venue would usually be Odsal Stadium in Bradford.

My dad was at the replay of a Rugby League Cup Final at Odsal when there were allegedly in excess of 120,000 people present, and the aerial photographs on the day would certainly indicate that.

Odsal is a vast, decrepit bowl formed out of a former household refuse tip, and in my day the terraces were largely formed of shale or burnt clinker, with railway sleepers for the standing areas. In midwinter the pitch would be a quagmire with poor drainage in the depression of the bowl, there was no floodlighting and it was generally a poor place. Despite the millions spent, or perhaps misspent on it by the Council in recent times, there is little improvement. Various plans to make Odsal the 'Wembley of the North' have come to nought and I do not believe there is the financial return these days to invest the £75 million that Bradford Council are currently talking of.

Notwithstanding all of this I loved the banter between opposing fans (no segregation in those days) on those old timber sleepers.

St Helens in those days had perhaps the most spectacular team, with names such as Coslett, van Vollenhoven, Murphy, French, Karalius and many, many more and I well remember a try scored which took the length of the field and involved interpassing with Murphy and his South African winger, whereupon 'van the man' sprinted some 80 yards to touch down under the posts with no-one putting a hand on him, brilliant stuff, the stuff of which boyhood heroes are truly made.

As age took over and my general fitness declined from average to below average in levels I took up the occasional invitation from Geoff Emmett at Rex Procter. Geoff moved along the chain from Assistant, to Associate, to Partner in the time spanning my period with the practice and thereafter with Morrisons and was to become the Senior Partner in the Bradford office, a close friend and eventually the Best Man at my wedding to Lena in the summer of 1981.

Geoff invited me to play the occasional game of football or cricket for Haworth Round Table and periodically to referee, or umpire the same codes for Haworth's Inter Table matches within their area, which encompassed a geographic span from Barnoldswick on the Lancashire border, through the Aire Valley to Leeds and Wetherby and Tadcaster and beyond. I was also invited to one or two social events and after a while was invited to become a member, joining some real characters. My early days of association with Round Table spanned the time my social diary was full, during 1976 in particular and I as I have said elsewhere often led me to leave Table meetings, twice each month, to make the journey across the Pennines to go 'clubbing'.

When I was invited to join, my membership involved some fairly deft footwork within the Haworth organisation, as RTBI (The Round Tables of Britain and Ireland) only allowed two members in each branch to have the same occupation and Haworth had a number of Surveyors, who were all reclassified pending my membership being ratified.

From 1976 for the following eight years I had an enjoyable time, particularly in the earlier years when there were some real characters in our particular Table membership. We had a reputation, particularly amongst the 'stockbroking' fraternity of Tables such as Leeds, Boston Spa and Skipton, as being a group of rough necks, a reputation that we rather revelled in, as we were often the underdog in many people's eyes, but this brings with it, as with most things in life, a certain togetherness which drives forward. Haworth for several years were particularly successful in organising a huge disco at Oxenhope, near our home village, to which we managed to attract the then stars of Radio One, such as Dave Lee Travis and Johnnie Walker. We were also the regular stewards of the entrance gates at the large and well known Keighley Show and our charity collection pub-crawl of

Haworth village and its surrounding area at Christmas was always a great laugh.

Each year, in October, we had the Round Table weekend, which was 'lads only', at some hostelry or other within the locality. My first such trip was to Boroughbridge, in 1976, which coincided with the end of one of the hottest and longest summers on record. We stayed in a motel complex, which has long since been demolished and removed. Our visit coincided with the first period of heavy rain after the scorching temperatures. The flat roofs of the building had cracked significantly and we found ourselves walking along corridors with large pools of floodwater, not that I can remember too much.

The weekend had started with me and Geoff Emmett driving to Doncaster to watch the Bantam's in action, secure a win and then scooting North along the A1 to the venue for the weekend. I remember consuming a huge amount of alcohol, but feeling alright, until breakfast the following morning where yours truly started a five hour vomiting session, only calmed by a hamburger consumed while watching Leeds United play Liverpool on the Saturday afternoon.

Subsequent weekends took in some picturesque countryside of the Lake District, the Peak District and North Yorkshire, and the camaraderie was brilliant.

In those days the main headline acts within Table were undoubtedly Gerald Hey, a Skipton Building Society Manager, who specialised in commercial loans, more generally to public houses or eateries. Gerald knew everyone, particularly those who could drink, and we had some hilarious times, prompted by him and others such as solicitors John Churchman and Colin Chapman.

Gerald's ultimate triumph was to return from a National Round Table rally to declare that he had made friends with some members from Banbridge Round Table in County Down, Northern Ireland and that we were going to instigate a twinning arrangement. Gerald had discovered that Banbridge was allegedly the birthplace of Patrick Bronte, the father of the famous Bronte sisters, who, of course, had settled with their parents in the Parsonage at Haworth, our home village. That connection and the fact that the Irish were drinkers was enough to convince Gerald that we should progress this arrangement and our first visit was arranged for the end of the first week of November 1978. There were some significant doubts about the trip, as Northern Ireland was in the midst of its troubles and generally not a safe place to be, but enough of us to fill three cars set off from West Yorkshire, took the ferry from Cairnryan near Stranraer to Larne and landed as darkness fell, in the late afternoon, fortified by several pints on the ship across.

We were met by a group of guys who became very good friends over the following three, or four years and taken to Banbridge, on the main Belfast/Dublin road, via the sights of the Falls and Shankill Road in Belfast, a quite scary experience.

After a day of leisure, seeing the sights of the hills and reservoirs around County Down and the lovely seaside town of Bangor, we donned our finest and mounted a coach to travel across the border through Newry, over the border and to a small town called Navan, north of Dublin. Here there was to be an Area Round Table dinner. We arrived, walked into the bar and, of course, our distinctive accents very quickly became noticed. Four rather rough and casually dressed individuals sitting at the bar insisted that they buy us the first two rounds of drinks. By this time I had developed a sense in strange places of not looking either side of me for the first five minutes or so after entry. Not entering into conversation with anyone and if after that time, no one had hit me then it was quite safe to proceed. I was extremely suspicious of these individuals who eventually said that they would have to leave but would be back. Back with what? I thought. Maybe the odd gun.

To my intense relief they returned ten minutes later complete with dinner jacket and black tie and announced themselves as members of the Round Table from the far south of Ireland and indicated at how pleased they were that we had made the effort to visit.

The following year the Irish returned to our home turf and after that I had one further visit to Ireland, spending a glorious day in the famous Crown Bar, across the road from the equally famous Europa Hotel. The Europa was the most bombed hotel during the troubles and I believe changed its name at one point in an effort to throw the terrorists off the scent. I was to revisit Northern Ireland, during the course of Morrisons acquisition of Safeway, and the self same bar, together with Store Operations Director, Mark Gunter many years later.

I enjoyed my time in Round Table but, like my membership of the Boy Scouts, many years early, I was never an avid, or 'anorak' type member. I could take it or leave it, and eventually after my year in the Chair, pressure of business at Morrisons dictated that I came to the decision that I should leave it. I resigned my membership of Round Table some two years of so before the throwing out age of 40.

Round Table today is a significantly changed organisation, which has had to deal with the passage of time, the competition of other activities and pastimes, and sadly, I believe, the less caring nature of us all as human beings. I enjoyed helping others, we had an association with a children's home in one of the Bradford suburbs and as I have said earlier raised money for their minibus and other things including Christmas presents and so on. We supported the Sue Ryder organisation and other local charities, and I believe it is somewhat of an indictment of today's society that people are not as keen to freely give their time to continue these worthy causes and support the urgent needs.

I thought long and hard about where this next section should be incorporated. After all, some of it is not sport and some of it is certainly not Round Table, but it would be remiss if I did not mention somewhere a group of fellow surveyors who have been in my life, even if only periodically, over the last thirty years.

In the spring of 1977, I received a circular from the RICS notifying me of that year's Residential Course for the Junior organisation. The Junior section of the RICS is open to all, up to the age, at that time, of thirty-three.

That year's course, which was to be held at Keele University, was on management and as I was targeting my progress through the Company I decided I should go.

Very nervously I arrived at Keele, having checked, on several occasions, the dress code for that evening's formal dinner, and set off to walk from my Hall of Residence to the President's sherry reception. My only previous experience of such events were having been sent by Ron Curry to an RICS weekend course at the College of Estate Management in Reading some years previously, and finding myself with senior partners of various organisations and somewhat out of my depth. At least here I would be with people of my own age and experience.

As I walked along the dark pathway I heard the pitter-patter of running feet rapidly closing on me, at which point a body jumped out in front of me and declared 'Hi, I'm Bob Dyson, what's your name?' Thus was the start of over thirty years friendship with the guy who was ultimately to become Senior Partner/Chief Executive of the large Manchester agency, Dunlop Heywood and in later life to move on to Jones Lang LaSalle.

Bob immediately adopted me a member of the Greater Manchester branch of the JO, as it was known, and there then followed some six years of riotous weekends, in York, Cambridge, Warwick and other locations, with a build-up of friendship which lasts to this day with other Manchester based surveyors, such as Alan Solomons, Jeremy Hobson, Steve Bramall, Malcolm Boyd and others whom I came to meet as a spin off, such as Lynn Garsden, Mike Guest, John Whalley and Bob Shaw.

If they converted me to joining them every year, I converted them to joining my crew at York races for the big meeting in August, and on one of these occasions, fortified by several glasses of champagne, we decided that we should bid for a racehorse, Malcolm Boyd being the so-called expert at all things bloodstock. Needless to say we failed but that fired us for our next great adventure. Greyhound racing!

We decided that greyhounds were infinitely preferable, at least on a cost basis, to the rather larger four-legged racing version, and got together a consortium to buy a dog. Malcolm Boyd was dispatched to the country of his birth, Ireland, to purchase such an animal and returned with the aptly named Kilgrany May. They must have seen us coming!

For the uninitiated, greyhound races consist of six dogs being released from traps and chasing an imitation hare around a course for whatever length of race is specified. Because only six dogs can take part at one time, each dog has to make a pre-race qualifying time, a bit like Olympic athletes. After some training, in Rochdale, our dog duly appeared at Belle Vue in Manchester and was set against a future greyhound derby winner. The only problem was that our dog ran wide on the bends and promptly deposited the future champion into the barriers, sustaining race career ending injuries. We decided that it was better to get rid of Kilgrany at this point.

Enthusiasm undampened however, we then entered our most successful phase with Blue Pants, aptly named because of the colour of her rear.

Blue Pants kept herself in dog food by consistently finishing second or third in races and actually winning a couple, until drama struck.

One afternoon whilst working away at my desk I received a rather excited telephone call from Bob Dyson, one of the listed owners, to say that he and Lynn Garsden had been called in front of the stewards at Belle Vue for reasons unknown. A second call later that day advised me that we had been told to withdraw our dog from racing as she was 'not genuine'. The full explanation of this was that she did not really know why she was racing and was in fact chasing the other dogs. The stewards felt that this behaviour would inevitably result in a fight on the track.

Bob had discovered that the reason for her two victories had been due to the fact the dog in front had stumbled near the winning line and our heroine had been unable to stop before crossing the line and taking the honours.

One rather pleasant upside to this episode occurred in the summer of 1980, when Lena and I were spending a week in Newquay, sharing a table with a rather elderly couple from East London. I remarked to Lena one morning at breakfast that Blue Pants was running that night. The husband of the couple, who constantly referred to each other as 'mother and father', heard this and I told him the story. 'Well then mother, as a holiday treat shall we put £5 on the lad's dog?' They duly did and Blue Pants duly obliged by winning her customary second place, so at least they were happy.

We did get a third animal, rather inaptly named Driss Will Win, but unfortunately she didn't, our trainer retired and we felt we were being short changed by the new man, and that brought to an end our dog racing career.

CHAPTER 15

By Bus and York Museums 1991–94

O N 1 APRIL 1991 WHAT A DAY! – we opened our 50th store at
Hillsborough, Sheffield, in the shadow of the famous football
ground.

Hillsborough Barracks had been built in 1854, as the standard
Ministry of Defence of the day fortified barracks from which soldiers
were to be sent to quell any civil unrest in the locality. This was a
massive site with walls and turrets around its perimeter and the old
barrack blocks, squash courts, officer's quarters and stables still intact,
but heavily ravaged by the passage of time. George Longden Estates,
fronted by a true Sheffieldite, Alan Hanwell, were looking to
redevelop, but other than part of the site being disposed of as the
headquarters of the Sheffield Insulation Group, under the guidance
of Sir Norman Adsetts, the site had remained derelict for several
years, indeed I had looked at it myself early in my time as a Main
Board Director.

John Stone, a Morrisons account architect with the John Brunton
Partnership at their Leeds office, knew Alan Hanwell extremely well
and had two or three attempts to persuade me to revisit the site.
Eventually he succeeded and two years or so prior to our opening I
decided that we should 'go for it'.

Alan Hanwell was duty bound to tender the site and I was
subsequently told, although I never knew whether it was true or not,
that we were the lowest bidder against Tesco and Asda, but we were
the only one prepared to keep the old stone-walled buildings, the
other two operators being more determined to pull everything down
and erect the corporate tin shed.

Our relationship with Sheffield City Council had never been great
going back to the 1980s when we first built at Darnall in the city,
but the prospect of someone taking a little bit of loving care to restore
their buildings persuaded them that we should be allowed to carry
out the alterations which I felt were necessary, and in the end we
simply threw a roof over the old parade ground, demolished some

buildings, but retained the majority, threading between some parts of the site a single deck of car parking to simply get the numbers up.

In subsequent times we further extended a shopping mall within the development and also built a transport interchange where local district buses could discharge their passengers onto the tram network which passes through the centre of Sheffield.

I remember on the day the tram was commissioned that Neil Kinnock, then the Euro Minister for Transport, alighted from the inaugural vehicle at Hillsborough with myself and Ken Morrison and marvelled at the work we had done. This was our fiftieth store, and one not to forget.

The store itself had an amusing side in that we decided, out of a surplus of space, that we would create a second-hand dealership within the store, and so at the back of the checkouts was established a unit called Granny's Attic, where you could simply go and trade in goods, which were then sold, a bit like a charity shop but without the charity. Unfortunately we quickly discovered that the unit was becoming very popular, arising out the fact that the local 'no-goods' were using it as a front to 'fence' stolen goods, and we quickly closed it down.

Being constructed of local stone and over 100 years old the site has maintained its image since construction and has seen the development of a significant amount of tenanted office space and a hotel.

The Hillsborough development contrasted steeply with the tin sheds of Stockton and the Parkgate Retail Park, at Rotherham.

Stockton was a huge retail park constructed on part of the old Stockton Race Course and a domestic rubbish tip, where Morrisons very nearly lost the services of their Property Director. Walking the site one day I was pointing out to the assembled group of consultants where the store entrance should go, mounting a pile of what looked like old refuse to do so. No less than five metres in however, the refuse collapsed to expose a burning pit of domestic refuse beneath my feet, and I was in it up to my knees and was sinking. Heat is a great motivator for speedy movement! Although the soles of my Wellingtons would testify otherwise.

Also in the year we developed a more locally sympathetic store in the North Yorkshire market town of Skipton, where we acquired the old auction market and created a store whose entrance replicated the old auction ring. The store had the spin-off of reducing the regular flood risks to the market town by culverting various becks as they traversed the site.

At the start of 1991, Ken had remarked to me that he felt that it was unfair that with the gathering pace of our development programme, I should be taking sites to the Board for approval which the rest of the Board had not seen. It was made very clear to me that this was no condemnation of my judgement, as up to then everything we had developed had been something of a winner, or at least not a loser. However, Ken felt that with the accelerating development pro-gramme and the expenditure which came with it we needed to be quite careful on where we spent our money and therefore proposed that future site inspections should take place with as many of the Board as possible, after an initial sifting of our opportunities by myself.

Thus dawned the day of the coach Board Meeting. Yorkshire Rider, as they were known in those days, more latterly to become part of the First Group, had a luxury coach, complete with galley, toilet and tables and we utilised this over the next two to three years to visit many sites. When the coach was not available, we sourced others, riding on various football teams' buses, including, on one occasion, the mighty Arsenal's.

This process allowed us to look at the competitors in an area as well as the sites themselves, and from 1992 onwards store openings often had a good smattering of sites we had bought 'off the bus'. The first of these was at Walsall, which we opened in 1992 and is built on the site of the former Walsall Football Ground.

We arrived at the site, parked up the bus and walked over the pitch, which by that time was redundant, the football club having moved to a new ground nearby. I remember the conversation well as we stood on the centre spot. Finance Director Martin Ackroyd, a fellow Bradford City fan made some remark to the effect that we ought to buy the ground simply to eliminate it as 'these bastards always beat us', so we bought, extinguished the ground, and I don't think the mighty Bantams of Bradford have ever won at the new ground either.

There then followed many amusing trips which resulting in stores being acquired for opening in 1992 alongside Walsall, at Mansfield, Kendal and Lincoln, in addition to the more local site at Oldham.

Walsall for me represented a major moment in my life on the Board.

I have recounted earlier the development of Market Street and paid what I think is an appropriate tribute to Bob Emmott, my colleague and 'inventor' of the concept.

By the time we were building Walsall I thought that the 'Market Concept', as it continued to be known, should be more of a Market Street, and organised that architect Bob Taylor, of David Lyons in Wakefield, the Project Architects, together with his Interior Designer, Tony Welch and my Project Manager, Vic Sephton should spend a day or so in York. I only briefly outlined my views.

The four of us trotted off to the Cliffe Castle Museum where there is a re-creation of a street from times gone by, included padded stuffed horses and carriages. We walked into the building, the other three still none the wiser and I asked them to look and note how the street varied. Each shop front was different to the one next door, roofs projected at different angles and the whole thing was broken up, tied together only with the footpath which ran along the front. I said that we ought to look at something like this for our Market Concept.

From the museum we then took a trip down the very famous shopping street of The Shambles and again noted, at real life scale, the differing elevations of the shops, the different colours and the total non-uniform appearance. This was what I wanted, but all to be wrapped up in current day regulations imposed by the Health Inspector and others.

To the enormous credit of my three companions that day I got largely what I wanted. A fish bar with a mosaic wall finish, the service counter replicating the marble slab of my childhood days, and so we went around the store, salad bar, delicatessen, bakery, cake shop and so on and so on. The only issue was I never told any of my Board Colleagues!

When handover came in February of 1992, the general consensus of the visiting executives of Head Office, each looking after their own area of the development from alarms to canteen equipment to purchasing and so on, was one of shock and awe, but very favourable shock and awe.

The Regional Director of the store was Mark Gunter, who was later to become my colleague on the Main Board, and his reaction was one of high surprise, but extremely favourable. This was tempered somewhat when I told him the rest of the Board were not aware.

The handover went very well, the store was finished to an excellent standard and I had even incorporated within the ceiling the equivalent of a shadow, which was to cause the effect of a footpath along the front of all the shops. Market Street, as it later became known was well and truly launched, at least in my view.

On the Friday evening, having driven home, my telephone rang and it was no less than Francis Robert Emmott, the creator of the Market Concept. The conversation went something like this;

Go . . . Walsall . . . you . . . wasting . . . we . . . and . . . from . . . the . . .

The many, many blanks in this conversation represent Bob's language, which I cannot possibly recount either from memory, or from its fruitiness, but he was not a particularly happy bunny.

The following day Bob made his journey to Walsall and Lena and myself were travelling to watch Bradford City, at home. When almost at the ground the phone in my car rang indicating Bob. I had described our conversation some fifteen hours or so earlier to Lena and I was expecting the worst. Answering the phone, I very quickly advised Bob that Lena was with me to which he responded 'I've been to Walsall, great, bye' and that was the start of the second generation of Market Street, which was to run for several years before, inevitably, modification further.

1993, saw seven more stores open, more in our heartland of The North, including the site of an old Brickworks in the Dewsbury Road area of Wakefield. This was a site that Ron Curry had initiated, but had been the subject of three separate planning enquires before we obtained consent, but I stood with it and in doing so won a bet from Keith Hutchinson, my colleague on the Board. Keith being a very devoted Christian, I refused to take his payment.

The year saw us develop at Tynemouth, in the North East, Blackpool, adjoining the airport, Shrewsbury and a replacement store for one of the original Whelan's units at Chorley, together with a second store for Bolton.

The year also saw us open a new store in Harrogate to replace the unit in the ill-fated Conference Centre. The deal to obtain planning consent saw us refurbish the old store, assist the Borough Council to generate new exhibition space and allow the Harrogate International Centre, as it is now known, to be launched on a firm economic footing. Much credit must go to Phil Willis, the then leader of Harrogate Borough Council, and George Crowther. I make no political point but Harrogate Borough council had changed control, to Liberal Democratic and these two gentlemen powered the Borough forward from its static narrow thinking of previous administrations.

Phil Willis later went on to retire as a Head Teacher at a Leeds school and became the MP for Harrogate, retiring at the 2010 General Election.

1994 saw us develop by the seaside at Morecambe and Scarborough, together with six other units throughout the north of England.

The Morecambe store was unique in that it occupied the site of the former railway station. In the days of steam the railway companies constructed their stations as near to the town centre as possible and Morecambe's was built almost on the promenade, out of which thousands of Bradfordians, over the years, disgorged themselves from the excursion trains to enjoy a day of candy floss and donkey rides. Scarborough was not dissimilar, though our site was out of the town, but the railway station there is still very, very central, whereas Morecambe's had been moved back down the track.

Morecambe was and to some extent still is a rather desolate seaside resort, its amusement park was subsequently closed and acquired by ourselves for the construction of non-food units, but unlike some places it is trying to redevelop. Today the promenade is neat and tidy with well kept and manicured grassed areas, and there is a nature trail of the various birds which populate Morecambe Bay on their various migration flights. Indeed, Morecambe Bay is a bird sanctuary in itself and the various puffins and other sea birds which we had created and moulded to the top of our protection bollards around the store entrance are tribute to this. I was also able to get the Company to sponsor various bird sculptures on the roundabouts around the store and on the new roads around the town centre, and ultimately we were able to sponsor the Eric Morecambe sculpture, unveiled by the Queen.

The unveiling, which took place some years after our store opening, brought me into contact with Her Majesty and His Royal Highness, Prince Philip, who came on a lovely day. Morrisons were asked to do the finger buffet catering for the assembled hierarchy of Lancashire, which was a great honour, and I am delighted to be in possession of a photograph shaking hands with my Queen, an unexpected surprise, as we had been briefed that this would probably not occur as Her Majesty quite often suffered from Repetitive Strain Injury through shaking so many thousands of hands over the years.

The Duke of Edinburgh was most amusing. We had mounted a small exhibition of our site, including the railway station, in which he took a great deal of interest. Having arrived by the Royal Train, spending the night just outside Skipton, the Duke of Edinburgh looked intently at the aerial photographs and quickly identified which our store was having driven past it earlier. I will not use his exact words, but he went on to regale myself, Ken, Lynne Morrison and Lena with his view of how the railways had destroyed most town centres in their time. He was probably right and fortunately his comments were made out of earshot of the accompanying press pack. A truly lovely day and another year, which saw us go forward.

CHAPTER 16

Pushing the Boundaries 'Darn Sawf'
1995–98

T HE FIRST YEAR IN THIS particular period of life was extremely
busy, with nine new store openings, including two major
schemes. The continuing process of Main Board meetings held on
coaches paid its dividends with faster decision making and earlier
progress on site, particularly in areas where other members of the
Board were not aware of the demographics or the competition.

In Darlington we had built and opened what was to be our most
successful store some fifteen years earlier, and Darlington always held
a soft spot for us. The Borough Council were equally encouraging of
our efforts, particularly the provision of the very high-class indoor
bowls club, who had in turn named two areas after those who had
helped most. The Ken Blundell suite, named after our then Deputy
Chairman, was a superb dining and function area with bars and so
on, the provision for which enabled the Bowls Club to hold national
and international tournaments, some of which were televised.

The Roger Owen Suite, which was to come much later, was on
the other end of the spectrum, a toilet block and changing area! Lena
often remarked that this was probably a fitting tribute.

The Borough Council in Darlington was anxious to develop a
large-scale site, but to incorporate within it various employment
opportunities and a good deal of industrial sheds. We were mildly
interested in the scheme, but Asda threw a lot of money at their site bid
and were appointed to carry out their development, which was when
the fun and games really started. Little by little and bit by bit, Asda
chipped away at their offer for the site, by demanding the omission of
various elements until, in the end, their true tactic, at least in our eyes,
was exposed when the site finished up with just a stand-alone, very
large Asda store. The Council decided enough was enough.

When this came to our attention Ken and I decided that we should
speak with the Council and thereafter was launched the second

175

Morrison Enterprise Trust, and we finished building out the development which incorporated a large Morrison store, numerous internal shop units, the Enterprise Business Start-up Trust, which I have described elsewhere and 100,000 sq ft of industrial sheds, which were built entirely speculatively and without one single tenant on day one.

The development became very popular very quickly and the industrial units, far from being a gamble, proved a very lively contributor to the Company's rent roll.

Darlington Borough had been keen on a piece of artwork and approached us about our contribution to this. After much negotiation and discussion and with my Development Director Chris Evenson in charge, we obtained lottery funding for a large sculpture, which would represent the town's industrial heritage in the railway industry.

Our original Darlington store had been built on the site of the Old North Road Locomotive Works and the Morton Park site, as it became known, was located not very far from the route of the original Darlington–Stockton rail line, where the first locomotive runs took place. Darlington, of course, is still a main line stop on the East Coast line, linking Kings Cross in London to Edinburgh and points further in Scotland.

This was where I first met the sculptor David Mach. David was born and reared in his early life in Dundee and is a very proud and quite tough Scot, famed for his short-term sculptures, including bundles of newspapers, coat hangers and the like, very few of which are ever permanent; but this particular project was to be.

The decision was made to create a sculpture of a locomotive which sped north and south on the East Coast line, replicating steam in its heyday, and the sculpture was to be of bricks.

David set to work on his ideas, which were eventually to be translated by skilled bricklayers from Shepherd Construction of York and supervised by a consulting architect, Tony Lightowler, of Fletcher Joseph, the architects for the main scheme. David Mach, at least to my knowledge, had never laid a single brick, but his instructions and ideas were carried out to the letter with 186,000 bricks forming the full sized image of a train appearing from a tunnel in full sized billows and clouds of steam and smoke. There are no curved, or special bricks in the sculpture, each brick to create the curvature being offset

21. *The Ben Cruachan hydroelectric scheme, on a school visit from Bingley, opened October 1965*

22. *Beep beep! Same bus but not me driving, the Hanson School of Motoring PSV, on which I learnt to be a 'knight of the road'*

23. Best man to my best mate, me and Keith on his wedding day, 1977

24. The flying machine! Shame about the brakes, me and special Morris Marina with MG engine, spring 1974

25. Lena's 'brothel on wheels', the purple Capri, with me and Keith Whawell in the Yorkshire Dales, 1977

26. *Former Rex Procter colleague Geoff Emmett is third from left in this motley crew of Round Tablers from Haworth and Banbridge, County Down, in the early eighties. The silver BMW on the right was the replacement for my ill-fated Rover*

27. *Never mind the Knights of the Round Table, what about the cavaliers? – charity collection, Christmas, 1978*

28. *I was reading the words on the card – honest! Eve of Newark store handover and fortieth birthday, October 1988*

29. *As rare as hen's teeth – A social gathering of the Morrisons Board, to celebrate Ken Blundell's retirement, together with wives. Side nearest camera, right to left, Ron Curry, with wife Caroline behind, Ken Blundell and Keith Hutchinson. Extreme rear of table, Colin Olivier. Side furthest from camera, left to right, Martin Ackroyd, Bob Emmott, Ken Morrison, me and John Dowd, with Lena between us*

30. One of the many visits to Euroshop. George Barker Refrigeration, Sales Director, Graham Mitchell, left and jazz pianist extraordinaire, Roy Prentice on the right, at Dusseldorf Industrial Club. Were we smiling at our miraculous escape, from the nightclub, the day before, or was it just admiration of Roy's pianist skills?

31. Glen's proud day, graduation from Nottingham University

32. Four years later and here comes Jason, leaving Cambridge, proud day number two

33. Long time friend Bob Dyson, of Dunlop Heywood and more latterly, Jones Lang, at one of our July Chester Evening race meetings – the girls were in the champagne tent!

34. *Another proud day, Glen and Helen marry, March 2002*

35. *Just happy! Jason, me, Glen and Lena, after the knot had been tied*

by as little as 6 mm from the next. A true work of art, which was unveiled by the then Arts Minister, Lord Palumbo.

Early on in the scheme, a meeting of the great and good representing the North Eastern Arts bodies was held in Darlington and David Mach arrived direct from a commission he was carrying out for one of the Swiss Banks in Lake Geneva. David replicated the archetype British tourist in his shorts and trainers and sat amongst the honorary members of the various arts bodies, some dressed in their finery for the meeting.

The maquette, or model, of the brick train was unveiled by David, and one very eminent female member of the Arts Committee asked David in rather 'toffee' tones, 'Tell me Mr Mach, what will I think when I see this?' David sat there for a minute, obviously not over enamoured with this particular member of North-East high society, looked her in the eye and with all solemnity said, 'Madam, you'll f****** shit yourself'. All credit to the Dowager, who did not bat an eyelid, but simply replied, 'Will I really?' I seem to remember swallowing my glass of water the wrong way and exploding into a fit of coughing, which did not help the situation.

Our other large scheme of the year was at Widnes. I had visited the site on the usual luxury coach with Members of the Board, to be greeted by actual tumbleweed blowing down the main street. Widnes is known for its production of chemicals, indeed the Rugby League Team of the town bears the same nickname, 'The Chemics'. We bid for the site and won it in competition for both our offer, but more importantly, the quality of our scheme. This was a town centre redevelopment, which was desperately needed, and we proceeded to construct road infrastructure, a new bus station, a large store, new market hall for the Local Authority, shopping mall and other features. As my Project Manager Vic Sephton remarked at the time, the Council loved us for treading where others feared to tread and revitalising the town centre.

I was not quite as pleased when some years later, Asda, one of our defeated competitors at the time, were allowed planning consent to develop a new store quite near us. But that's the way it goes.

Other sites developed during the year were at Burton-on-Trent, Doncaster, Bulwell, a run down area of Nottingham, Tamworth, Huddersfield, Bilston, in the dirty West Midlands which is now being so well redeveloped, and at Cleethorpes, on the east coast. We were very busy.

As a consequence of our activities through 1995, the following year was very quiet in terms of new build, indeed, I don't recollect that we opened any new stores, but concentrated instead on extensions and refurbishment, carrying out such activities at no less than seven stores, rebuilding petrol filling stations, adding to the rent roll by constructing additional non-food units on existing sites and also buying in the freeholds of two of our existing stores. Spending the money in long-term investment.

The year was also a minor landmark in that corporate governance caught up with us and Ken relinquished his role as Managing Director and appointed John Dowd to the position, a situation which John was to fulfil extremely well, until his life was cut tragically short, after a relatively short illness.

The other key part of the year was to see Bob Stott to return to the Company as Buying Director, and he was later to become Chief Executive.

1997 saw us open four new stores, largely in our operational area at Cheadle, in Stockport, Sunderland, Ecclesfield in Sheffield, Northampton and Middlesbrough. In addition we replaced an earlier store at Heywood, near Rochdale, rebuilding the old store and disposing of it to the Irish textile operator Dunnes.

This work was accompanied by major refurbishment projects on what was becoming a treadmill operation at a number of stores and extensions, and additions of filling stations on a random basis through the estate.

The opening of our store at Cheadle in February 1997 was somewhat unique in our board decision-making process. We had famously visited the site on one of our, now noted, coach trips sometime previously, the site being operated as a non-food base, alongside one of the main roads into Manchester and at the intersection of another main artery into Stockport. The Board had quite fancied the site, although it was rather tight, but the asking price, which was in the region of £11 million, was off-putting and I remember Finance Director Martin Ackroyd arguing against it.

My Development Director, Chris Evenson and myself were convinced that this would be the number one store if we purchased the site and carried out the development, and there was also the possibility of additional rental income from the remaining non-food units, which could be remodelled. I remember walking the site and sitting on the 'luxury' football coach on the way home in a dismal mood, with the rejection of most of my colleagues ringing in my ears.

Even the coach transport that day was not one of the best we had used and upon investigation by Ken the driver advised that it was used by non-league team Northwich Victoria for its away matches. Ken's response was 'I bet they don't win many'. I certainly did not feel that I had won one that day.

A few days passed, we gave back word to the vendor and Ken came to see me. Setting aside the finance calculations, he asked what I thought the sales figure would be for the store, which was significantly in advance of any other projections. I told Ken that we had now formally rejected the site with the developers, to which the response was 'I agree with your assessment, let's get it bought and tell the others later.'

After a certain large meal of humble pie, we managed to acquire the site, which promptly shot to number one in our sales figures and remained there for a very long time, being reinforced with a subsequent extension and major revamp. A very sound purchase indeed, and a very good example of the 'grocer's nose' triumphing over the accountants' bald figures. In my experience most account-ants will find a reason for not doing almost anything, including breathing.

The following year saw us spring forward again with no less than ten store openings and also the launch of our second regional distribution depot, at Northwich in Cheshire. The site also incorpor-ated a second major produce pack house to supplement the facilities which we had operated for some years in Bradford.

The 1998 stores saw us re-launch no less than four units, which had been acquired by from Somerfield or the Co-operative Group, in its various forms, these being at Boroughbridge, in North Yorkshire, a second store in St Helen's, Hull, and Chingford, in Essex.

The Morrison build stores were at Halfway, on the south side of Sheffield, Brampton, near Rotherham, Banbury, Anlaby, in Hull and Retford in Nottinghamshire.

The last of our new stores that year took us well and truly beyond our existing boundaries, in Erith, on the south bank of the Thames.

Erith was another site where the tumbleweed and a rather arthritic fox met us on a Board visit. The site was large at 20 acres and also included the added 'bonus' of a very heavy-duty concrete pier which extended into the Thames. Erith saw the start of my relationship with the Bexley Thameside Partnership, which I have recounted elsewhere.

The site had been previously owned by United Newspapers and was used for storing newsprint in the days when newspapers were printed in Fleet Street in central London, but had become redundant when the printing operations moved to better facilities at Wapping, but the pier came into its own, as newsprint in those days was imported from Scandinavia. The ships were unloaded into riverside warehouses and then train or lorry took the newsprint up to London. We set about refurbishing the pier, taking out the old railway lines but retaining the old railway turntable at the end of the pier, which was used on opening day by the Mayor of Bexley Borough to turn his Mayoral car around. The locals now have a very useful fishing pier, which is well liked in the community.

The new distribution facilities at Gadbrook Park in Northwich were extremely helpful for all this additional floor space which had been created, although we had been trying to locate an addition distribution centre west of the Pennines for some six years previously, and this brought me into contact, or rather conflict, with the noted Neil and Christine Hamilton.

Mr Hamilton was the MP for Tatton, who famously lost his seat to the former BBC Journalist, Martin Bell, 'the man in white' in the 1997 election, when Hamilton was implicated in the cash for questions scandal of the 1990s. The seat is now held by the Chancellor, George Osborne.

Neil Hamilton had been the constituency MP from the formation of the seat in 1983 and I met him and his 'lovely' wife towards the end of 1992, at which point he was some sort of Junior Minister, a position that he repeatedly laid on me, during our meeting.

We had identified a 200-acre site for our depot and it was the ambition of Ken and myself to redevelop the rest of the site and 'make a bob or two' for the Company, much as we had done with our initial distribution site at Wakefield, some years earlier.

Unfortunately, the site was not allocated in the Vale Royal Planning Strategy and we knew we would have a fight, but the Local Authority were very supportive of our plans as it would bring in much needed jobs into the area. The local village of Lach Dennis however had different ideas and had enlisted their MP, as is perfectly normal. We met in Winsford and I outlined the Company and the scheme and the investment and the job creation and everything else to Mr Hamilton, who said, that he would take my comments on board but could not possibly influence the outcome of any planning decision in his role as a 'Minister of Her Majesty's Government'. This may have been his position, but it certainly was not his wife's. The lovely Christine waited until the end of our meeting and then proclaimed very loudly, very forcibly and directly to me 'Put it this way Mr Owen, we don't want you here and we are not going to have you.'

Two, or three weeks later I received, anonymously, a copy of a letter which the Minister 'who cannot interfere' had written to the Secretary of State, John Gummer, indicating that this particularly planning application should be called in for a public enquiry and stopped. I was furious at the nature of Mr Hamilton's dealings and we made it known through our legal representatives that this was simply not on. I always suspected that the Junior Minister's involvement may not have stopped with that letter.

Our application was called in, was rejected and we then spent a fruitless eighteen months pursuing a further site at Newton-Le-Willows, further north of the M6 motorway, which was similarly called in by Mr Gummer, notwithstanding the fact that would have brought back into use a derelict and unused colliery, again creating much needed employment.

Eventually, we came back to Northwich, on a site immediately adjourning our first rejection, and I have always comforted myself with fact that despite the delays there was at least some poetic justice, for the eventually shamed MP and his wife.

Throughout 2009, we have had major incidences of the MP expenses row and quite frankly my experience of the House of Commons through Mr Hamilton gave me no surprise at all to see what went on some fifteen years later.

At this point I should say something about Morrisons and its Board.

The public perception of the Morrison Board was that it was a very calm and consistent place to be, yet in actual fact, the records show that particularly through the 1990s there was a significant turnover in this most elevated of positions in the Company.

I joined the Board in February 1987 on the day that Bob Stott resigned and left, to return ten years later and thereafter become Chief Executive before his retirement. Other colleagues at the time of my joining were to retire. Ken Blundell and Ron Curry being two, and perhaps the most notable being Ken himself in March 2008.

Ken Blundell and Ron subsequently passed away as did active colleagues John Dowd, who was to become Managing Director, and Keith Hutchinson, who had been an extremely good buyer on the wines and spirits side. Both John and Keith suffered with brain tumours and eventually this was to claim them both. Extremely nice guys, who were a pleasure to work with and who had the respect of many.

Through the 90s we saw the arrival and indeed departure of others.

Colin Olivier had been with the Company before I joined in 1975 and was something of a business systems guru. Colin was brought back shortly after I had joined the Board to head up the Company's IT function, and having made some changes, then departed.

Brian Barnfather had been the Deputy Manager of our store at the Merrion Centre within Leeds City Centre itself when I joined the Company, and had progressed to Store Manager and other positions on the retail side. I was always somewhat surprised when Brian was brought onto the Board as Distribution Director, a position which I never thought sat well with him, and his tenure on the Board was short lived.

Bob Emmott and Martin Ackroyd who joined the Board on the same day as me both left for different reasons and I have commented on Bob elsewhere. Martin Ackroyd was a sound guy who, in my view, was more than capable of growing as the Company grew organically, but unfortunately when things went wrong after the Safeway acquisition he was very much in the firing line and paid the ultimate price. I still see Martin occasionally at our beloved football club, and I detect that there is a lingering feeling of bitterness about the way he was treated.

Martin and myself figured in one of the strong debates at Board Meetings. These debates often took place and Ken very frequently used the expression that we could 'do as you like and speak as you like in this room, but when those doors open we are together', very sound comments and the togetherness took us forward, even through the disagreements and rows.

The row which was to feature Martin Ackroyd and myself figured on the first character named in this book, Rod Smaldon. Rod had made his mark on the company and was very good at gaining the ear of the right people. For a short time he was placed in charge of the IT function, a function with which he had little experience but made the right noises, and when Board appointments were being discussed, Ken and John Dowd, to whom Rod reported, were in favour of appointing him to the Main Board. Martin and myself, who had grown up knowing the man slightly better, said that we were both totally opposed to such an appointment, it would bring the Company no benefit whatsoever and that we felt so strongly that if an appointment were made we would have to consider our positions and in all probability resign. The appointment would, in our opinion, have been a disaster for the Company and in particular for the day-to-day business.

Having heard our views I believe Ken and John spent some time thereafter analysing the strengths and weaknesses of the individual and did not progress an appointment. Rod Smaldon was then to leave the Company and I understand at his leaving drinks do, blamed myself and Martin for his departure.

I have briefly touched on the passing of my former boss. 1992 and 93 were not good years for me from a personal point of view, although the Company and my own progress continued to flourish.

On New Year's Eve, 1992 my own father died after several months of illness. He had started to show failing health some three years earlier, but had secretly been struggling for some time before. Taken ill whilst on holiday with my mother, he was later diagnosed with prostate cancer and his last months were spent between hospital and then the Sue Ryder Care Home, at nearby Ilkley. I don't feel that mum ever came to terms with my father's illness and indeed may have been in denial about it, but he slipped away peacefully in the early hours of the eve of the New Year. Gone was a man who had made many sacrifices, I am sure, for me and the rest of my family. A quite, peaceful individual who quietly got on with life and never bothered too much about the lives of others, simply because he did not regard it as his business.

Over the previous three years or so Lena and I had taken to going out for dinner once a month with Ron Curry and his wife Caroline, an event, I think, which all four of us looked forward to. Ron was no longer a Director of the Company and I believe used our dinner dates as a means of keeping up to speed with what was going on. Lena and I were regularly regaled with Ron and Caroline's biking stories and their caravan trips. They had made a super home out of their bungalow at Hawksworth on the edge of Ilkley Moor, and we often laughed about the funny side of our job.

One of Ron's final brushes with the infamous Arnold Marriott had been when he was building a walled garden and was looking for a number of circular features to adorn the brick piers of his boundary wall. 'Anything to match red brick', was the instruction given to Arnold, the demo man. I well remember Ron turning up at work one morning, cursing Arnold, who apparently had arrived at the house in the very early hours and had tipped a number of sandstone spheres in the drive. The spheres were the wrong size and the demolition man was promptly ordered to remove them.

Not daunted by this, Mr Marriott said he would get some more and I remember curiously driving to work one morning, idly listening to the radio report of some sandstone spheres having gone missing from the boundary wall of the Queen Mother's Scottish residence at Glamis Castle. Ron arrived at work, gleefully, to inform me that he had had a new delivery, and I often wonder where those spheres came from. I know Ron was somewhat concerned for a few days afterwards!

Having taken our summer recess from the monthly dinner date, I arrived home one evening for Lena to advise me that she had received a telephone call from Ron and that he wanted to speak with me urgently. This was around mid September of 1993. I called him back.

Ron, in his usual forthright manner said, 'There is no easy way to deal with this, so I am just going to tell you and put the phone down.' I agreed. 'I've not been well during the summer and have discovered that I have cancer and I am dying. I don't want you to see me in this condition, so this will be the last time we speak.' The telephone went down, we never did speak again and some two months later I was to give the address at Ron's funeral, at the village church at Esholt, near Baildon, the original set of Emmerdale. My 25-years-plus association with one of the well-known figures in the Property and Construction World was over and although we did not always see eye-to-eye, indeed far from it, I did feel that I had lost a very important and influencing part of my life.

At Ron's funeral I said that he often liked to describe himself as 'hard but fair'. I remember the sharp intakes of breath when I said that this was not true and that Ron was 'hard and unreasonable', but only with those who could not understand his way, or accept his way of working. Ron had a lot of great sayings, one of which was, that he would explain something once and if the recipient did not understand he would explain it again, if something needed explaining for a third time he would start to think that he had the wrong person. A phrase I often used, over the years, with my own staff.

For some time prior to 1993, Ken's wife, Edna, had also been suffering with cancer, and suffered an agonising and slow decline. I vividly remember Ken, his sister Joan and brother-in-law, Ken Blundell, sitting behind me at Ron Curry's funeral and Ken, in hushed tones, telling his sister that things were very bad, so much so that Joan Blundell rushed off with Ken to their home. In mid December, some six weeks after Ron Curry's funeral, Lena and I were at another. Edna Morrison was a very homely, warm person. Ken's second wife, she was very much into the business and had been the first critic of Bob Emmott and myself and our attempts to create the Market Concept in 1985. I remember with some mild amusement, my first contact with her. At that time Ken, Edna and family lived at Farnley, just outside the West Yorkshire town of Otley, in a really nice house with long drive and several garages. Ken's eldest daughter Andrea, by his first wife, was very keen on show jumping and very competent at it and the house had stables and other facilities, but Mrs M thought it time that the drive be resurfaced. Ron Curry stepped up and volunteered one of our tame surfacing contractors and I was put in to bat to arrange the work, which was duly carried out and completed.

The week after Ron Curry asked me what I was doing on Saturday morning, I replied, 'working, as normal' and he suggested that I visit the Morrison house to look at the finished surfacing. I remember the briefing well.

'If you get through the back door, you've done well, if you get a cup of tea, you are the star, if you stand on the outside door mat, you're in trouble.' I arrived and stood on the outside doormat!

Edna, her face quite stern, came to the door, greeted me and told me that her car had been in the garage most of the week, would I like to help her get it out. I marched across the newly surfaced drive and tried to open the door to the garage, only to find our contractor, Brian Wells, had surfaced up to the door and there was no movement. Mr Wells was promptly summoned and the work reinstated, but not a good introduction to the boss's wife.

I was delighted in more recent years when Lynne Dent, who at that time was a partner in our legal advisors and who had acted for me on many property issues, advised me that she would have to give up the Morrison account as she had become involved with Ken, and ultimately, they married and added a further two children to the Morrison family. I was delighted for both of them and although since retirement I have not seen much of either I know that Lynne is putting her skills to some benefit as Chairman of the Governors of the Bradford Grammar School.

CHAPTER 17

The Brink of Greatness
1998–2002

FOR ME, THESE FOUR YEARS were pivotal to the future and, at that time, unknown scale of the business going forward. This was the period which saw us actively engaged in acquiring competitors' stores, extending our distribution network both in geographic and physical terms, re-positioning our production facilities, extending and refurbishing stores at a rapid rate, and looking at physically new areas for expansion, of which the most notable was north of the Border.

In addition, although I was not to know it at the time, we also became involved in the prelude in the acquisition of Safeway, which saw us approached by two of our competitors, Asda and Tesco. They were looking at acquiring Safeway, but knew they would have to divest a significant number of stores to competitors in order to comply with Competition rulings.

1999 also saw the centenary of the business started by Ken's father as a market trader and we managed to open our hundredth store in our centenary year, in Nelson, East Lancashire, not much more than twenty-five miles from our home base.

For my own part the period also saw the consolidation of some of my non-Morrison activities. I had been invited to join the Boards of, firstly, the Bexley Thameside Partnership, a London Borough Quango. Made up of Public and Private sector Companies and organisations, it was established to look at regeneration and invest-ment, within the London Borough of Bexley.

Secondly, I was invited to join an organisation in Newcastle, which went by the rather inglorious name of Fish Quay Redevelop-ment and again was a Public and Private sector, arts based, organisation set up with the specific purpose of redeveloping the old Quay near to the mouth of the mighty River Tyne as an arts and artists complex. In both cases I persuaded the Board that membership

187

of these organisations would be a good way of increasing the Company's profile, and my offer to be the Company's representative was readily snapped up.

In the case of Bexley, I spent three years spanning the development and thereafter trading period of our store at Erith. The commitment to the two bodies was not significant, although I did attend bi-monthly Board Meetings of each, which meant travelling, but I generally managed to link in the meetings with visits to nearby stores, although at that time the Erith opening in October 1998 was a giant leap for Morrisons to the south, our nearest store being at Northampton some fifty miles north of London.

Bexley was a fascinating time, I well remember introducing the Partnership to the concept of Enterprise Development, which I have mentioned elsewhere.

In a nutshell, however, the Company had been responsible in developing various nursery industrial units, backed up by the central services associated with clerical functions and also organising the provision of business development programmes for those eager to start up on their own. The scheme had worked very well on a small basis in our own city of Bradford and had later been extended to a hundred-acre site on the outskirts of Darlington. Both schemes, of course, were adjacent to a large retail store.

My fellow Board Members at Bexley, eager to see the Darlington experiment in the flesh, caused me a very hectic two days in the beginning of 1998, when, following the late finish of a Board Meeting Thursday evening, I was on an early train to London the following morning. A short commuter ride to Bromley, collection by car, journey to the terminal of Gold Air at Biggin Hill, and thereafter a private flight for six of us to Teesside, where the airport was situated some two or three miles from our Darlington site.

Upon arrival in the North East we were collected by my own Centre's Manager and PA, given a tour of the facilities and a presentation on the Enterprise Trust which existed there and thereafter we flew the return to Biggin Hill, train to London and home in time for tea! – or not quite.

The Darlington Enterprise Trust format was very much admired by my colleagues from the south and formats of it were adopted later.

When I left the Bexley Thameside Partnership, I was presented with a signed book of the district and later invited to the Bexley Borough Council civic dinner as a guest of honour. Much is made of the cold, or warmth of southern against northern people, but the presentation at my final Bexley Board Meeting, brought a quite large lump to my throat. I had been adopted and accepted as a 'player' in their team.

My experience at Newcastle Fish Quay, more accurately Tynemouth, was not as successful but warm nevertheless.

I have always had a great admiration for the people of the North East, dating back to my early contact with the bowlers of Darlington some years earlier and people from the old Durham, and now Teesside and Tyne and Wear, are no exception. Bright, warm, humorous and willing to share, you are more often than not made extremely welcome and my time on the Board of the Fish Quay Partnership was no less than I would have expected.

The rather large scale rebuilding of the old fish processing sheds was, in my view, hijacked by the design team, and although things may now have changed, was to my mind a classic example of the Lottery Commission's failings in its early days.

Having taken advice from the Lottery Commission the Fish Quay Partnership were strongly recommended to appoint a London based architect, who had apparently set himself as an expert in Lottery Grant Application type schemes and proceeded to make, in my view, a total pig's ear of it. The scheme turned out significantly over-budget and the production of information was far too slow.

I would have much preferred a Newcastle based architect who had some sympathy for the lovely surroundings of the river mouth and the history that goes with it.

Having trodden the site of the former Armstrong Vickers Gunnery works back in 1987 I had a lot of feeling for the River Tyne frontage and have subsequently marvelled at the construction of the 'blinking eye' bridge, the Sage Centre and other wonderful schemes.

Standing at the mouth of the Tyne and looking upstream, the old navigation towers, which showed the the way into the River from the North Sea, are still standing and the whole thing has a warm feel about it. London architects with a view to having their fees paid by the Lottery Commission, irrespective as to whether the project went ahead or not, were not the solution, and ultimately the Fish Quay Partnership fizzled to a halt.

I visited the site some months before I retired and was sorry to see that not much had been made of it, at least not as much as should have been.

1998 saw us open ten stores, of which five had been acquired from competitors and rebuilt or remodelled. Major refurbishment was also carried out to six existing stores and minor refurbishment on many others to bring them into line with current merchandising regimes.

In addition our fresh food facility, Farmer's Boy, opened up on a new site less than twenty years after its original had been built, not half a mile away, such was the expansion of the volume of our product and ranges.

The new Farmer's Boy was a big disappointment to Ken and me. My Construction Director David Wade and others from the construction team had been left very much in a delegated position of designing and building the new facility and Ken and I had decided to take a back seat, given that the Company was becoming so large and you couldn't 'have your finger in every pie'. The result was a disappointment and Ken and I spent several months thereafter beating ourselves up on the basis of 'if only'. Eventually, after much heart rending and many minor alterations, Ken and I decided that we would have to make the best of it, the factory settled down and with many subsequent modifications and extensions is now a corner-stone of the Company's fresh food production business, very much linked in to the three abattoirs units at Turiff in the Highlands of Scotland, Colne in East Lancashire and Spalding in Lincolnshire.

During 1998 we also witnessed severe competition and aggressive marketing campaigns throughout the industry. Whilst many of our competitors introduced their own loyalty schemes, Morrisons contented itself with a promotion on fuel called Morrison Miles, which is running to this day.

Additionally the OFT (Office of Fair Trading), called an enquiry into the state of the industry, one of many which was to blight our operational activities over the next ten years and which, frankly, have achieved very little indeed. Equally the stance of Central Government regarding planning consent for food stores remained difficult.

By 1993 I had roughly doubled the number of retail outfits that I had inherited when I joined the Board, from 33 to 60. In May of that year, I had made a very bold statement to the Board that in every six-year cycle the number of stores would double. By 1993 we would be operating 66 outlets; 1999, 130; and 2005, 260. I did say at the time that this would necessarily require some corporate activity in the form of acquisitions and some of our programme at this time was going down that line, as evidenced by the 50:50 mix of new build and acquisition stores the previous year.

Little did I know what was to come in 2004.

When quizzed what I would do after achieving the 260 stores by 2005 I, rather flippantly, replied that I would retire and again, this almost came true. My strategy for 2005 also included seven major Regional Distribution Centres (RDC), but did not include any site acquisitions in Scotland.

With the Owen luck, one month after my famous 1993 statement, John Gummer, the then Secretary of State for the Environment, issued his first planning edicts, in the form of Planning Guidance notes, which sought to control the development of food retailing and retain it in town and city centres. This was a complete mystery to us, as the Government's assumptions that food retailing was essential to the vitality and viability, as they called it, of towns and city centres, was strange at a time when factory outlets and other non-food developments, previously the life blood of town and city centres, continued to get consent out of town. We campaigned that the Government stance on planning was, of itself, anti-competitive.

In 1999, the Company celebrated its centenary and also the opening of its hundredth store at Nelson, in East Lancashire. What a way to come from the market stalls of West Yorkshire, set up by Ken's father.

The rate of store openings for this year was less than previously, but nevertheless we managed to open five, including the relaunch of one building and one modernised store acquired from the Co-operative Group in its various guises.

Perhaps the most unique aspect of the centenary year stores was to open in Letchworth. This is a sleepy town of middle-class, Home Counties England, most noted for the fact that it was the very first garden city, founded in 1903, by Ebenezer Howard and was therefore the world's first garden city and one of the first ever new towns. Letchworth's development inspired other projects, including one nearby at Welwyn, and I understand that Canberra, the Australian capital city, was inspired by its design.

The design of our store had to be something special and we managed to marry it in with an existing building on part of the site on one of the main streets of the garden city, giving us many problems, not least of which was to satisfy the Garden City Heritage Foundation and its Director Stuart Kenny. Mr Kenny had been a big thorn in the Company's side, along, it has to be said, with many others in his time at Leeds City Council, who had conspired to stop us developing on a site in the Kirkstall District, and in the process had cost the Company in my estimation, £7 million.

Still the development went ahead and I was extremely pleased with the result, but towards the end of the project, my mind turned to our customary piece of art and we discovered that there was no sculpture or bust of Ebenezer Howard anywhere in the town. We elected to have one done and set in a quiet seating area outside the store entrance. Mr Kenny's reaction, as I recall it, was rather harsh and somewhat furious, but we would not give way and the bust of the great man himself attracted much favourable comment from the inhabitants. I always suspect in cases where Local Authorities are not too suited with one's efforts that they are perhaps rather peeved that they did not think of the idea themselves!

And so the decade and the Millennium came to an end. The following year we were to open the Kirkstall store in Leeds, which was probably my second thumbing of the nose at Mr Kenny.

The Millennium year saw us open eight new stores, which included acquisitions from the Co-operative Group, at Dereham, near Norwich, Rhyl and Ipswich and other acquisitions from Somerfield at Hyde, in Greater Manchester. The Kirkstall development, in addition to the efforts of the Council itself, was thwarted by the invasion of a group of 'tree-huggers' at our Head Office, and this gave rise to some very serious security issues, which I addressed in the new HQ building some six years later.

Ken and myself were in his office one day when a small group of people, many of whom were later identified as objecting to the then proposed Aire Valley Motorway link, literately invaded the building and walked into his office. Dirty boots on his desk, feet up all around and a refusal to move.

No less than five 999 calls to the police produced no action whatsoever and word went around the building, with the immediate assembling of a group of Morrisons heaviest.

The police eventually arrived and cautioned us! Their excuse was, that if we were to adopt a robust approach to removing people from our building, then we would be arrested, notwithstanding the fact that the people themselves were trespassing. Ken and I were livid and Ken later rang the then Deputy Chief Constable of West Yorkshire Norman Bettison, later to become Sir Norman, and protested. The response of the police force on this occasion was to give Ken the top man's x-directory telephone number with a request that if such an invasion occurred again, Ken was to contact direct and action would be ensured. We wonder about the police and that particular incident did not do my particular confidence any good.

I always admired Ken for his calmness in those events. By now he was past normal retirement age and I felt that the stress of the invasion might have some effect on him, but within an hour or two he was back to his normal cheery self.

The following year saw us open a further seven stores again, dotted around the country from Barry and Rogerstone, in South Wales, to Jarrow in the North East and another replacement in Bradford of one of our first generation stores at Thornbury.

The Jarrow development was interesting in that it saw another piece of artwork, where we recreated in a bronze sculpture the famous picture of the Jarrow Marchers, setting off to London. We even managed to get the daughter of the family pictured carrying the banner in so many newspapers and journals to unveil the sculpture, which was a classic Graham Ibbeson.

Graham had been responsible for the famous bronze of Eric Morecambe, which the company had sponsored, in the comedian's hometown and which had been unveiled years earlier by the Queen. His works stand proudly, in my mind, with that of the Scottish born sculpture David Mach, who was responsible for our full size brick 'train' at the Darlington development, to be seen by motorists journeying along the A66 between Stockton and the A1.

The Jarrow Marchers brought tears to many eyes that day, on the 65th anniversary of their famous march.

The stores in South Wales brought me into contact, all be it accidentally, with another personality of slightly higher profile.

Sian Lloyd is the well-known face of independent television's weather forecasting. I met Miss Lloyd at a reception at the Foreign and Commonwealth Office in Whitehall some time prior to the two stores opening and was introduced to her by the Leicester MP Keith Vaz, whom we had had some dealings with on potential regeneration issues a number of years earlier. Left alone with the redoubtable Miss Lloyd, she advised me that she did not shop in supermarkets, preferring the local grocer, as supermarkets were the death of the high street. I then discovered that she did 'occasionally' shop in her local Tesco store at Penarth, which, 'as you know darling, is the posh part of Cardiff'.

I had indeed been in the particular store, whilst looking at sites in and around Cardiff, and clearly Tesco at Penarth was potentially a competitor. I regaled Miss Lloyd with the story that one of my colleagues had accidentally knocked a cup off the table in the Tesco cafe, the shattering of which had caused three of the customers to have a heart attack, such was the age profile of the store customers. She chose to ignore the comment. Upon leaving she walked some three or four metres away from me, turned around and said that if I wanted anyone to open the two South Wales stores, she would be available. 'Email me darling', were the last words I ever heard from Miss Lloyd.

CHAPTER 18

Oh Dear, We Are Big – 2002–05

T HE YEAR OF 2002 WAS TO BE SIGNIFICANT, in more ways than one.
Most significant of all, it saw the marriage on 9 March of my
eldest stepson, Glen, to Helen, whom he had met whilst sailing round
the world on the Robin Knox-Johnston Clipper trip of 1998/99.
Their individual backgrounds are elsewhere in this book, but we had
a fabulous day, topped off, if that were possible, by departing on a
holiday ourselves the following day.

Earlier in the year I was busy pursuing planning consent for a third
Distribution Centre, to be located at Burton Latimer, near to
Kettering, where we had opened a store some two years earlier, and
I suppose things to come should have been flagged in my mind, when
Ken announced that he had arranged with David Webster, the
Chairman of Safeway, that a few of us should visit their new flagship
store at Plymstock, a suburb of Plymouth, in Devon. In mid-January
a group, including Chief Executive Bob Stott, flew by charter plane
from Leeds to Plymouth. Peter Derbyshire, a pilot I was to come to
know over the following years, flew us in a rather aged twin engine
turbo prop which, unbeknown to us all, did not have its automatic
levelling devices working, and when Bob Stott departed his seat to
become 'hostess' for the morning and serve the drinks, his weight
transfer immediately lifted the plane another 150 ft in a solid climb.
Bob returned to his seat on all fours and never moved again for the
rest of the day!

Plymstock had been created to wow the City Analysts and no
expense had been spared, as we were to find some two years later
when we acquired it for ourselves. There were coffee shops, reading
areas, tasting areas, sample kitchens and so on and we cynical
Yorkshiremen seriously questioned the cost and duly reported it back
to our colleagues on the Board.

Quite early in the year we were well into the new store
development programme which saw new build stores at Grays, Essex,
Kings Lynn, Cambourne, near Cambridge, Redcar, and Byker, on

Tyneside, together with the opening of a former Safeway store at Enfield, which we had acquired from B&Q. We also rebuilt one of the original Whelan's stores, acquired in 1978 at St Helen's, which had formerly been the site of an engine shed, retaining the railway themes.

The Cambourne site was especially interesting as it is the site of a new settlement, and when I took the Board there, on a luxury coach trip, I was expecting them to take one look at the empty fields and reject the site. At that time there were a few houses and a village school, but we knew what was coming, took the plunge and developed what has become an extremely successful store.

By now I was making regular trips to Scotland to look at and deal with the acquisition of new sites, following our earlier excursions as a Board which committed ourselves in developing in a new 'country'.

Additionally, throughout the spring Lena and myself were engaged in attending Morrison Long Services Awards, which we always enjoyed and threw ourselves into with some enthusiasm. In those days, of course, only Morrison employees with more than 25 years service were entitled to the Award, which took the form of the presentation of Share Certificates, or a gold watch, at a hotel in Bradford. We hosted the recipients and their partners for the weekend, commencing with a reception and a presentation during Saturday afternoon, dinner and a show at the famous Bradford Alhambra Theatre in the evening, after which the time was their own. Subsequent to the Safeway take over, of course, this has become a much bigger proposition with three, or four different events now being held and with the event itself becoming re-gionalised, although those based in Yorkshire, take advantage of the splendid new Head Office building, with photographs of the recipients draped artfully over the office escalators being a particular feature.

Spring also saw my visit, for the umpteenth time, to the three yearly EuroShop Exhibition in Dusseldorf and the pleasant reception of HRH, The Princess Royal, to accept a charity cheque at our flagship store in Bradford.

2002 was also a significant milestone in my support for Bradford City, and although I have spoken about my beloved club elsewhere, chronologically, I should mention now that April saw a testimonial game played for one of the clubs iconic servants, Stuart McCall, who had played at the club for two spells, starting as a young man and then returning in the twilight of his career, after several years success with Glasgow Rangers and Scotland.

The match took place at the end of April and was attended by an almost full house of some 25,000 at the Bradford Stadium, over half of which were from Glasgow. This made for a fantastic sight and atmosphere, with our Scottish friends largely fuelled by the journey's consumption of alcohol and a mass raid on the nearby Tesco store. The game itself, or more particularly the events around it, brought into sharp focus for Lena and myself just how things do not change in sport and religion. Hosting friend Archie Gilroy, from our steel subcontractors Bone, in Glasgow, together with his son Steven, we shared a table of ten for lunch in the nice dining facilities in the ground. Lena and I were the only English on the table and sitting next to two Scots, who were obviously together, my inquisitive wife questioned the emblems on their ties, which appeared not to be Glasgow Rangers. The question was met with a straightforward response of 'mind your own business' and Archie explained to us afterwards these were Orange Lodge ties and that our visitors were not from Glasgow, but were from Northern Ireland and it was better not to say too much more. I was to find out more about Northern Ireland several years later, as I have documented elsewhere.

The year passed with regular trips to Scotland, looking at sites, watching construction start and thereafter travelling the rest of the country with our new store development programme.

In midsummer the Produce Board of the Company decided that given the expanding volume of trade we needed to look at fresh facilities. The Dutch Bos Brothers whom I had met in 1986 were looking to retire and offered to sell their business to us, an offer which was subsequently taken up and completed, but we very quickly realised that the facility at De Lier near the Hook of Holland was not big enough to cater for future capacity and volume requirements and in any event the property was leased and the lease would be expiring shortly.

In August myself, my Main Board partner, David Hutchinson and Produce Director, Chris Walker flew to Holland, looked at the existing facility and looked at a couple of sites nearby. This started a process of visits throughout September and October, culminating in me making a presentation to the Produce Board, with a recommendation for a site adjoining the Hook of Holland ferry terminal. The site was far larger than my original brief had anticipated, but I argued successfully that given future expansion of the Company, we ought to be looking at a position whereby we could build larger facilities, even if in phases, without having to move offsite again. My recommendations and costings were accepted and I returned to Holland in November to meet with the Rotterdam planners.

In November, I cannot remember the exact date, I received a telephone call from my colleague, Martin Ackroyd the Finance Director, who said that I was required to go with him to a meeting in Nottingham the following Sunday. I cannot remember the exact date, but it may have been the 10, or 17 November. Upon asking why, I was met with a very vague answer, but we duly drove the seventy or so miles from Bradford in which time Martin told me that we had been approached by Safeway, to acquire their business.

Our clandestine meeting took place in a Nottingham hotel and I very quickly realised that either the Morrison Board were not fully aware of the point which any process had reached, or that the Safeway side were trying to bulldoze a deal through, as all sorts of discussions took place, which would lead the uninformed observer to think that the two parties had been 'at it' for several months. As far as I was concerned this was virtually the first I had heard of a singular Morrison-Safeway deal, although as I have recalled elsewhere, we had been interested on two separate occasions previously, but with other operators. It appeared that Ken had been in discussions with David Webster for some time.

Following this initial meeting there followed a period, which was to change the course of the Company forever. Weeks of negotiation followed and the Company's first offer for Safeway was made on 9 January 2003. I well remember this, as we were all summoned to London the previous evening and were in place in the offices of ABN-AMRO, when the announcement hit the Stock Exchange on opening at 7.00 a.m. All hell broke loose on the news channels and in the Market, as everyone had been taken by surprise.

My long time friend Bob Dyson, who was Chief Executive of famed Manchester agents, Dunlop Heywood, called me, and not knowing his number I simply answered with my name. The voice on the other end loudly proclaimed 'I've just heard the news and nearly crashed my ******* car'. Bob, always an enthusiast, went on to extol how pleased he was to hear the news and how much he hoped the deal would come off, but there was much to do yet and all this on top of routine, indeed, the following week saw me in London with our competition solicitor on the Monday, Swansea and Newport, by private plane, on the Wednesday, Scotland on the Thursday and Friday and then working on sketch schemes for our produce pack house in Holland the following week.

As soon as our interest in Safeway was known, we were swiftly followed by announcements from Asda, Sainsbury, Tesco and private finance organisations, each signalling their intentions of a counter bid. We believed that we had been used as a stalking horse and the Safeway Board promptly withdrew its recommendation to accept our offer.

Over the next few weeks we had many discussions with the Office of Fair Trading (OFT) and hoped that clearance would be granted for us, but this was not to be the case and in late spring the OFT referred the case to the Competition Commission, for what effectively became known as the '2003 Grocery Inquiry', which affected the whole industry and its suppliers.

Hours, days and weeks were spent giving evidence to the Inquiry and it was interesting to see just how far advanced Morrisons was in its hands-on management compared with our competitors, the most graphic example of which was the one-day public hearing when all appeared, one after the other, to put their case before the Competition Commission investigation went into private, individual hearings.

Contrast the styles of Ken Morrison, Sir Peter Davies, of Sainsbury, Terry Leahy of Tesco and Tony De Nunzio, of Asda. Ken spoke from the heart and with intense and deep knowledge of his Company's business, the other three spoke from scripts written by their PR people, which came out as having nothing whatsoever to do with the inquiry and more to do with marketing their businesses. I believe that day in itself was a particular PR disaster for Sainsbury's and Asda and we had in any event decided for ourselves that Tesco were too big to be allowed to take any part of Safeway, unless they made massive property disposals. In September of 2003, the Competition Commission reported and cleared Morrisons, only to bid for the Safeway business, subject to the compulsory disposal of fifty-two stores. These stores occupied locations within the traditional heartland of Morrison activities, in West Yorkshire, the North East, Lancashire and in other odd cases elsewhere.

I had previously forecast to the Board that we would have to divest of some thirty-seven stores, but had not taken into account that the Competition Commission would require us to dispose of some smaller stores which did not really hit my radar at the time. We were delighted with the outcome.

On 15 December, 2003, we made a second offer for the Safeway business which valued it at £3.35 billion and given that the private finance parties had withdrawn, the deal was uncontested and completed on 8 March the following year. Unfortunately the twelve month delay caused by the OFT/CC enquiry had led to the deterioration of an already ailing business and this made subsequent integration and the recovery process all the more difficult.

From clearance to March of the following year the Morrison business focus turned its eyes to Hayes in Middlesex where the Safeway Head Office was located. Most of us on the Board were familiar with the Safeway properties over most of the country, having looked at them twice previously in association with proposed bids from Asda and Tesco, which would have seen us taking a significant number of properties.

Over New Year, I took Lena to Scotland, having promised her New Year's Eve in that country. Heartened by the prospect of Hogmanay on Princes Street, in Edinburgh, she accepted my invitation, but was dismayed when we caught the 4.15 flight back home to Leeds and spent New Year's Eve in what has become a traditional way, in our house, on our own, with a glass of champagne. Lena still recounts the day we spent trekking around the perimeter of Safeway's' various depots, in preparation of the acquisition.

8 March 2004 was an earth-moving day. Prior to the take-over Morrisons was operating 127 stores, and overnight we acquired a further 496, ranging from the outer islands of northern Scotland, through the Isle of Man, Northern Ireland, the Isle of Wight and as far south as Gibraltar.

On acquisition a substantial proportion of the acquired stores were not considered appropriate to the Company's long-term strategic vision. This view largely came from the trading side of things and was set against the Morrisons one price, national pricing policy for all products except petrol, and our IT systems did not have the facility to introduce multi-pricing, even given the fact that the Safeway system did. We therefore decided on a disposal programme in addition to the programme which had been imposed upon us by the OFT.

At the same time senior staff from Morrison were parachuted into the Hayes Headquarters, animosity ranged over a large area, which was generated by what we found to be typical Safeway management and management style.

I remember on 8 March the entire Morrison Board was assembled at Hayes and we walked into the auditorium, where in three sittings the entire HQ staff at Safeway had the news broken to them. The format took the basis of a brief few words from David Webster, the Safeway Chairman, who, frankly, could not get out of the building fast enough, together with several of his associates and their rather weighty severance cheques.

After David's few words, up stepped Ken with typical Yorkshire brusqueness and welcomed the assembled faces to 'the Morrison family'. The shock/horror which spread across those faces like a wave cannot be described in words. The stunned silence was immediately followed by a ripple of conversation and it became very clear to us on the top table that the Safeway staff had been led to believe that it was they who were acquiring Morrisons and not the other way round.

Ken spoke at some length and for those who knew him, his words were very well put, but for those who were not from Yorkshire they were badly received, I have to say, through no fault of Ken's. As the third group of people departed the auditorium the consensus view of the Morrison Board was that we were in for a rough ride and a long hard road. These people were not going to be cooperative and clearly had been used to a soft life where they received bonuses, basically, for turning up for work. All of this was to change and Ken had given them much food for thought.

Prior to the actual acquisition being completed I had held informal and confidential meetings with the team I believed would take us through the subsequent conversation programme. These were well tried and trusted sub-contractors based in and around Bradford and comprised Mitton Mechanical Services (heating and ventilating), Andrews (terrazzo flooring), Johnson Brothers (suspended ceiling), George Barker (refrigeration), NG Bailey (electrical), Abraham's and Carlisle (shop fitting), Butterfield Signs (illuminated signs) and Pitts (electrical contractors).

I explained to them all that the prize at stake here was too large to lose, that the eyes of the City would be on us, that criticism was likely to be rife, that questions were likely to be asked as to whether Morrisons could swallow such a large meal, and that for their case in particular I was not prepared to allow them to bite off more than they could chew.

I encouraged them to become managers and enter into alliances with other like organisations in their particular industries, sub-contracting work, but that they would be responsible for the standards, qualities, performance and delivery, on time and at cost. This was to be one of the big adventures.

I involved in all this my own Construction Director, my Services Manager and my Maintenance Manager, as we had seen the level of decline in the Safeway estate over the previous twelve months from 'not very good', to 'abjectly poor' and Graham Carter, the Mainten-ance Manager, would in particular have his work cut out.

We agreed as an initial platform that key members of the team would visit the so called Safeway mega-stores, which comprised locations at Plymstock in Plymouth, Thamesmead in South London, Gamston in Nottingham, and Stratford-Upon-Avon, together with two other locations in Scotland. We aimed to have all these inspected and our initial views on paper, or at least thought through, prior to the big day itself, and this was duly delivered.

At this time, Lena and I were actively involved in buying property in Spain and trips there were the last thing on my mind, indeed looking at my diary for February, prior to the acquisition, I had trips to Spain for three days, followed immediately by trips to Holland for the produce factory work and then trips to Scotland. Life was a round of climbing on and off aircraft.

If nothing else, Safeway senior management had been very keen to extol the virtue and protect the position of their senior management team.

My overall and lasting view of the Safeway Board and its senior
management group, was that they were a set of arrogant individuals,
who thought they were god's gift to retailing and who operated on
a different planet, let alone different level from their Morrison
equivalents. We were to find that this hunch was further backed up
by the fact that within a very short time of the acquisition most of
the senior management of Safeway departed with their tails between
their legs. The Safeway Board, of course, departed similarly, but
somewhat better off financially.

One such meeting which illustrated to me the paucity of the
Safeway set up was when at the end of January 2004 I flew to
Heathrow and met Finance Director Simon Laffin, together with his
Property Director Fernando Garcia Valencia, and was virtually told
that I would be making a serious mistake if I did not appoint him in
place of my own staff. The man himself had been brought into
Safeway, by its Chief Executive, Carlos Creido Perez, had a massive
salary, school expenses, free trips to Spain on an unlimited basis and
all the other perks you could think off on the one hand, yet on the
other hand his English was poor, he clearly had no knowledge at all
of English planning or construction systems, and I decided there and
then that this would be the first departure, a departure, that when it
came, was taken with good grace and extreme politeness.

By now the works to the new produce pack house in Holland
were on site, we had cleared all the hurdles of local authority and its
greater metropolitan partner, Rotterdam City and had negotiated a
contract for what was to become phase one of the pack house with
local developers and builders, Van Mierlo, who were based very close
to our Hook of Holland site. The brothers Van Mierlo, Bert and
Wim, together with their Site Manager Stefan Kamp, were exceptionally good to work with. The unfortunate thing from my part was
that all my Project Managers were committed to existing development programme work, or were about to be committed to the
Safeway programme. Our other consultants were likewise committed
and in the end, after much thought, I turned to the Senior Partner
of our Quantity Surveyors, Rex Procter, Bradford Office, Geoff
Emmett. Geoff, you will recall, is a name from my very early days of
private practice and someone who I worked through Round Table,
and indeed was my best man in my marriage to Lena. I decided that

Geoff should act as Employers' Representative on what was, at that time, Morrisons' only design and build project. Geoff would keep costs within lines of the specification and I would pay periodic visits to the site meetings, which eventually I did, on the basis of every other meeting. More later.

Ken had a famous line: 'never trust a Dutchman', and constantly warned me that these people, whom he had not met, would eventually come up with some large-scale claim. It never materialised and Van Mierlo's attitude and approach when we had to launch phase two before phase one of the project was complete, as a consequence of the Safeway acquisition, was extremely accommodating. We ended up with a superb result all round and I believe friendship on top of that, which was a major bonus.

Shortly after our acquisition of Safeway I was in bed at a hotel at Hayes, very near Heathrow, when at 4 a.m. my internal phone rang and I was greeted by my colleague Mark Gunter, the Store Operations Director, with the news that our store in Winsford, in Cheshire, was ablaze and that we were likely to lose it. This was all I needed on top of all the other problems, as I had discovered some very unhealthy issues within the Safeway property department, which resulted, ultimately, in many of the staff either leaving voluntarily, being dismissed, or becoming the subject of police investigation. All sorts of malpractice appeared to be rife and issues were not helped by the fact that, as with many other sides of the business, the property maintenance business had been outsourced to a national firm of surveyors, E C Harris and Partners, who were acting as a call centre. I very quickly terminated this contract and brought the work in-house, where we had it fully under control, and I sincerely hope that Morrisons never go that way, as it is a recipe for disaster.

In our conversation in the early hours of that morning, Mark and I agreed that I would get in my car, which I had fortuitously taken with me to London, and drive up to Winsford the following day, where I was met by a scene of disaster, but a scene of hope given the absolute spirit of Morrison staff throughout the group.

The fire had been large and intense and had destroyed the store warehouse, but fortunately the level and standard of construction and the excellent maintenance of elements such as fire stop doors, had prevented the blaze doing anything other than smoke damage to the rest of the unit. We were open again within a week or so of the fire, a member of staff was arrested, charged and subsequently served time at Her Majesty's pleasure for the offence of arson with intent.

By now we were entering into negotiations with the OFT regarding the requirement to dispose a number of stores and we fortuitously and, if I say so myself, skilfully argued with the OFT that in four of the locations, where we had to divest stores, we would swap the divestments and dispose of the Morrison stores through the process and keep the Safeway stores. The Safeway stores to be retained were at Ripon in North Yorkshire, Southport, Chester, and Bramley in Leeds, and these four stores were the first to be converted to Morrisons, all at the same time and all within a month of the acquisition being completed.

We then set about a programme whereby we said we would test the water further, by the conversion of one of the mega-stores at Milton Keynes later in the year, and then the programme would roll out of three stores conversions each week, from the autumn of 2004 running through to 2006.

At this point my Construction Director David Wade together with Retailer Paul Pleasance, Fresh Food Director, Tim Robinson and Merchandise Director, Amanda Lomax got in a car and eventually drove round all 220 plus units. Below them was a team who would go around the stores and produce what were called 'red line' drawings, indicating what that team thought could be done. The red line drawing was inspected, approved, or rejected and the drawing brought forward for final drawing office treatment.

At this point Mark Gunter and I introduced at Mark's suggestion a regular get together to go through the drawings as they came forward in batches, and by the time the project was completed, at the end of November 2005, Mark and I had seen every layout drawing of every store, and on some occasions more than once, when we initially rejected the plans proposed. This level of attention at Main Board level was, I believe, unprecedented in almost any business you would care to name and laid the foundation for a successful turn-round of the old Safeway business.

Having set up a good contact with the OFT and our Case Supervisor Bob Gaddes, I undertook to hold regular meetings in

London, to update them on the disposal process and other aspects of the business.

I believe that this regular get-together served the Company well and created good will. Civil servants, once they have made decisions, very often do not get to see the end result, but by our regular conversations they saw what was going on, had the odd humorous note injected and finished our relationship in good spirit.

Our commercial disposal programme was helped as early as July 2004, when Somerfield took 114 smaller stores off us, as this led itself to a separate OFT enquiry which I headed up, and we successfully disposed of the units.

During the course of 2004, having discovered the effects of the delay on the Safeway acquisition and the detrimental decline to the Safeway business, we were faced with an unprecedented period of profit warnings and ultimately, of course, this led the Company to declare its first, and only, loss. It also led, sadly in my case, to the demise of my former colleague Martin Ackroyd, the Finance Director.

Martin had been with Morrisons when I joined in March 1975. He was, like me, an avid Bradford City fan and we enjoyed many away trips together and pints in pubs, and had been fellow members of the MCC, the Morrison Cricket Club.

Martin was, and remains, very much a homespun Yorkshireman, having lived in the Bradford area for most of his life, and I was very sad, as indeed was Ken and the rest of the Board, to see him go, but the City demanded a sacrifice for us being 'bad boys' and unfortunately Martin had to be it. He has subsequently gone off and become something of a mini property developer in his own right, with properties in the North East and Devon, and when I see him on the increasingly rare occasion at football, seems to be in good spirits, but clearly regrets that he left the Company on the terms he did.

With the conversation programme progressing well and some of our financial situation resolved, the City were keen for us to comply with corporate governance and at this point, Ken had no alternative than to give way to the City, and in May 2004 appointed Duncan Davidson of Persimmon Homes and David Jones of Next as Non-Executive Directors. Ken often said that he would value a good checkout operator against a Non-Executive Director any time and appointed the two concerned largely because he knew them both, although Duncan Davidson was only to remain in the Company for less than a year, departing in March 2005. Duncan's very clear idea of Board Meetings based on his Persimmon experience was that you met the night before, had a very heavy dinner with plenty of wine, had a brief Board Meeting the following day, followed by lunch and then depart from whence you had come. The state of Morrisons demanded a little more than that.

David Jones was a completely different character and very quickly made it clear that he took his Non-Executive situation very seriously. There was clearly friction between Ken and David from day one, not helped by the fact that some issues relating to business process in the Morrison boardroom found their way into the columns of the daily newspapers. Ken always suspected that David was the source of this information, but equally the other suspected that the reverse was the case. I have no view for obvious reasons, at least for the purposes of this book.

Towards the end of 2004, David Jones witnessed at first hand one of the first of the clashes, which took place in the boardroom.

Ken, buoyed by the success of our conversion programme, prior to its temporary cessation for Christmas trading at the end of 2004, wanted us to accelerate to five stores conversions each week and was anxious to work through holiday periods and so on.

We had a team out in the field, which was training the former Safeway's staff into Morrison ways, re-merchandising stores and so on, and Ken's request, which, I always suspected, was made on the back of lack of full knowledge, was not really capable of being met.

This came to a head in a Board Meeting in the late 2004 and in an effort to be peacemaker, I suggested that if the rather significant amount of property maintenance were taken out of the conversion programme and dealt with separately and ahead of the main conversion works, then we could accelerate the programme to four stores each week. I can see now the look on Mark Gunter's face across the boardroom table at my comments, which had not been discussed with him.

After some to-ing and fro-ing, we agreed that this would be the way forward, I released my maintenance team to simply 'carry on, as fast as you can' and we redrew the programme to four conversions each week, starting at the end of January 2005 and completing on 25 November the same year. We completed on time and at cost. For week after week we had 36 conversion sites under some form of contract at any one time.

Although we managed to complete, the programme was not without casualties. Many people suffered personally through tiredness, or even exhaustion in some cases, many marriages were put under strain and for my part I felt that the prize was too big to lose.

In June, Lena and I went away to Bermuda for two weeks and I spent much of the first week thinking over the issues which lay ahead. So much so that at one point my wife thought I was in some sort of trough of depression, but at the end of these days thinking I had made my mind up and immediately upon return called a meeting for all our suppliers, sub-contractors, consultants and my own team involved on the construction side of this massive conversion programme.

Prior to that meeting I summoned my Construction Director, David Wade and advised him that within immediate effect I would be taking him off the responsibility for all new build construction and that all his project managers would report to me direct and that David would concentrate totally on the Safeway conversion project. He was not best pleased by this, but there was no option, the prize was simply that large.

Subsequently at a Board Meeting, I advised my colleagues of my decision, told them that I did not want any discussion about it, but to a little surprise I received wholesale compliments on the decision taken and the full support of the Board, a gratifying experience which was rewarded by the delivery of the programme.

When 25 November of 2005 arrived and the message came that the last four stores had opened, Lena and I had decided in advance that we would treat all the staff, both in Head Office and in our regional offices, to a drink, champagne for the grown ups and orange juice for the juniors, and that this particular toast would take place at 9 a.m., the very moment the last four stores opened.

I invited Chief Executive, Bob Stott and Ken to join us in my drawing office where everyone assembled, I said a few words and included everyone from the office clerk, who had dealt with an increasing mountain of post, to the senior men who had been at the arrowhead of the operation. Everyone, either by name or by section, got a mention.

Fortuitously, Bob joined us as I got to my final sentences, which were somewhat broken by what I thought and felt was a very emotional moment. Those reading this who have staff working for them, or simply team mates who are thought a lot of, will understand what it is to present yourself in front of forty or fifty people who all rely on you day after day for their jobs, their well being and everything that goes with working as a team, looking at you bright-eyed with anticipation and knowing that they have done the job. This makes for emotion and Bob fortunately jumped in and completed, in his own way, my last few sentences.

Although I had invited Ken to join us, even for an orange juice, he refused, with the reason that, 'there is too much still to be done'. I thought then and still do now that for the sake of ten minutes this was a rather churlish reaction and I know it would have meant more to my staff for him to be there, than for him not to be there.

And so, 2005 blew out. We had seen the Company increase from a turnover of £1.78 billion to £4.94 billion and the share price increased from 69p to 251p, although there were blips along the way.

What we now had to do was deliver. The new Finance director, Richard Pennycook, had been in place for several months and had seen the closing period of the conversion programme, and subsequently had set about putting in place an optimisation programme, which would bring the Company further together, especially with our Safeway inherited staff and systems. Richard saw this through in the coming months, in a manner in which I do not believe he has ever had the credit for.

CHAPTER 19

Never Trust A Dutchman 2005–06

I BRIEFLY RECOUNTED IN CHAPTER 18 my work 'abroad' in Holland. This had started in 2002 when the members of the Produce subsidiary had decided that we should seriously investigate and thereafter proceed with the acquisition of our former Dutch supplying agents Bos Brothers, who were based at De Lier, near the Hook of Holland. I have recounted elsewhere my brief dalliances with Bos Brothers, when in the 1980s I was a guest at one of the Dutch auctions, with my colleagues of the day.

Bos Brothers were occupying a leased warehouse and some adjoining properties at the chocolate box village of De Lier, about 8 km from the Hook of Holland ferry terminal. They packed product for Morrisons and shipped it on the overnight ferry into Lincolnshire or Harwich, often using the services of local contractor Visbeen, known locally as the 'Rotterdam cowboy'. Visbeen is a massive haulage company, possibly on a par with our own Eddie Stobart, or the French, Norbert Dentressangle. The Bos property lease was coming to an end and the brothers had decided they had had enough and subsequently sold out to us, whereupon the Morrison way of thinking took over. We did not want a new lease, the property gave little room for expansion and it was decided that we should build new premises.

I undertook two trips, with my colleague David Hutchinson and Chris Walker who at that time was the Produce Director, and eventually they settled on a site, but my view was that it wasn't big enough.

David Walshaw, who had been a long time architectural consultant with his various practices but had semi-retired, was persuaded to join me on a visit to the selected site to look at a feasibility study. I very quickly decided that the site would not be big enough for future expansion and that to proceed now would be very short-sighted indeed. Instead, I selected an adjoining site with room for expansion, both in the short and medium terms and after a number of meetings with Rotterdam Council, we agreed terms through local developer, builders Van Mierlo, to proceed.

My first trip to Holland had been through Liverpool, with Easy Jet, but in the meantime a new operator came on the market, Jet 2.com, who amazingly had a base and their main operating centre at our local airport, Leeds Bradford.

Their schedule had two return flights each day, the outbound at 7 a.m., which was a lot more comfortable than the KLM feeder flight one hour earlier. The return evening flight was difficult given the uncertainties of the length of site meetings, so it was very quickly agreed that this would be an overnight stay, for the duration. Fortunately, I did not attend all the site meetings, so was spared the 'grief' of having to eat out in what is quite a nice city.

David Walshaw was to help me over the coming months with various feasibility studies for the larger site and ultimately we made a presentation to the Hook of Holland Council and its elected Mayor, Theo van Eyke. I took much admiration from the way Local Government operates from this scheme. We reorganised Local Government in 1974 and did away with many of the Urban or District Councils in favour of the large Boroughs, or Metropolitan Councils. I think we lost a lot.

In Holland the old system still applies and although Rotterdam, in this case, are the overseeing body, the Hook of Holland had the final say on issues such as planning consent, and Mayor Theo was not impressed by our first attempts.

After a very serious presentation in the local town hall, Mr van Eyke pronounced that this was a landmark site: 'it is the first and last thing people will see in my country and it's not good enough', he said. Theo was not the usual local councillor we find in the UK. No disrespect to anyone because, of course, we live in a democracy, but the ordinary man in the street who might be a bus driver, local nurse, local college lecturer, or whatever does not have the business acumen, and local government today is a business just like anything else, although, of course, it is invariably not run as one, but should be.

Theo van Eyke was a businessman. He ran a large painting contractors and I believe also did some paint manufacturing. When I say a large painting contractor, this is not one that employs 30 or 40 people and comes round to paint your house. This is a painting contractor who has the contract to repaint all the containers which pass through the adjoining Europort container terminal. Containers that circle the world continuously. He was elected for four years and he knew what he wanted. Ultimately, he got it.

Ken's famous quote of 'Never trust a Dutchman' never really came through either at this point, or later in the chapter.

On my first overnight stop, with David Walshaw, we arrived at our hotel just off the centre of Amsterdam, for David to proclaim he knew the area, having been twinned with a local Round Table during his time of a member of Skipton in the Yorkshire Dales. We checked-in and asked the receptionist about local restaurants, she pointed us in the direction of an Italian, Bice, which is a worldwide franchise and has a good name. David decided he knew better from his Round Table days and having settled in we went for an early evening beer, to find his favourite restaurants, of which there were two, allegedly.

After walking for a hundred yards or so from the hotel, David said he was sure he was at the spot, but the restaurant was no longer there. No problem, we will go onto the next one, and so it went on, David failing to find his fillet steak target on both occasions.

During conversation over our second beer it emerged that David had been in these restaurants only during his Round Table time. For those of you in the know, Table membership ceases at the age of 40 and David, at this point, was 62. Restaurants change hands and shops change usages!

We settled on the Italian and like two genuine British tourists arrived at 6.15 p.m., ignoring the 'open at 6.30 p.m.' on the door, eventually gained the attention of the waiters and asked if we could book a table. The answer was yes, what name?

'Owen,' I said. 'Ah,' said the waiter, 'Michael Owen!'

For some reason, unbeknown to me, I declared myself to be the famous footballer's uncle, the nearest connection I could get, being that Michael's father, Terry, had once played for Bradford City.

There then followed a series of visits which became gradually more and more intense and I found myself the subject of scrutiny from Claudia, the waitress who served coffee and the sweet trolley and who pronounced herself Holland's number one fan of one Michael Owen – oh dear.

Subsequent visits led me to researching the England star's injury problems and so on until there came the crunch, when Claudia asked if I could get a signed photograph.

My various travelling colleagues over this time had taken some delight in the fact that I was digging a hole and had not yet thrown away the shovel.

Towards the end of the project I took Geoff Emmett, who had been our representative and was Rex Procter's Senior Partner/Consultant, at that time, Mike Taylor from Mitton Mechanical Services, and David Walshaw, the original feasibility architect, over to Holland to look at the completion of Phase one of the project and get a feel of the standards as independent observers. Dinner was arranged for the Bice restaurant and I spent all day being ribbed about my impending death at the hands of the sweet trolley waitress – little did they know.

After a tiring day, pre-drinks in the hotel bar saw no respite, and tension for the other three built as we walked the short distance to the restaurant, whereupon I pulled from inside my raincoat pocket a framed, signed photograph, with a dedication 'To Claudia', all organised by my PA Glynis, who had contacted Liverpool's training ground and obtained the necessary, thereafter having the prized picture framed by her sister. The faces of the other three were a picture. Apologies to Michael for misrepresentation.

The project in Holland went very well and in the beginning of May 2005 Ken and the rest of the Produce Board, accompanied by various others, went to the formal opening of the unit, which now transports such a volume of product to the UK each night that Stena Lines started an additional ferry vessel. In addition to provided extra employment for the Hook of Holland, we have also increased the volume through the small ferry port, and Mayor van Eyke's words about the company and what we had delivered on official opening day were extremely warming. Geoff Emmett settled the final account with the Dutch extremely amicably and minor works of a remedial nature were carried out promptly and without argument, what a difference to the UK. 'Never trust a Dutchman,' said Ken, well I would certainly trust these ones.

Throughout the rest of 2005, we were extremely busy, with a major concentration on Scotland. By now the Safeway estate was well through the process of conversation to Morrisons, which is recorded elsewhere and which would finish in November of that year, but we were busy developing a Morrison built estate, having committed ourselves into the Safeway acquisition. The course of the year led to store openings at Hamilton, Auchinlea, Cardonald, Paisley, Livingstone and Stroud in Kent.

The Scottish units were very varied, not in their quality or type, but the locations at Cardonald, a run-down suburb of Glasgow, and Paisley were Safeway throwbacks, where the sites had been acquired, in both cases, at absolutely exorbitant figures and we simply had to build them out.

Auchinlea is situated next to a junction on the M8 motorway, which link Glasgow to Edinburgh, in an area called Easterhouse, which has a very bad reputation, but is now rapidly improving with our development and the adjoining development of a large non-food park, known as Glasgow Fort.

Paisley was very interesting, in that it was formally the site of one of the mills in a town which gives its name to a specific type of weave, and the site was witness to the competitive nature of the food retail industry. The site was originally accessed by a timber footbridge, which had decayed over the years, but which we subsequently refurbished and became an attraction, (in addition to the old mill buildings) to, no less than HRH The Prince of Wales, who opening the adjoining apartments and was very complimentary about our style of architecture. Shortly after Safeway acquired the site they discovered that Tesco had bought the land which formed one bank of the adjoining river across which the bridge, decrepit as it was, spanned. Tesco clearly felt that this would be the main site access and their purchase would result in a stranglehold. Not to be. Design of the highway network required a new bridge and Tesco's purchase was rendered worthless.

Don't let anyone tell you that the food retailers club together to create a monopolistic situation. We were at each other's throats, and this remains the case now, despite several OFT investigations over the last 10 years.

'Never trust a Dutchman', part two arrived during the middle of 2006, and contrary to Ken's earlier views we went and appointed a Dutchman as our new Chief Executive.

Bob Stott, who had been Chief Executive and had steered the

Company through much of the rough water surrounding the Safeway acquisition with some success, was to retire and Marc Bolland was appointed in midsummer, I had my first discussions with him at the beginning of July and he eventually took up his post, joining from Heineken, the Dutch brewers, in September.

Very shortly after the announcement of Marc's appointment, on 27 July to be precise, we had a particularly stormy Board meeting. Ken by now had embarked on his almost manic pursuit of his dislike for the staff canteen at our new Head Office, and that afternoon the Board were to host a 'family' visit around the new building. This was to include Ken's sisters, his family, a number of retirees and the widows of John Dowd, Keith Hutchinson and Ron Curry.

Having met Marc Bolland almost three weeks earlier, I had done some research of the Heineken man and established very clearly in my own mind that the Board structure in terms of its Executive make up would be changed.

Having been suitably angered by the exchanges relating to our new and subsequent award winning building, the discussion moved to our new boss who, to my surprise, my colleagues seem to have little knowledge of.

I announced that in my opinion Marc would change the set up of the Executive Board and that this would in future comprise a CEO, Finance Director, to be Richard Pennycook, and Operations Director, to be Mark Gunter. When questioned I said that was based on my analysis of Mr Bolland's Board structure at Heineken, and further added that this would lead to the exit from Main Board level of myself, David Hutchinson and Marie Melynk. David was responsible for the fresh food operation through produce, the food factories and the abattoirs and also responsible for distribution. Miss Melynk was responsible for trading and marketing.

My pronouncement caused quite a stir with one of my colleagues and my forecast was to come partly true when, upon his arrival, Marc said that once David Hutchinson had retired the following year, he, and his position, would not be replaced at Main Board level and the same would apply to my position upon my retirement. Miss Melynk was to remain on the Board, but in fact departed the Company in early December 2006 due to ill health, and the legal reasons around that departure prevents me from saying more.

Marc Bolland was like a breath of fresh air. Smart and debonair, with a true marketing personality, he was fluent in six languages and had become very well connected throughout his area of operation with the Dutch brewers. Like us, Heineken were a family firm and he was used to dealing with the likes of Fred Heineken, a set of circumstances which I am sure, stood him in good stead throughout his career in Morrisons in his dealings with Ken.

The City were taken by surprise by the appointment and were initially very sceptical, as he had no food retailing background, but I suspect the best indication of the size we had become was given as to how he set about the task. Consultants were brought in on branding, consumer focus groups were held in various places throughout the country and Marc, much to Ken's dismay and not a little upset, unveiled a new branding for the Company, including a change in logo, the change of the Company's colours, the change of transport fleet and new marketing slogans. There then took place a massive programme to re-brand the stores, starting with a new build at Speke in Liverpool, which opened in July 2007. The re-brand was then fed back through all the existing stores, including the 220 odd units we had converted from Safeway, not two years previously.

I think, and it is my personal view, that Marc Bolland deserved a lot of the credit he received for effectively taking the company forward, in terms of its image, its marketing and its trading position. Much credit has been given to Marc for the revival of the Company, post Safeway. Whilst the re-branding credit is undoubtedly his, I believe the Company was well on its way back before he joined. All stores had been converted, the distribution network was being upgraded, stores were being extended and had been extended with dramatic trading results, but nevertheless Marc's contribution was without doubt the icing on the cake.

I enjoyed my time with him and was not surprised when he resigned in late 2009, to join Marks and Spencer. A position, he told me, he could not afford to pass up, as it was a once in a lifetime opportunity. Indeed, I understand that I perhaps owe my newest Directorship at Bradford City to Marc, who was initially approached for the position, but passed it sideways to me. I think his knowledge of football would have been most welcome at the Coral Windows Stadium, BD8, particularly his connections with the Dutch footballing fraternity, where he was used to rubbing shoulders with the greats like Cruyff, Van Basten and so on. Instead, in a rare error of judgement, he chose to go and watch Leeds United rather than the Claret and Amber of Bradford!

'Never trust a Dutchman' – there may be some you can't, but the ones I have met you definitely can.

CHAPTER 20

The Big Decision and Massive Change
2006–08

I STARTED 2006 EXTREMELY TIRED, but with a very good feeling. After
all, some two months previously I had overseen the completion of
the conversion of some 220 former Safeway stores to the Morrison
brand, the biggest exercise of its kind ever carried out and completed
in British retail and, probably, British construction history. My team
had every right to hold their heads up high, and they did. For several
months after the completion of the exercise they bounced around like
youngsters, while at the same time completing and maintaining the
existing workload of continuous commercial disposals and of course,
the ongoing organic growth of the Company through new site
acquisition and construction.

For my part, I found myself increasingly thinking about the future.

Lena and I had discussed retirement periodically for the previous
eighteen months. My previous boss, Ron Curry, retired at fifty-eight,
although he was to spend the next three years, or just less, remaining
on the Morrison Board as a Non-Executive director. This in the days
before corporate governance stopped such appointments. Ron had
retired when the Company had a portfolio of 33 stores, and times
were slightly different in 1987. After his retirement I told him, on
more than one occasion, that I thought fifty eight was too young an
age to be finishing, but by this time Ron had remarried, to Caroline,
who was some thirty years his junior, and I could appreciate the
reasons why he wanted to spend more leisure time with his new
young wife. This does not stop me thinking, however, that there
were a few years of a very experienced career that were wasted and
lost to the Company.

I had earlier flagged to my fellow Directors the fact that I did not
believe that I would be working up to the, then, Company
retirement age of Directors, of 62. My announcements at the time
were greeted with indifference and not surprisingly so, as the

Morrison Board had something of a record of pretending that bad things were never happening, but in my case, bad for the Company, or not, I was determined that I would be going. The two of us discussed at what age and had agreed that 62 was too late as 'you never know what's round the corner' and at 58, as in the case of my old boss Ron, was too young. We also discussed the fact that I needed to keep active in some form of other and I agreed that I would pursue Non-Executive Directorships where I thought I might obtain a position which was both interesting and enjoyable, but at the same time rewarding to me. The reward in financial terms was not the main thing, I had been well looked after by Morrisons, in terms of pension and general remuneration, and over the previous twelve months I had been awarded a significant salary increase, which not only benefited me directly, but helped my pension fund. We both had shares in the Company which were clearly subject to market fluctuations, but which we both believed would stand us in good financial stead in the future, so in many respects life was not pressured.

After several discussions around the dinner table or in front of the television it was agreed that I would retire on my 60th birthday.

At the beginning of September 2006, the Company had a major change of philosophy, when Marc Bolland joined as Chief Executive from the Dutch brewer, Heineken, not unlike Morrisons, a family-owned and operated business with a dynasty type situation involved and, as Marc was to tell me, a head of family who was not always the easiest to get on with.

The first thing Marc did upon his arrival was to ask the Board to prepare and submit a simple document, indicating where they personally felt they would be and where they also felt the company would, or should be, by 2010, effectively a three/four year plan. I was about to leave for my customary September break in Cyprus and was under a little pressure to produce a meaningful 'one-pager' as Marc loved to call them, however, the work itself was easy. I started by telling him that in October 2007, he would be receiving my resignation and that in October the following year I would be out of the door. The die, to some extent, was cast, but much was to happen between the now and the then, as I was about to find out, in the next roller coaster period of Morrison life.

Through 2006 we continued apace with the remnants of the former Safeway estate to be dealt with and the new store opening programmes to continue and plan.

Through the year, we opening four new build stores including the redevelopment of a Safeway at Crowborough, East Sussex. The expenditure of a significant capital amount on this site was frowned upon initially by the Property Board, but having convinced them that Safeway had laid out significant money on site acquisition the scheme went ahead, and although its opening was less than grand in terms of unfinished work, I am pleased to say that, along with many of my hunches and retail feelings, the store proved an absolute winner.

Through 2006, we successfully disposed of fourteen smaller stores that did not have a future with the group and at the end of the disposal programme, in my time, as I have said elsewhere, I had recovered almost exactly 50% of the purchase price of Safeway, making this truly the 'deal of the century'.

Other more fringe but equally important elements were taking over.

Finance Director Richard Pennycook had pioneered and launched the group Optimisation Plan, which was to bring various things into line with common systems and practices to those run by Safeway formerly. Richard worked very hard on this and set them out in March of 2006, and all targets were achieved within the year.

Richard developed into an excellent aide to the incoming CEO, and as I conclude this book he was very much 'in the frame' to succeed Marc as CEO during 2010. From a personal point of view, I very much regret that Richard did not get his chance.

Two non-mainstream issues were exercising me at the start of 2006, over and above the normal workload.

Firstly, there was the issue of the Company's replacement Head Office, also to be named Hilmore House, in honour of Ken's mother Hilda. This is a brute of a building, at over 330,000 sq ft, with some 1,200 car parking spaces and situated on three levels with interconnecting escalators, lifts and staircases.

Planning for the building had started some six or seven years previously, but as with a lot of things 'Morrison', because it did not have a bank of checkouts earning money it was always a little bit on the back burner until the twelfth hour when then, generally speaking, all hell broke loose to get new facilities into place. The Head Office was no exception to this rule.

Over the years we had had several working groups at Board level, including the late John Dowd, Chris Balaam, the IT Director, Martin Ackroyd, the former Finance Director, the rest of Board from time to time, and principally myself.

In the end the scheme landed fairly on my shoulders and I well remember one particular Board Meeting, when I was discussing in animated style what I thought we needed in terms of special requirements, costs and so on, for the site, which we had acquired from Bradford Council. I ploughed on through numerous pages of notes and became increasingly conscious of the fact that there was no feedback, comment, coughing, or anything else from my colleagues. When I looked up, I discovered I was virtually on my own in the boardroom, each of the others having decided that it was time for a pee.

In the end I decided I that I would take the scheme on myself, in and amongst all the other duties that were being performed, in particular the Safeway acquisition and integration.

Michael Helliwell, a very loyal and trusted architect who had carried out many store schemes for the Company, was entrusted with this prestigious scheme, which had a construction build estimate of £56 million. This was to be Mike's swan song and he announced on more than one occasion that he would retire at the end of it. Being in his mid seventies, no one would argue with that.

The scheme featured everything that was good about Morrisons: traditional materials, energy management, sound internal build and something to last. We recruited people who were new to our team, most notably TSK, the space planners and interior designers from Manchester, a Facilities Manager in Fran Smith, who reported directly to me and who had had experience with the transport group Stagecoach and a big Leeds law firm, and they were all meshed together to form a great team providing information to Shepherd Construction, of York, who are well versed in constructing quality buildings.

Fran and myself, worked through all the details of the scheme, starting at the front door, with the uniforms for the Receptionists and

Telephonists, looking at colour schemes for the staff canteen, which I named 'jd's', in honour of our late Managing Director, John Dowd. Cutlery, crockery, uniforms for departmental facilities staff were all discussed, dissected and then agreed upon. Implementation was then left to Fran and my Project Manager, Mark Oxley and they did a super job. I have heard of other corporate moves which have involved a literal army of management to accomplish, but they basically did it between the two of them, with a little guidance from me.

When the time came for the move, we left a period of almost a month between the building being finished and the first staff moves, during which time we conducted on-site induction visits and meetings for 1,400 staff, and then started moving them, one department each day. The exercise went like clockwork. Until the complaints started.

All companies have a minority of people within them who regard themselves as self-appointed experts or, putting it slightly harder, prima donnas who think they know everything, but know nothing, or at least very little. Morrisons' Head Office staff were no exception, and we immediately ran into problems of people bringing their kettles and their other bad practices from the old buildings. At this time the Head Office operation had been spread between three or four different locations around Bradford and Wakefield and it was inevitable that different standards would be applied.

To counter this, I requested that Ken and Chief Executive Bob Stott be in attendance every morning in the first week, when department after department moved. Ken and Bob were great and supported me to the hilt, with Ken personally confiscating equipment that was not needed. The message soon got back to the others, 'don't bother bringing it', and so between April and June of 2006, the people moved and the reception from them regarding standards was tremendous.

Unfortunately, there was then to begin a rather unfortunate period in my relationship with Ken. Within a very short time Ken, prompted by others, started to make criticisms about various aspects of the building, it was too hot, it was too cold, the toilet flushes did not work properly, and so on. I knew that this was mostly coming from one of my colleagues, who I will not be naming, but on it went.

After a while Ken turned his criticism to the canteen, which had been meticulously planned by our own catering people rather than my facilities management team. Ken hated it with a passion I have rarely seen from him and numerous meetings were held to find out who was responsible. Ken, unfortunately, had a habit in the time I knew him of going first from one person to another getting opinions and then quoting them back at you without those expressing the opinions ever being present to be challenged, and so it came with the canteen. My own staff and my own Board colleagues couldn't believe it, and indeed my Non-Executive colleagues could not believe it either, and went out of their way to praise the building. Indeed, Deputy Chairman Sir David Jones called me the night before our first Board to say that Ken had invited them as a group to look around the new building and David had not seen anything quite like it. He was overcome with the standards and the quality and went out of his way to tell me, which was extremely good of him, and this was repeated the following day by all my Non-Executive colleagues. My Chairman, unfortunately, never really reciprocated or repeated those observations on his own part.

The ill-fated canteen was so successful that it drew a company subsidy, which was significantly less than the rest of the group. Morrisons subsidised all works canteens and the rule of thumb throughout most of my career was that the subsidy amounted to 50% of the costs. In the case of the new Hilmore House the subsidy got as low, in my time, as 20%, which I thought was a major achievement, but clearly not good enough, and in the photograph album which was presented to me on my retirement, my Project Manager Mark Oxley says of the Head Office 'award winning building, but I have it on good authority that the chips in jd's have never been any good' – what a damning indictment of Ken's views, views which were to bring me into a little conflict with him the following year.

I was so appalled by some of the treatment I received about the Head Office that I determined that the only way around this criticism was for the building itself to win an award. Morrisons had never been one for actually entering awards, preferring to be given them on merit, but I was so upset with what I thought was unjustified criticism that I entered the scheme and subsequently won the RICS

Yorkshire Property Awards, for the best new scheme. The judges said we won by a 'country mile'. Other entries by other parties to the contract were not quite successful, but we did manage to reach National Finals in several elements, such as interior design, planning and the like.

The second major diversion for me during 2006 revolved around a Safeway store in Northern Ireland. I have described elsewhere my strategy for the Safeway estate, post acquisition, which was largely accepted and implemented by the Board.

Safeway had built a new store at Bangor, in County Down, as part of their twelve- or thirteen-store Northern Ireland estate, and one of the outstanding legal issues when we acquired the Company was the threat of a prosecution for alleged illegal tipping.

As I had found from the pre-acquisition investigations, Safeways Property staff, indeed almost all Safeways central staff, never did anything themselves if they could get a consultant in and pay them to do the job, whilst drawing a nice little salary at the same time, and Bangor was no different. Minutes of Site Meetings were circulated to a whole host of Safeways staff but not one of them went to any site meetings. That is one good way of making sure that you cannot be blamed for something if it goes wrong, and that was the whole philosophy which seemed to operate within the Company, as well as the department.

The Northern Irish equivalent of the Department of the Environment, were prosecuting the Company, along with four other parties, arising out of work on the new Bangor site. It seemed that inspectors from the Northern Irish Government had followed a vehicle from the Bangor site to a farm some ten miles distant and observed the materials from the site was being tipped into an old bomb crater.

Consequently, a prosecution was being brought against the main contractor Gilbert Ash, the client, ourselves, the earth moving contractor, the haulage contractor and the farmer upon whose land the alleged contaminated material had been tipped. All this had proceeded through the Courts to a situation where it was set for trial, in front of a judge in Belfast Crown Court.

Numerous visits took place during 2005, with myself and Company Secretary Jonathan Burke, and ultimately Jonathan was bailed to appear at the Crown Court on trial, the reasoning at that time being that our Counsel did not want a Main Board Director in the dock.

The trial was set for Downpatrick Crown Court and was to be a trial by jury in May 2006. I appeared for the Company, in a case that was initially set to last four weeks.

I was appalled at the lack of effort and attention that had been paid by the Safeway staff to the issue, but as hardly any of them were left within the business we had to go it alone. I spent a full day touring the area, running from the site at Bangor out to the tip and so on. The farmer ran a wholesale and retail meat business from his farm, but I could not get access to the area where the alleged offence had taken place. Being a Surveyor and classing myself as smart, however, I examined the local Ordnance Survey Map and found that there was another farm with a track looking across a depression onto the site of the alleged offence.

Driving up the track to the farm I was met by a rather unruly looking gentleman, complete with shotgun. What does one do when faced with speaking to an unknown quantity in an English accent, driving a hire car with English registration plates? My stomach churned quite a few times. Added to this the site was close to the 'bandit country' of the Troubles.

Having established that I was on the wrong land and naming where I wanted to be I was promptly told to f*** off and the gun barrel was clicked into place. I don't think I have ever driven so quickly down an unmade road as I did that day.

By the time we got to court, I had commissioned aerial photographs of the site and spoken to the world renowned Turf Research Centre at Bingley, not many miles from my own Head Office. They confirmed without even examining photographs that the failure to grow grass over the area of the infill bomb crater was due to methane and that this could only be coming from the deterioration of household waste and not virgin soil.

I went to court armed with the soil records from the Safeway site, which showed virgin clay and no fill, the aerial photographs, and the case against Morrisons collapsed within a day. The whole episode reminded me of something akin to the excellent novel *Belfast Confidential*.

Ultimately, the farmer and the two contractors for earth moving and transport pleaded guilty, I claimed our costs for the case and was paid them by the three guilty parties, together with a message that it would be better if I did not go back to the area! The whole prosecution could have been avoided if the Safeway Management had been more proactive.

Having being to County Down in my Round Table days, I did take advantage of one day off between the case against Morrisons collapsing and the sentencing hearing back in Belfast, to travel along the coastal route from Larne, around to Giants' Causeway and then back on the motorway. What a lovely country Northern Ireland is and my journey reinforced my views, formed on a visit with Store Operations Director, Mark Gunter prior to the Safeway acquisition, that the Troubles have been a major tourist disaster for the country, a disaster that I hope they can overcome in the years to come.

Throughout 2006 I was heavily into travel, if it had not been Belfast for the Court hearing, it was the South West and Gibraltar, for our planned store extension in this outpost of the Union Jack.

Looking now at my diary, I wonder how I achieved such journeys as a trip to London in the morning, meetings back in Bradford in the afternoon, trips to Belfast the following day and then flights to the South West, for site visits, followed by flights to Aberdeen for Scottish store visits, all in the course of a week. This was punishing and as the clock ticked into summer, I found myself increasingly thinking about the future.

Marc Bolland decided very quickly that although there were star performers in the business, for example we won the Seafood Retailer of the Year, we ought to concentrate on our real points of difference, by looking at healthy eating and organics and so on.

Marc, very sensibly, announced that there were many strengths in the business, but also challenges that needed addressing. The Optimisation Plan instigated by Richard Pennycook was paying off, the opening of the new Head Office had brought people together, and Marc wanted to start on a programme and path of profit recovery, so the Company could position itself for the future.

This led to the declaration of what Morrisons was going to be, and it was going to be the 'food specialist for everyone'. This encapsulated a number of building blocks to be put in place, revised systems, additional training and so on and so on. Marc undertook a number of customer panels throughout the country and made it very clear that as Chief Executive he was going to push this through, come what may.

In early December 2006, Marie Melnyk, who had become Managing Director prior to Marc's arrival, left the business. Marie had been with Morrisons longer than me, but now left the company on health grounds.

Through 2007, the performance of the Company was very strong. Turnover hit £13 billion, debt fell dramatically, largely as a consequence of receipts for property and increased sales, and all this against a background of opening eight new stores through the year and numerous extensions.

Following Marie Melnyk's departure prior to Christmas of the previous year, another of my colleagues David Hutchinson retired in June 2007, also on grounds of ill-health. David had served twenty-one years with the business and had become a close friend, although we did not always see eye-to-eye. I had been delighted to help him with his fresh food property issues, extending existing pack houses, building new pack houses for produce in the wake of the Safeway acquisition and so on. David was very good company and was cruelly robbed of a long and happy retirement when he passed away, the short period of eight months after his retirement.

Numerous management groups had sprouted through the organisation to deal with the various issues which faced us, and I became Chair of the Environment Group, on CSR issues. Our targets were to cut the Company's carbon footprint and other issues to do with this, becoming more energy efficient and so on. Life remained challenging with the continuing chore of travel.

We had taken a decision to retain the store in Gibraltar, although in my original plans, pre the Safeway acquisition, this was one for disposing of, but we did not receive any offers which matched our valuation, and in hindsight I am mighty glad we did not.

Our site in Gibraltar occupies one of the few pieces of flat ground and is absolutely prime. Being a major employer and a major player in the Gibraltarian economy, the Government were very concerned as to whether we were staying or going, and several meetings were held in 2005 and early 2006 to assure the Government of our intent. Building work on three extensions to the store commenced in 2006 and although we had planning consent for some additional retail units on the site, the government became very concerned about the effect this may have on Gibraltar High Street, which housed a lot of UK names, such as Marks and Spencer.

They stepped in at the beginning of April to stop us building these units and an indication of my diary is that on 10 April I left Leeds/Bradford Airport at 3.45 a.m. for a meeting in Gibraltar at 9.00 a.m. local time, from where I then flew back to Bristol and had a meeting in the afternoon at Bridgewater to discuss our planned, final, major regional distribution centre, flying back from Bristol to Leeds on a scheduled flight at 6.30 that evening. Those were the sorts of days I put in.

Criticism about the Head Office, and in particular its canteen, had not gone away, and it was an issue of some concern of Marc Bolland, on my behalf. In the end I took a rather major decision and arranged to meet Ken on 11 April, the day after my epic journeys to Gibraltar and the South West. I had previously discussed, with Marc, my feelings and I told him what I was going to tell Ken. His reaction was sympathetic and supportive, but at the same time was one of 'Do you really want to do this?' I did.

I met with Ken and told him to his face, that after thirty two years working for the Company I felt that I no longer had a relationship with him, arising out of the issues with the Head Office and in particular its canteen. I said that I thought the criticisms were both unfair and unfounded and as I was not prepared to accept them and as he was clearly not prepared to accept anything other than the position he had taken it was my sad duty to tell that I would not really be entering into any further discussions and that if any discussions were to take place I would be conducting them with Marc.

Ken's reaction to this was not untypical. When serious trouble struck, Ken, by his own admission, always ordered a cup of tea. His other move, invariably, was to change the subject and in this case, taking advantage of my previous day's labour, he pronounced that he thought I had been looking very tired over the recent weeks and perhaps I was a little emotional and overstretched. I had seen and heard this tactic so many times over the years and simply let it go.

I think the 11 April will always go down as a black day for both of us. I had admired and continued to admire Ken for all that he had done and achieved, achievements which far outweigh anything that

I had ever had done personally, but his criticism was beyond the pale, not just for me, but for the effect it had on my staff, and the award for the building did nothing to assuage that situation and the hurtful nature of it all. Indeed, Fran Smith had left the Company and was equally upset by the criticisms.

Prior to all of this and indeed Marc Bolland's arrival we opened one store in the previous year at Leyland, on the site of part of the famous truck and bus manufacturer, and in keeping with my personal dictate of recording the past, there is a very attractive bronze sculpture of a Leyland worker ladling molten steel into a casting block for a new engine, located on the edge of the site.

Our first store opening under the new Chief Executive, was at Swadlincote, in Derbyshire, a town centre scheme, which I took Marc to look at the week before it opened. He was very impressed with what he saw, but by this time had already embarked on his ideas for rebranding the Company.

This was a very interesting day for me, as I had my new boss in the car for several hours and we visited the new store, followed by a trip to the former Safeway unit at Chesterfield, which was at that time being extended, in the first of probably three or four such moves which have transformed it into a top trading store. I explained to Marc how we carried out such operations and continued trading and we looked at some of the Managers' numerous requests for further extensions, some of which were ultimately carried out and completed.

I had planned for Marc a trip to the Morrisons store, at Hillsborough, which in its time was our 50th to open. The unit is situated less than a mile from the Hillsborough Football Ground and is unique, in that the building dates back to 1854, when it was constructed as a barracks unit, complete with turreted walls some 900mm thick, and sits in a conservation area.

On our way to the site, Marc proclaimed that he was hungry and could do with an 'English pub meal'. This proclamation was made as we dropped into the bowl which is Sheffield city centre, and I pointed out to him that the pubs in this area would be eminently suitable, if he fancied a fight. This quickly refocused the hunger!

On arrival at Hillsborough with its impressive buildings, Marc said he could not believe what he was entering, even less so when we walked into the store itself. I had constructed the sales area on what was the site of the former drill parade by simply roofing it over, and the old turrets and towers were left in situ to form the internal walls of the new store, through which were threaded the various aspects of Market Street. We took a walk through the rest of the development, to look at the attached shop units, offices and relatively new transport interchange, which I had built to link the outlying villages with the Sheffield Tram System, which, in itself, passed through the centre of Hillsborough. Ken and myself had been passengers on the first tram, along with the European Transport Minister, Neil Kinnock, when it was opened, Mr Kinnock taking great pleasure of alighting and walking with Ken and myself to look over the site of our store, proclaiming himself utterly amazed.

Hillsborough is one of my more unusual, but nevertheless bright, spots. We won the site in competitive tender with two of our national rivals, whose plan was simply to demolish the buildings and replace them with the corporate tin box. Alan Hanwell of developers, George Longden, was a Sheffield, born and bred, fan of the barracks and refused to let this happen, to his eternal credit, and I think we completed a super job.

After a short break at Hillsborough, Marc's hunger pains recommenced and we stopped at the Red Lion pub above Hillsborough, on the Barnsley Road, for a well-earned break. I learned much about him in those few hours, some of which was to come back and bite me in November 2006, when we opened a relatively energy efficient store in Cardiff, in a large regeneration area, which Marc said he positively hated, although trade had proved otherwise since its early opening weeks and the completion of other residential developments around the site.

The Cardiff store looks across the bay to the posh area of Penarth, home, as I was told to my face, of the self proclaimed queen of the weather forecasts Sian Lloyd.

My differences with Ken aside, 2007 was a big year for store openings and, it has to be said, one of my lowest points.

Never afraid to take on regeneration sites, or sites in deprived areas, we had some real challenges that year, with new developments in Speke in Liverpool, Johnston, near Paisley, Hartcliffe in Bristol, and the town centre of Wednesbury in the West Midlands. All of these had their problems of either society, or previous use, but we managed to do an excellent job on all of them and the Speke store saw the incorporation of the first raft of Marc Bolland's rebranding exercise, which, I have to say, is significant step forward, but not liked by Ken.

Out went to the traditional yellow and black of Morrisons and in came a softer green to replace the black. Market Street was upgraded and revamped from my last effort in 1993 and the new format was rolled out into all the stores that followed at Johnstone and Dundee in Scotland, York, Hartcliffe and Wednesbury in England and Llanelli in South Wales.

The Dundee store was a belter. Located on a superb site, immediately adjoining the main road North, from Perth to Aberdeen, it was large, well exposed to the public and easily got at, subject only to some fairly significant roadworks which were to become the bane of my life over the latter months of that year.

The A90 is a major trunk road to the North of Scotland and as such falls under the control of the Scottish Parliament and its Transport for Scotland arm. The Local Authority were relatively small contributors and our scheme envisaged the replacement of no less than three mini roundabouts, with a complex traffic light system.

I have never been one to openly criticise my staff, but I do believe that my Project Manager, Paul Taylor was let down by his immediate senior, Construction Director, David Wade and myself.

Transport for Scotland were typical 'play it by the book' officers, who were not going to let anything spoil their normal routine. The roadworks were redesigned on several occasions and then ultimately given the go ahead, or so we had thought. Upon this situation arising, I pressed the button to start the store construction and as work progressed rapidly on site I became aware that all was not well with our Scottish colleagues. The scheme was changed again and then again and all the time the clock was ticking against a planning condition which said we could not open the store till the roadworks had been completed.

Regular questioning of my two subordinates led to a gradual decline in confidence that the matter was going to progress to a successful conclusion, and I had advised the Board accordingly.

As summer moved towards autumn, I realised that many of the meetings which had been ongoing to resolved our problems had been attended by my Project Manager but not his boss, and I reached the reluctant conclusion that if real progress was going to be made, I was going to have to involve myself. There then followed a series of meetings with Dundee City Council and others, which led to an improvement in relations, but not in progress.

Between us Dundee City Council had said that they would cooperate as far as they could, and alternative routes to the stores were determined, leaflets issued to the prospective shopping public and the store handed over in perfect condition for pre-trading stocking and training. I thought I had got matters back on the right track, but was extremely annoyed with my Construction Director and wrote to him. I believed that my Project Manager Paul Taylor had literally been 'hung out to dry' and had received an inappropriate, if not non-existent level of support.

I remember that David Wade took exception to my letter and threatened to respond in like terms, but never did, in my view an admission of guilt.

Lena and I went on holiday, as usual, to Cyprus in September, planning to return on the weekend of 29/30 September, the day before the Dundee store was due to open.

On the Thursday I received a telephone call from my Development Director and number two, Chris Evenson, to the effect that we had received a letter from Transport for Scotland, indicated their displeasure at our projected opening, a letter which he indicated he was going to ignore, and I agreed.

The day after, we received a summons to appear in the Crown Court (or Scottish equivalent) on the Saturday prior to opening, and at that point Transport for Scotland were granted an injunction to stop us opening. The brown stuff well and truly hit the fan and I returned to face the music.

Immediately upon my return I said to Marc Bolland that this was an issue of my making and I would sort it out, and many conversations followed with the City Council and Transport for Scotland, including the Deputy and First Minister's Offices of Parliament. Words were obviously spoken and there was an immediate softening of approach, to the extent that all the parties concerned convened a meeting at the store on 18 October.

My work since returning from holiday had not slackened. I had an appearance in front of the Competition Commission, meetings with the local authority in Bridgewater, one of several strategy meetings for the future with Marc Bolland and two days in London, which led up to the fateful meeting in Dundee.

During my second day in London, I became concerned that matters with the various authorities might not be handled properly. David Wade had developed an unfortunate habit, for which he had also developed an unfortunate reputation outside the Department, of going missing when the big issues occurred. David had taken to booking snap holidays, or being on site with one of our numerous store extensions at the other end of the country, when big issues were being debated elsewhere. Initially I had taken this to be a lack of ability to prioritise and decide what was the most important issue, and indeed he had half suggested that he needed to be somewhere else when the key Dundee meeting was to take place, a situation that I promptly corrected with him.

Nevertheless, the anxiety gnawed at me and during the afternoon prior to the meeting I arranged that I would fly to Scotland the following morning, which left me departing my hotel in Central London at 5.30 a.m. and flying from Farnborough to Dundee, swearing my PA to utter secrecy, until I landed in the Scottish city.

The meeting passed off well and we were ultimately able to open the store 29 October, some four weeks behind schedule, but with the road works still incomplete for another four or five months. Disaster it was, but major disaster was averted. As my Project Manager Paul Taylor noted in my farewell photograph album, 'nice store, shame about the holiday, not our finest hour'. The holiday reference referring to my hours spent on the telephone whilst in Cyprus trying to salvage the situation.

I was not present at the Dundee opening, myself and Store Operations Director Mark Gunter journeying to South Wales for the Llanelli opening.

We arrived late Sunday evening, at a hotel which was in the middle of nowhere, but extremely nice. Having had a late dinner, we both retired to the bar and Mark, quite an accomplished musician, took to playing the piano, which was situated in the hotel lobby area.

To this day I still smile when Mark recounts the tale (I was sitting in the bar), of being approached by one of the hotel staff of dubious

gender and asked if he 'did duets'. Mark in his typically forthright
Northern way answered, 'not with you, f*** off'. We laughed about
it for some time the following day, on our journey north from the
new South Wales store.

Immediately on my return from the 'thumbs up' Dundee meeting,
I wrote my resignation letter to Mark Bolland, 21 October being my
birthday and occurring on a Sunday and me requiring twelve months
notice. The letter duly went in and the die was cast. There then
followed a period of what, to me, was sadness mixed with happiness
and tinged with more than a little bitterness.

The bitterness concerned my Deputy and Development Director,
Chris Evenson.

Chris had joined the Company in 1984 and was my first member
of staff to be promoted following my own elevation to the Main
Board.

In November 1987, I promoted Chris to the Board of Management as Development Director and he took over from then onwards
all the Company's site acquisitions issues, estate management issues,
and became the focus of the Company's development programme
and rental income stream. He did it superbly well, grew into the job
and became utterly respected throughout the property world and
through the Company's various property professionals and consultants. I had been recommending him to the Board from as far out as
2006 and before Marc Bolland's arrival and I continued to do so at
regular intervals thereafter.

To my shock and horror in 2008, I was told by Marc Bolland that
an external appointment would be made, more than likely that Chris
would be considered for the job alongside other candidates. In answer
to my various questioning I was told that Ken, incoming Chairman,
Sir Ian Gibson, Marc himself and my other executive Board
colleagues 'didn't fancy Chris much'. The main reason for this
appeared to be that he was not a 'Roger Owen'.

Indeed, Chris was and remains a quiet individual, but highly
competent, very professional and one who gets on with job. His part
in the post Safeway break up was and remains inestimable. His part
in the development programme, which became my legacy when I
departed, was equally tremendous and one which twelve months on
still provides the Company's development stream in most part.

Ultimately, Chris was not rewarded the top prize and I was delighted to hear from him, some months after my own departure, that he had been offered a super job on exactly the same terms as his Morrisons employment and had taken it. We speak very occasionally and he is now a very happy individual whilst, as I complete this book, I discover that much of what I and my predecessor, Ron Curry, had taken thirty-four years to build, has been effectively demolished, in thirty-four weeks. The end result might be improvement and I hope it is, but that will be for others to judge.

I was and remain very sore about the treatment which Chris received and it led to more than one emotional conversation between us. I am sure that Chris believes me when told I had no part in the circumstances in which he found himself and I believe that he has already had the last laugh.

My final full year in the old Company saw nine new store openings and the first batch of smaller stores, under 25,000 sq ft trading area, being situated in Giffnock, near Glasgow, Northallerton and Blandford Forum, the latter two being former Safeway stores which remained closed from our acquisition some four years earlier.

We also opened former Co-op and Somerfield stores at Clifton in Nottingham and Gorleston, to add to the new build programme of Kidderminster, Whitefield, near Bury, Granton, near Edinburgh and Holyhead. The Kidderminster store was unique in that it was the first retail store to obtain an excellent BREEAM (Building Research Establishment Environmental Assessment Method) rating for its build standards and consideration of the surrounding environment. An award which has been repeated in 2010 with the rebuild of a store in Halifax.

Against all of this our extension and refurbishment programme continued apace and towards the end of 2008 we agreed terms for the acquisition for almost forty stores from the Co-Operative group, following their acquisition of the Somerfield Group. In November of 2008, I presented my Property Strategy to the full Board and proclaimed that in addition to the proposed acquisitions, there was a development programme going forward which would give my successor an easy ride for the next two years. Met with scepticism by my colleague Susan Murray, I was compelled to start naming the units, at which point a hail of protest that 'we believe you', came forward from my colleagues, and so the legacy was left.

CHAPTER 21

Bradford City – Disaster and Pride

I RECOUNT ELSEWHERE THAT WHEN Lena and I married, I inherited two young men, who had been away from day-to-day male contact and influence for seven years of their young lives. My parents both took to Glen and Jason immediately and of course, very shortly after our wedding in July of 1981 the new football season started and the boys were anxious to go.

Lena herself comes from a very sporting family where her father and brother were both involved in local sport over the years, brother-in-law Brian having played in the same cricket league as myself but in a higher Division and with more skill than I had, judging by the number of mentions he always seemed to get in the Monday evening paper review of the weekend's events.

Lena said she was determined to play a part in this 'new sporting life' and pursued her interest in sport by joining the boys and my father with me at Valley Parade. At that time the ground was unchanged in many ways from my first visit, some 28 years previously, with the exception that it was even more dilapidated, with the main stand being a timber structure with a small standing only paddock directly in front of it.

Lena deemed that Jason, at the age of 9, was not suited to stand in the paddock with me and his elder brother as the language was somewhat more 'fruity' and she did not want him exposed to it for a few more years, so it was decided that Jason along with mother and granddad would sit in the stand and myself and elder brother Glen, would occupy the paddock, and this situation persisted through three or four years of ups and downs familiar to all Bradford City fans, until the season 1984/85.

The club had a very good year with some excellent young players such as Stuart McCall, who went on to play for Everton, Rangers and Scotland, before returning to the club to take it into the Premiership and then became manager. Stuart was side by side with club captain Peter Jackson who was later sold to Newcastle and thereafter came back to Valley Parade and Huddersfield Town, before going into management, first with Huddersfield and then Lincoln, Greg Abbott who later went into local management and is currently manager of Carlisle, John Hendrie, who went on to play for Leeds, Middlesbrough, Newcastle and thereafter managed Barnsley, and the redoubtable (or notorious) Bobby Campbell, a hard hitting centre-forward with no little skill, whose goals, along with those of fellow striker John Hawley, a signing from Leeds United, propelled us to promotion.

We had already won the Championship prior to the last game of the season, scheduled for 11 May 1985, where Lincoln City were to be the visitors.

My family, in my opinion, had more than its share of good fortune that day from more than one direction.

Shortly before half time in a largely uninspiring game on a bone hard pitch, there were some cries from the crowd behind of 'burn it down, burn it down, burn it down'. Turning to see what the fuss was about I observed smoke coming from the end of the main stand, the old timber structure, furthest away from my standing point.

The smoke rather quickly started to thicken and people started to move from the stand. All of what followed was vividly recorded by Yorkshire Television and their commentator John Helm, a local Baildon boy, in terms and images far too graphic and painful to recall here in detail.

People very quickly realised that there was something at that point potentially serious going wrong, I turned to my dad and Jason in the stand and beckoned them to me. Things then happened in a surreal whirl. My dad, who at that point was in his seventies and not in the best of health or mobility, was starting to make a move to the back of the stand and the exits, but Jason, amazingly, persuaded him to come forward. Before I knew it Jason had hurdled the low wall, which separated the seating area from the paddock, straight over the top of my head almost into the arms of his brother.

By this time I could see the flames licking up as far as the roof of the stand and hear the cracking of burning timbers. The heat was starting to hit my face, even though I was a good fifty or sixty metres away from it. My father slowly made his way down the stand towards me, following his grandson, with the obedience and discipline of a child following its parent.

By now the smoke, the heat and the flames were all gaining volume and ferocity. I told the two boys to vault the wall onto the pitch; fortunately we were standing on the half way line. I told them to walk across the pitch following the half way line until they met the wall on the other side and there to wait for me.

I then told my father that he would have to climb over the wall; the flames by now and the heat were becoming closer and more intense. He protested for a short time then realised there was no option, first sitting on the wall and then swinging his legs over to collapse on top of me to the lower level and then repeating the action as we scrambled onto the pitch, thereafter to safety.

I did not turn round until we both got to the waiting boys. I did not need to, I could see the horror on Glen's face in particular, but turn round as I eventually did I saw with my own eyes the utter hell which had broken out behind me and at that point became aware that my somewhat receding forehead was stinging from what turned out to be a simple minor heat burn.

I cannot describe the images of seriously injured people being carried on advertising hoardings or simply wandering in a daze, but one individual in particular always strikes me hard. This young man walked passed me, apparently shocked and stunned, dressed, as I suspect most of us were, in some form of anorak quilted jacket.

As he walked past I saw that the entire back of his jacket was off and his skin was just a mass of red, raw blood.

I very quickly decided that we should get away from the ground. My father was very quiet and I was frightened of a heart attack. As it turned out he was more concerned that he had lost his flat cap climbing over the stand wall, and his only injury was a burst blood vessel where I had rather roughly man-handled him onto the pitch itself. The boys were quiet.

In those days we did not have mobile phones and it took us some time to get to my mother's, whereupon we made the various telephone calls to reassure Lena in particular that everything was ok. That night the phone never stopped ringing, firstly, my boss Ron Curry and then others. Fortunately, Jason was to go away with his school the following Monday and missed all the subsequent publicity, inquest and recriminations.

We were very lucky. I have not mentioned Lena in this, but

shortly before the final match she underwent a serious operation and although back at home and recovering well she did not attend the game that day.

This was not for want of trying, and she had a conversation with her Consultant Surgeon, John Clayton that this was biggest day in the history of the club while she had being watching. John's rather icily accurate refusal was along the lines of 'if there is a serious incident, such as a fire and you have to get out quickly, you will haemorrhage and most certainly bleed to death. You are not going'. I suspect that if Lena had disobeyed those instructions, a situation that was highly unlikely, the consequences would have been dire.

On the other hand and the second stroke of fortune was the presence of Jason in the stand with my dad. It was he who persuaded his granddad to come with us and not make for the exits where many were trapped and died. I believe that my son's actions and the conviction of my dad that he should be with us, saved his life.

Others were not so lucky, 56 people died and almost 200 were injured. Many more were injured mentally rather than physically and still bear the scars of that day. One of these was Ernest Normington, who died aged 74.

I had known Mr Normington, by sight, from a very early age. He was employed by the former Shipley Council as a dustbin man, who did the rounds of our house. Like my dad he was also a keen gardener, supplementing, I suspect, his council wage by selling his produce from his allotment around the adjoining streets to our house. When I was in my teens and in possession of a paper round I delivered papers to his house, even though it was immediately next door to the paper shop. This was a proud man, who did the best he could for his family during his working life and died enjoying his favourite football club. He was sitting one row behind my father when the fire started, and he went to the exits.

The Bradford fire spurned various reports on ground safety, which have subsequently been implemented. The ground was rebuilt and then rebuilt for a second time, when the club achieved its success of promotions up the pyramid and eventually to the Premiership, in the spring of 1999.

One of the highs on the way to that was to win our League play-off at the old Wembley Stadium when the whole family, including girlfriends, minus my then deceased father, were able to enjoy the moment. The lows have followed with successive relegations and administrations, but support has never dwindled.

I recounted earlier how I became involved in supporting my beloved Bradford City and it seems to me that there have been too many years of mediocrity.

Bradford City were the first winners of the more modern day FA Cup Trophy in the season 1910/11, when they lifted the new cup after a replay, the expensive piece of silverware having, rather curiously, been made by the famous Bradford jeweller, Fattorini. Since that day it rather seems to me that there have been three or four generations of under-achievement, under-investment, and an almost inbred sense amongst 'Bantams' fans of the acceptance of failure. We almost wallow in it, and therefore when success does come, they are highs indeed.

Many Bradford fans will tell you that because the ground is built on the site of an old well, the Holy Well, there is some form of jinx on the ground and on the team itself. I am not a great believer in this, merely the fact that whilst Bradford had made its fortune in the past out of textiles, the hard bitten 'wool barons' were so tight with their money that they never really put it back into the community, in the shape of either of its football teams or its Rugby League team, the result of which being that my team have seemed to me to have struggled from financial crisis to financial crisis over the last forty years.

At the last minute on several occasions the club has been saved from going under by one benefactor or another, or just the simple passing of the hat around the supporters. For a short period in the early 1970s Ken Morrison himself became a member of the Board, I suspect more to act as a credible link between the club and the banks than for his support, having many times told me that he is a Rugby League man at heart.

For all but the last ten years or so my beloved City always seemed to get the bad decisions, always seemed to get the ball that hit a divot and went into the net, or always seemed to be playing on inadequate pitches, at Valley Parade, with no money. Is this just me being an avid fan and recounting what most fans think applies to their team?

Football has, however, provided me with some happy days watching the team. I can remember my first away trip at the age of

36. Hillsborough – opened April 1991 – our fiftieth store and a superb conversion, of an 1854 Barrack building

37. Interior of Hillsborough

38. Enterprise Five, Bradford, opened October 1987 – one of the early Market Streets in the largest store in the group

39. A more modern day Market Street. Willenhall 2009

40. *'Bring me sunshine' – Eric Morecambe sponsored statue on the promenade of his birthplace*

41. *After unveiling Eric, Her Majesty met the other Erics. Ken Morrison is behind the Queen, with Lynn Morrison, full face and Lena hidden under my chin – what a day*

42. 'The train now arriving' – David Mach's brick masterpiece steams into Morton Park, at Darlington

43. The Jarrow March becomes more than just a picture in the paper. Graham Ibbeson's bronze sculpture was unveiled by the daughter of the banner carrier's on the sixty-fifth anniversary of the march leaving town – not a dry eye to be had

44. *The third store at Victoria shopping centre, Bradford, opened in 2000, after its predecessors in 1961 and 1969*

45. *Bet you can't get your trolley round this lot of trouble – Safeway, Downpatrick, Northern Ireland – typical of the way no one in that organisation seemed to bother about anything, except bonuses*

46. *'Never trust a Dutchman' – the brand new produce depot, at the Hook of Holland*

47. The New Corporate Headquarters, opened Summer 2006

48. *The Hilmore House winning team, left to right, David Wade – Construction Director, Fran Smith – Facilities Manager, Glynis Wilkinson – my P.A. and Office Manager, Mark Oxley – Project Manager and me holding the award*

49. *The last 'team', pictured in 2007. Standing left to right, Production Director – David Hutchinson, (fondly remembered), Chairman – Sir Ken Morrison CBE, Chief Executive – Marc Bolland, me, Trading Director – Martyn Jones. Seated left to right, non-executives, Paul Manduca, Susan Murray, Nigel Robertson, Store Operations Director – Mark Gunter, Finance Director – Richard Pennycook, non-executive – Brian Flanagan*

50. One year after joining the Board

51. One year before leaving it. Draw your own conclusions

ten or eleven on the supporters' coach to Doncaster for a Friday night match and coming home defeated, but happy that I had seen my heroes playing on 'foreign soil'.

There have been many interesting Cup trips, the *Bradford Telegraph and Argus* famously once ran a special train, when the Bantams made an away FA Cup tie at Arsenal. What a day that was. Leaving Bradford Interchange with a full cooked breakfast and a lunch before arrival at Finsbury Park, then the match, a 2-0 defeat, and the return home, with dinner and wine — simply super.

Other not so happy trips stick in the mind, none less than the many journeys I have made to Grimsby, usually for a night match, usually in the middle of winter and usually a journey home defeated, sometimes heavily, and freezing cold, with the blast of the easterly wind straight off the North Sea, occasionally accompanied by snow. Equally trips to Walsall were never particularly happy and it gave me great pleasure to take the Board of Morrisons to the old ground at Fellows Park and buy it for conversion to a Morrisons Superstore. If Walsall's hero and one time manager Alan Buckley had usually managed to put it over the claret and ambers, then at least the Bradford grocer got the last laugh in extinguishing the unhappy memories.

There are so many memories, going back to the days when teams such as Workington and Southport, now a distant memory, but still playing in the lower pyramid were visited. My mate Keith and I dropped in to Workington after a camping trip to Scotland one year, to see the Bantams victorious 3-1, in an early season fixture, and similarly I later visited Southport, in what I believe was their last season in the League, together with my former colleague Martin Ackroyd and others from Morrisons to see the team win 4-1 on a balmy Friday evening. But they got their own back when I succumbed to food poisoning from one of the rather dubious hot dogs. Or perhaps it was the several pints of local bitter after the victory.

All football fans can relate to these sorts of stories.

Prior to crowd segregation, indeed many years prior, I used to occasionally go to away games with my father if the distance was not too great and we regularly went to fixtures at places such as Rotherham, Halifax, Hull, Oldham, Doncaster, and most noted of all, Barnsley. These were the days when fans could change ends at half time, and at Barnsley there was always a pitched battle between the fans around the halfway line, when the claret and ambers took on the mining fraternity of South Yorkshire.

Michael Parkinson the famous broadcaster and journalist used to have a column in the *Sunday Times*, where he regularly wrote of the sporting heroes of South Yorkshire. Michael was no mean cricketer himself and I believe played Yorkshire League cricket for Barnsley, alongside or against the likes of Freddie Trueman, Geoff Boycott and many others. Michael's real pride however was the red and white of Oakwell and he recounted the many stories of his old heroes, in particular a central defender who rejoiced in the name of Skinner Normanton. I don't remember this individual but I do recall others such as goalkeeper Harry Hough, who later came to Bradford to play for our enemies, full back 'Spud' Murphy, and other uncompromising defenders such as Barry Swallow and Duncan Sharp. These seemed to me to be men who were hewn out of the 'black gold', which was cut literally under the feet of those who stood on the Barnsley terraces. Rough and rugged, taking no prisoners and very much befitting the description that famous old comedian of South Yorkshire, Charlie Williams, gave himself. Charlie was a central defender with Doncaster Rovers for a number of years and in his words 'I couldn't play, but I could stop those who could'. It seemed to me that on every visit to Barnsley my beloved team came up against eleven such individuals and possible a further fifteen thousand on the terraces.

Other Yorkshire teams had similar heroes, or villains. Hull City had Billy Whitehurst, a rough tough centre forward who would take man and ball and put both in the back of the net. Sheffield United had Keith Edwards, who seemed to reserve his best goalscoring escapades for Bradford City. Bradford Park Avenue had Bobby Ham, who was the most hated player at Valley Parade, until he swapped sides and transferred to us and became an instant hero. I have personally known Bobby for some years now, having been involved through Morrisons with his Construction Company, run by him and his brother Alan. Bobby tells a story that encapsulates even full time professional football of thirty years ago.

Bobby and his brother Alan both played for Bradford Park Avenue, Alan not quite as successfully, but nevertheless went on to play for almost all the non-league clubs around West Yorkshire and district, extending to clubs such as Gainsborough Trinity and many others. Bobby on the other hand, was an ace goal poacher and played in his early career alongside another Bradford Park Avenue legend, Kevin Hector, who went on to play for Derby County and England.

Bobby tells a story of him and his brother starting up their construction business and so keen were they to succeed that they were working all hours. Alan, a part-time professional, had more time to run the business and Bobby joined him when he could.

On one particular Saturday Bradford City were at home, as I recall, to Tranmere Rovers. Bob and his brother were working on a house in the Wrose area of Bradford and the instructions given by the Bantams manager Bobby Kennedy was that on match days at home the players should stay in bed late, have a light lunch of beans on toast and be at the ground at 2 p.m. Not so for the brothers in the fledgling Ham Builders, as it was rather unfortunately called at the time, later to change its name to Ham Construction.

Come Saturday morning, off went the two boys in their van to do spot of plastering, which overran. Bobby had very sensibly left his clothes at the yard where the business was based, but as Alan swung their truck around the Five-Lane-Ends roundabout at Idle, home of the curiously named Idle Working Men's Club, Alan managed to put the overhanging ladders of the truck through the front window of a bus. There then followed a long wait whilst the appropriate inspector was called, details were taken and so on, with the clock ticking. They made it back to their yard, where Bob had no time to wash but simply changed and set off to the ground, late. Because of the timing he was unable to get through the traffic for what was quite an important game and ended up abandoning his car and running the remaining distance to arrive at the ground five minutes late, covered lightly in plaster dust and looking to manager Kennedy as though he was rather ill, gasping and sweating at the same time. When questioned about his pallor and breathlessness, Bobby said he thought he was coming down with a touch of flu, but would be fit enough to play in such an important game. He went on to score two goals; Bradford secured the points and eventually, I believe, were promoted, or very close to it. That sort of thing would never happen today when players are cosseted in hotels, even in the lower leagues, for the night before a match, home or away.

Now as we enter the 25th anniversary of that disastrous day of the fire, the club is in good financial shape, is jointly owned and in July of 2009, I received a phone call from the Chief Executive, David Baldwin to ask me if I would be interested in joining the Board. Many years ago I would have jumped at the chance, but 34 years of experience and 22 years on the Board of a PLC teach you to be a little more cautious. I went along and met David, was interested and accepted the offer.

At the end of July 2009 I joined the Board, basically as a non-executive Director, but with responsibility under my title of Commercial Director to try and bring in more money to the club and at the same time review expenditure. Things have not moved as quickly as I had hoped, but I am constantly advised by colleagues that this is what happens in football and football is different from any other business, so I suppose I have to be patient.

I regard my appointment and the wearing of the club tie as a tremendous honour, a compliment to my reputation and to many degrees a dream come true, but the dark days of 1985 will never be forgotten. The week after the fire a short verse appeared in the *Bradford Telegraph and Argus*, written by a lady from Clayton in Bradford called Gaynor Shutt. I do not know this lady, but the verse struck home with me.

I have kept that verse in my wallet for the last 25 years. Every so often, perhaps every four, or five months I glance at it, it reminds of how lucky my family were that day, it reminds me of the grief suffered by so many normal families and it reminds me of Ernest Normington, an ordinary working man, just like the gardener Tommy O'Hara who I have spoken about earlier, normal people doing their best.

I keep the verse and I read it to remind myself of where I come from and how important it is to retain humility.

I hope for better days for my club and I hope that I can be part of it.

Today my heart is heavy.
It is broken into two,
My God! All Bradford's broken
And there's nothing we can do.
We had to sit beside our screens

And watch as hell broke free,
We heard the desperate cries for help.
The screams of agony,
This day of jubilation,
Which the devil has made wild,
My fears were for the safety,
Of my husband and my child,
And when they fell into my arms,
So shocked at where they'd been,
Demented by the terror,
And the horrors they had seen.
Where to begin? Where do we start?
How do we count the cost?
Who where the young? Who were the old?
How many lives were lost?
This town of ours is deathly,
Just the rustle of the trees,
This town of ours is steeped in grief,
Poor Bradford's on its knees.

Gaynor Shutt – May 1985
Come on City!

Epilogue

SO WHAT NOW? HAVING SPENT the first day of my retirement attending the opening of a new store at Rothwell, in South Leeds, followed by an interview for the Morrison Company magazine, I realised that tomorrow would be the first day of the rest of my life, to use a hackneyed phrase. A number of things needed prioritising.

Firstly, my mother who was approaching her eighty-seventh birthday was not in great shape. She had failed in health for some time and especially from the late summer of 2005, when she became quite depressed. Lena and I, having thought we had got her through this, relaxed somewhat, but discovered that she had stopped taking some medication months prior to my retirement and that this lack of medication was again affecting her lifestyle. Meals were being missed and most important of all, her short-term memory was failing, as dementia set in. We realised that this could not go on and commenced a search for a Residential Care Home.

Mum had taken respite care on two or three occasions whilst we were on holiday in previous years, but had not enjoyed the experience at all and her pride was an obstruction to her acceptance that she needed help, so help had to be imposed upon her.

Residential Care in this country is very variable both in terms of quality and price and often the two do not go hand-in-hand, as we found during a swift trawl through local agencies.

At the same time, Lena had indicated that she felt we should take a holiday 'in the sun' for a few days, and we had made a booking to go to Dubai. This is a location we had never visited or even passed through and our initial plan was to spend time there on route to, or from, Australia. The clock was ticking, but we were able to secure a place for my mother at a Care Home in a leafy area of Shipley. Ironically the location is not more that a 100 metres from the house where my Grandmother started her life in West Yorkshire in service to one of the textile families – my, how the circle turns. As I complete this book the lady, together with my late father, to whom

I owe so much, is now somewhat restlessly settled in her new surroundings, but life will never be the same. Scans have shown that she does not suffer with anything quite as serious, or as devastating, as Alzheimer's, and her quality of day-to-day living is good, being cared for, fed and having people there if anything goes wrong. But this is not the lady who embroidered the lovely pictures, was so vibrant in her Church and social life, which makes the finale of her presence with us all the more sad.

Lena and I have jokingly said we will take ourselves off to Switzerland when the time comes, or maybe the rather callous laws of the United Kingdom will have changed in respect of voluntary euthanasia.

On a more cheery note, my first year of retirement, following our trip to Dubai, saw us enjoy the Orient Express from Venice back to London, spend some five weeks, in three visits, at our house in Spain, which we have now managed to get somewhere towards the order that we want, two full weeks in Cyprus and a week with our friends Christine and Michael Taylor at their relatively new house in Florida, an experience which we both enjoyed, although sitting in an air boat without the engine running in the middle of Everglade wilderness was rather unnerving, as you have no idea what is swimming alongside you!

Our travel plans are now, family issues allowing, to travel to the major tennis events, the Grand Slams and the Masters tournaments throughout the world, in the first instance, and throughout Europe for the Masters tournaments, taking in the sights and sounds and smells of the various cities. Australia has always been an unobtainable destination with my work commitments, but sometime soon that vast country and its neighbouring New Zealand may see the arrival of the Owens.

Lena has said for some time that money is to be enjoyed, we have both worked hard for what we have and are extremely proud of our achievements, so upon retirement I 'splashed the cash' and became a boy racer with the purchase of a Porsche 911 and replaced my fourth or fifth E-Class Mercedes with a new CLS. A major extravagance for a humble Yorkshire lad.

I had said for some time prior to retirement that I would like to pursue the avenue of Non-Executive Directorships, and indeed during the course of 2008, I had taken some 'further education', with a recruitment agency, to educate myself back into the stream of applying for jobs, interview techniques and so on, notwithstanding the fact that over the years I had interviewed probably hundreds of people. I was approached in the late autumn of 2008 to join an AIM listed company providing Health Care Properties, but after four interviews with just about every member of the Board, the Chairman apparently decided that one of his mates was better persuaded to take the job. I bear no grudge against this as it gave me an extremely valuable experience.

At the end of 2008, I was interviewed for a Non-Exec role with the Olympic Delivery Authority, to fill the vacancy left by the resignation of Sir Howard Burnstein, the well respected Chief Executive of Manchester City Council, who had, at this point, gone off to be Chairman of the Blackpool Regeneration Company, a Board position for which I had previously applied and then withdrawn.

Deciding that 2009 would be a year where, at least, I should get my name in front of people, I did circulate, before my retirement, some twenty five copies of my CV to various recruitment people and was told by the man who taught me the new methods, not to expect too much immediately, as Non-Exec jobs were like buses. There would be a long gap then three would come along together, and in any event at this point the recession was biting hard.

Whilst on holiday at our house in Spain, in June 2009, I received a call from a recruitment agency asking whether I would be interested in a Non-Exec position with one of the country's leading sports retailers, JJB Sports. This company was being chaired at the time by my old Vice Chairman at Morrisons, Sir David Jones, he of Grattan, Next and Morrisons fame, and the day after we returned to England I went to see David, for whom I had always had some degree of respect at Morrisons. He greeted me in the JJB boardroom, with the words 'I hope you are going to join me, to sort out this f****** mess'. My interview went well and I was invited back to meet the Executive Directors, which represented something of a major culture shock.

They appeared disinterested to the point of distraction, and when David appointed his Senior Independent Director, I was advised that the person concerned wanted other Non-Execs with experience. Clearly, I had none, but at that point I had decided to advise the recruiters that I was no longer interested in the job, as I really felt I could not work with the Executives. When you are in a fight and with your back to the wall, as we quite often were at Morrisons, you have to have a team which is together and battling for the common cause, and I was not convinced this would not be the case in Wigan.

I mentioned earlier, in July of 2009, I received a call from David Baldwin, who is effectively the Chief Executive of Bradford City Football Club, my lifetime heroes. David, whom I knew by sight but little else, asked me if I would be interested in joining the Board. We had a talk, I had a think, I asked lots of questions and eventually decided that I should accept their offer, which, for any Bradford City fans reading this book, I can stress is unpaid and I receive no expenses.

I was now to transform from the average supporter who sits in the stand and moans about the Directors, into being a poacher turned Gamekeeper, and my, what a shock I got.

Bradford City, in conjunction with, probably, no more than five other clubs at the most, have no debt, have not drawn on their bank facilities, but simply have no cash. This is life in the raw where every penny counts, where the breakdown of the lawnmower, two days before a home game, is a major issue.

I am charged with trying to bring some extra revenue to the club and at the same time cutting costs, and at the time of finishing this book, I have been spending, on average, two days a week for five months trying to achieve some success. Things move, but not half as quickly as in my previous job, and it is frustrating for me, as I believe that I am constantly not doing enough. The compensatory factor in all of this is that at least life is very amusing. I work with two Co-owners Julian Rhodes and Mark Lawn, who have sacrificed much of their personal time and wealth to keep a football club alive. This in one of the largest cities in the country, with a substantial fan base and average crowds of twice that of the rest of the Division we play in. Bradford City should be Championship level or even better and I look forward to the days when the club I have supported for all but the first five years of my life are back in a position in which they can be proud of and where heads can be held high. I shall be trying all I can to make this happen.

So then, one Non-Exec job of a type achieved and now, as I finish this book, other offers are coming to me, but in the meantime there is a massive job to be done within the City of Bradford itself. Bradford has been badly let down by its Quango Regeneration Company, the Council itself and the Regional Development Agency, Yorkshire Forward. These three bodies between them are responsible for utter and complete chaos in the City, no master plan, no execution and apparently, inadequate, inept contractual arrangements with developers, leaving Bradford on the cusp of life and death.

I believe that politicians, both Westminster and local, should be flogged publicly for what they have failed to achieve, and the Officers of the Council who have clearly little ability should be drummed out of town.

My ambition for Bradford is to have an elected Mayor – I know there can be good and bad – and to have the city effectively put into Special Needs by Central Government, until such time as its infrastructure and development strategy can be resolved.

Bradford started its slide to oblivion in the sixties, when it tore down its old buildings, this, in stark contrast to its neighbour, Leeds, who retained theirs and now have a vibrant thriving shopping centre.

Much is made in Bradford of its diverse population and yet the areas where the large concentrations of immigrant population is located suffer low levels of educational achievement, bad health, high levels of car crime, lack of car insurance and so on. In my view there had been too much settlement in Bradford of members of the former Commonwealth countries. William Hague of the Conservative Party has described Bradford as rich for immigration. The BNP have said that Bradford has not experienced immigration but colonisation, and whilst I agree with nothing much that these people put forward, I have to agree with the latter. Bradford has indeed been colonised to a significant and substantial effect.

In parallel to everything that has happened over the last fifteen years, or so, in Bradford the city has not been helped by what, in my view, is a collection of the most inept and inadequate Elected Members and Officers of the council. I make this judgement based on my significant travels around the country and abroad and my numerous dealings with many and varied Local Authorities.

The city centre of Bradford now resembles a bomb site with no prospect in the immediate future of development . Buildings which could be put to use, such as the famous Odeon (formerly Gaumont) cinema are in disrepair, instead of in active use as a concert hall.

The much vaunted new shopping centre is in terminal delay, allegedly caused by the credit crisis of 2008 and onwards, yet this centre was supposed to be up and running by the end of 2007, which meant that tenants and deals should have been done at the peak at the property boom. Local politicians swallow the story of the crash, and it would appear that there is no provision in the contract for termination of the developers' agreement for non-performance. This particular surveyor would have been out of a job if he had ever put Morrisons in a similar situation.

As I finally finish this book news comes of the Government of the day's proposal to create a high-speed west coast based rail link to London, with a leg across the Pennines. Bradford has two dead-end stations which need linking so that the City can be on this high speed trans-Pennine link, but the Council poo-poo it. Other towns, such as Huddersfield, who will be on the link will benefit and Bradford will sink further into the mire, which is why I and others are working at a plausible scheme to link the stations and link in the new shopping centre, if indeed it ever gets built.

Oh for that elected Mayor!

I believe that I very quickly severed my links with Morrisons, a task, if that is the right description, that I had set myself and was determined to achieve, although the Company through its Board have been very kind and Marc Bolland in particular has seen to it that one of the suites within the conference/meeting area of the splendid offices has my name on it as a lasting reminder. This is a great honour to me to have my name within the building named after my former Chairman's mother and a building which carries only one other reference to the past in that the staff canteen is named and branded 'jd's', in memory of my former colleague and Managing Director John Dowd, who sadly passed away, long before his time.

Marc invited me back for lunch in August of 2009 and was keen to have me back on a regular basis, but I said to him at the time that I did not want to be the albatross circling the ship.

My final business-type contact prior to finishing this tome came out of the blue at the end of November 2009 when I received a call from my former colleague and close ally, Mark Gunter, who, as Store Operations Director, was my chief 'client' within the business. I provided the ammunition for his business in the form of building stores for him to operate.

Mark advised me that he, Chairman Sir Ian Gibson, and Marc Boland, had been talking about me that day, having attended the re-launch of a former Safeway's store, long since converted at Welwyn Garden City. The first day's trade had been exceptional, a reflection on Morrisons' rapid growth and increase of Market Share, and apparently remarks had been passed as to what a legacy I had left for the two years following my retirement in the form of acquisitions and sites under construction. Apparently, Sir Ian, supported by Marc Bolland, had suggested that a phone call be made to me to tell me of the store's success, and so it came.

Barely forty-eight hours after the very kind gesture, driving along I was surprised to hear the news that Marc Bolland had resigned and was going to take the top job as Chief Executive of Marks and Spencer. Marc had been connected to this position by rumour for several months, but had denied it, however, now here was the proof. I called Mark Gunter, to be told that MJB, as he was sometimes known, had arrived at the office that morning, and promptly resigned. and as things turned out the Dutchman departed Morrisons prior to Christmas 2009.

Two days after the news I wrote to Marc and told him how much I had valued his contribution, as a Shareholder, as a retired colleague watching from afar and as a colleague in his time with the Company. Marc Bolland joined Morrisons in September 2006 and was leaving some three and a quarter years later.

In my email I told him that I was surprised, but not shocked, given that the average lifespan of Chief Executives today is not the old job-for-life scenario, but more likely to be somewhere between three or four years in tenure terms. Marc called me within fifteen minutes of receiving my email and we had a lengthy chat, particularly bearing in mind that he had much else on his plate to deal with. I wish him well in what he clearly regards as the top job in British retail, I am sure that he will be successful. Many have made much of the fact that he has no experience in this area. I am sorry, but he had no food experience when he joined Morrisons and didn't do too badly there.

The business pages of the following week's Sunday papers were full of what I regard as rather 'unfortunate' comments attributed to Ken Morrison. I am not sure if Ken has made these observations or not but at least he stopped short of his famous quote to me, heading up one of the earlier chapters, 'never trust a Dutchman'. I trusted Marc Bolland and I believe in the modern days' world of the boardroom Morrisons have little to chastise him for.

So now I go off, to make the best of what I can for my City, my football club and most important of all, my family, for what remains of my time. I hope that this will be many years of fun, enjoyment and continued activity and variation in the lives of both Lena and myself.

I hope that I have delivered everything that my parents in the past and my family in recent times might have expected, and just as importantly I hope that you have enjoyed reading about it, warts and all.

I await Jennifer Saunders' call.